D0880000

Children & Television

To ARTHUR NADEL
For his development of prosocial programs for children, wise guidance to friends, and willingness to share his creative talents with others.

Children & Television

Images in a Changing Sociocultural World

GORDON L. BERRY
JOY KEIKO ASAMEN

Copyright © 1993 by Sage Publications, Inc.

All rights reserved. No part of this book may be reproduced or utilized in any form or by any means, electronic or mechanical, including photocopying, recording, or by any information storage and retrieval system, without permission in writing from the publisher.

For information address:

SAGE Publications, Inc.
2455 Teller Road
Newbury Park, California 91320

SAGE Publications Ltd.
6 Bonhill Street
London EC2A 4PU
United Kingdom

SAGE Publications India Pvt. Ltd.
M-32 Market
Greater Kailash I
New Delhi 110 048 India

Printed in the United States of America

Library of Congress Cataloging-in-Publication Data

Children and television : images in a changing sociocultural world / edited by Gordon L. Berry, Joy Keiko Asamen.
p. cm.
Includes bibliographical references and index.
ISBN 0-8039-4699-6 — ISBN 0-8039-4700-3 (pbk.)
1. Television and children—United States. 2. Pluralism (Social Sciences)—United States. I. Berry, Gordon L. II. Asamen, Joy Keiko, 1953-
HQ784.T4C47 1993
302.223'45'083—dc20 93-973
CIP

93 94 95 96 10 9 8 7 6 5 4 3 2 1

Sage Production Editor: Judith L. Hunter

LIBRARY
ALMA COLLEGE
ALMA, MICHIGAN

Contents

Preface

Children today live in a multimedia world. It is a world composed of media forms that are now part of the total culture in which a child is born, grows, and develops into an adult. It is also a world in which the United States is well on its way to being truly universal in its cultural diversity. Against the backdrop of the media explosion and changing cultural landscape in the country, television and other electronic media are becoming more important than ever as a type of noncertificated teacher of children.

Television programs with their images, portrayals, and creative story telling are more than passive entertainment. Whenever television is on in the home, it teaches the young viewers something about themselves as well as about individuals and groups who are different. The social, psychological, and educational constructs inherent in the teaching and learning processes of television, and how developing children learn from them are the foci of this book.

In this book we approach these psychosocial and sociocultural constructs of television and children from a multidisciplinary perspective. Although the general framework of the content is research based, we also present concepts related to general practices that students, researchers, teachers, public interest organizations, broadcasters, and other groups can utilize to better understand the role of this medium in the life of the child.

As senior editor, I would like to express my special thanks to Dr. William (Bill) Cosby, that master teacher, and Lou Scheimer, a friend and mentor, for inviting me years ago to work with them on a television program for children known as *Fat Albert and the Cosby Kids.* This program stimulated my research in the field of media and social behavior, and this book is a continuation of that early work. In addition, there have been a number of broadcasters, such as Judy

Price, with whom I have planned and debated the issues associated with prosocial programs for children that have provided me the opportunity to apply the research related to human behavior to the real world of television programming. As always, Juanita Berry deserves special thanks for her support during the development of this project.

As the co-editor, I wish to acknowledge the continued support of my parents, Keigi and Kiyo Asamen.

Both editors want to thank Cathy Dawson, Sarah Kincaid, and Grace Hong in the Communications Processing Center of the Graduate School of Education for their patience in the preparation of the manuscript. Equally important, we have appreciated the assistance received from the people at Sage Publications.

Gordon L. Berry
Joy Keiko Asamen

Introduction

Television as a Worldwide Cultural Tapestry

GORDON L. BERRY

Television is a medium that has made such an impact on U.S. society and the world that we are always creating metaphors to describe its role and place as a communicator. Although it is indeed correct to view television as a "window to the world," a fitting metaphor that relates most closely to the thrust of this book is to also see it as an audiovisual tapestry on which is being woven a complex and ever-changing national and international set of images that are hung on the small screen for all to see. It is a tapestry of highly creative, and not so creative ideas, thoughts, languages, life-styles, and sociocultural portrayals decorated into varicolored patterns of entertainment, information, and social messages that, like the metaphor, frequently transfers meaning from the object it ordinarily designates to one it may designate only by implicit comparison.

The social messages of television are so ubiquitous and yet so complex that the role they play in helping developing children (also adults) learn about themselves and an array of people, places, and events are not fully understood. One might argue that it is the very nature of this ubiquity and the real or imagined power of this medium, especially in the lives of children, that has caused so much critical attention to be drawn to it over the last 35 years. And yet, the attention that television has received should not be surprising to a society that always rallies around any new institution-like phenomena that can potentially compete with the traditional agencies of socialization such as the home or family, the school, and religious organizations.

We are protective of children because we recognize that they are not little adults, but developing boys and girls who have special needs. It is no wonder that this tapestry of program content draws both negative and positive criticism from adults who recognize that they are charged with the responsibility of socializing the young. In this connection, one can only imagine that even with the advent of the printing press, those individuals who did not get their news and entertainment from whatever was the so-called popular culture of that day must have been a little suspicious of this new print communicator. After all, the newly printed works could inform and provide reading material for children that would not always be under the control of their parents and teachers.

Even today, those parents, teachers, researchers, and intellectuals, who primarily get their information from print, computers, and other sophisticated media sources, still look with a jaundiced eye on this common piece of furniture with a screen in it. A common piece of furniture that must always be evaluated for the content that comes from it. Our evaluation process and criticism must, however, be based on informed response and analysis.

Clearly, television today does have a great deal of systematic study directed toward it. Nevertheless, scientific inquiry of any secondary cultural socializer of children must stay under the microscope. On this point, Adler (1971) wrote:

> If this country has a unifying culture, it is the mass, popular culture; and today, television is the most vital expression of that culture. We need television criticism which is neither simplistic nor patronizing, criticism which will provide both a language for describing what appears on the screen and standards for discriminating excellence from mediocrity. (p. 3)

The chapters in this book seek to recognize the important influence of this medium on children inside the United States and beyond its shores. The content reflects the notion that television is a vital expression of the culture, and a type of audiovisual *National Geographic* whose images and portrayals move the child through a series of experiences from which some of them begin to use it as *one* vehicle for securing information and shaping their worldview. A worldview, in this context, is broadly composed of the child's attitudes, values, opinions, and concepts, as well as how the individual thinks, makes decisions, behaves, and defines events (Sue, 1981).

Clearly, we must be careful in attributing too much to television when the acquisition of attitudes and values are discussed because it is only one factor in the equation associated with the child's belief system. At the same time, everyone concerned with children who are growing up in a more diversified country and world must be aware of the role this medium plays in a changing social, economic, political, and general cultural landscape. Some aspects of the cultural diversity can be seen in the 1990 U.S. Census. These projections show that by the year 2000, more than one third of the population will be racial and ethnic minorities, and by the year 2010, racial and ethnic minorities will become a numerical majority. Documented immigrants, undocumented immigrants, and refugees are now more numerous than ever before; last year, one in every four students in California lived in a home in which English was not spoken (Sue, Arredondo, & McDavis, 1992). This "diversification" of the United States can be seen to be more dynamic by the data that show that the population is increasingly aging, people with disabling or handicapping conditions are seeking more opportunities, and women presently represent one of the growing groups entering the labor force.

It is chilling to think that just as the United States is becoming universal in its population, groups such as the Anti-Defamation League, the Los Angeles County Commission on Human Relations, and the Urban League are reporting an increase in hate crimes and other social unrest. These social conditions and behaviors, I would argue, are not exclusively related to television or other media, but to people and events that are part of a challenging and changing world.

As I noted earlier, in this book we approach the social-cultural issues of television and the developing child from a multidisciplinary perspective. Such an approach appreciates the complexity of identifying all of the variables associated with the social, cognitive, and behavioral influences of this medium because of their relationship to those personal attributes that the viewers bring to the content of television. In this respect, television, properly used, can be a marvelous medium for children who are wise consumers of it. We must all know of its ability to communicate correct and incorrect social messages, as well as to portray both positive and negative sociocultural experiences. At the same time, we must appreciate the ability of television to open the world to children in a matter of seconds and expose the beauty of humankind's few differences and many similarities. This is the sociocultural tapestry of varied views from which this book is woven.

References

Adler, R. (1971). Introduction: A context for criticism. In R. Adler & D. Cater (Eds.), *Television as a cultural force* (pp. 1-16). New York: Praeger.

Sue, D. W., Arredondo, P., & McDavis, R. (1992). Multicultural counseling competencies and standards: A call to the profession. *Journal of Multicultural Counseling and Development, 20*(2), 64-88.

Sue, W. S. (1981). *Counseling the culturally different: Theory and practice.* New York: John Wiley.

PART I

Television and the Developing Child in a Multimedia World

Children today are growing up in a society driven by various forms of media. Although children of every generation have always been faced with changes taking place around them, the media explosion today presents special challenges because television and its electronic relations seem to play a role, albeit one sometimes difficult to identify, in the socialization process.

The chapters in Part I are designed to provide the reader with a point of departure for understanding the developmental impact of television on the social, psychological, and educational dimensions of children growing up in a world where television, as well as other media, are the norm. Given the ubiquity and power of this medium, these chapters serve as the psychological foundation for the other chapters in the book.

John P. Murray analyzes the experiences of the developing child in a multimedia society by identifying what he refers to as the "current media ecology of childhood"; he continues by explaining why children with television are living in a world very different from that of previous generations. Drawing on the historical media gaps between today's children and those of the past, Murray argues that the central role that television plays in a multimedia environment for children results from the fact that television, unlike all other media before or since, reaches them at a much earlier age and with greater intensity. Whatever the psychological and educational powers of television on children, Murray sees some hope in recent debates and new legislation to bring about more collaborative effort among researchers, educators, broadcasters, and public policy specialists to develop a national telecommunications plan that will ensure a broad range of television programs targeted to the needs of children at various ages and stages of development.

The position that the decade between the 1972 U.S. Surgeon General's Report on Television and Social Behavior and its update produced much of the initial research on how children's cognitive development modifies or influences their understanding of television is advanced by Catherine N. Doubleday and Kristin L. Droege as the springboard statement for their chapter. They focus on some of the special cognitive processes and understandings that the child experiences at various developmental stages (preschoolers, young children, and older children). This analysis is an invaluable next step from Murray's work because it establishes a point of departure for understanding what children are learning from television and the implications of the learned information for a particular developmental stage.

Early television research, as observed by Murray, Doubleday, and Droege, focused on content that was very much represented by the issues of violence, advertising, and some other areas such as racial and gender stereotyping. Marguerite Fitch, Aletha C. Huston, and John C. Wright, acknowledging the early research, turn their attention to the forms of television and their effects on attention, comprehension, and behavior. In their chapter on television forms and children's perceptive reality, they move a step further by shifting from a theoretical examination of the cumulative effects of forms independent of content to a more contextual approach that considers the whole television stimulus. That is to say, these researchers propose that some formal features have come to be associated with certain types of content in ways that activate schemata for specific program genres. These genre schemata are how children organize the world of television. The authors then present support for the theory that children develop and use schemata about program genres to guide them in organizing and processing their television experience. This chapter expands our knowledge of developmental stages as they relate to how and what children comprehend from television programs based on their perceptions of reality. Significantly, this is a chapter that has special model building, research, and practice implications for many other aspects of the book.

Patricia Marks Greenfield and her colleagues present a chapter that explores both commercials and imaginative play. The significance of this chapter becomes clear in a book of this type because of the need to understand from a research perspective the relationship between program-length commercials and imagination. The findings of this study suggest that television, as well as television-based toys, are potent cultural tools for developing the symbolic representation of mental events. The implications drawn from the results offer major challenges for product-based programs and research in the area of imaginative play.

Parents, educators, and mental health workers, according to Dorothy G. Singer, are concerned about television's effects on the imaginative and creative capabilities of children. She approaches the issues of creativity and television in her chapter by assisting the reader in understanding the distinction between imagination and creativity. Imagination she describes as a possible precursor to creativity in that a child who has been skillful in imagery and fantasy spinning will possess the essential ingredients necessary for the creative spirit. Creativity, on the other hand, is seen as the ability to generate new ideas and to think about things in original and different ways. By exploring current research on creativity, as well as pointing out the methodological problems associated with studies in this field, Singer provides a compelling set of ideas for understanding the role that television plays on creativity.

James A. Anderson and Milton E. Ploghoft offer information on children and media education. For these researchers, one part of media education fosters the observation of details, their sequence, and their relationships in a purposeful manner to arrive at an understanding of the ideological structures, themes, values, claims, evidence, and their warrants, as well as narrative elements such as motivations, plot lines, characters, and characterizations. The chapter covers the state of the new knowledge on media education with a caveat that it is a subject that is undergoing a revival and potential change.

Gordon L. Berry rounds out the discussion in Part I with a chapter on television in the school curriculum. He makes the point that ready or not, schools must assist children to be wise consumers of this medium. He provides for the reader a set of principles for bringing television content into the classroom, concluding with challenging the classroom teacher to assist children to become visually literate.

1. The Developing Child in a Multimedia Society

JOHN P. MURRAY

To suggest that children growing up in the 1990s live in a very different world than the one their parents or grandparents experienced as children is not only to state the obvious but to *understate* the obvious. Although many of the parents of young children in this last decade of the 20th century grew up with television, some of these parents—and almost all of the grandparents—lived in a world without television as a source of information and entertainment.

There are, of course, other changes in the information environment in which children live today. The current media ecology of childhood includes computers and video games, VCRs and laser discs, and ever-changing audio systems with computer interfaces that *could* enhance the integration of both education and entertainment in a multimedia society. However, that integration has not yet occurred and its potential remains a matter of some conjecture. Still, it is not an exaggeration to suggest that television is one of the core components of a multimedia society that has dramatically altered the nature of childhood and the development of children.

The central role that television plays in a multimedia environment for children results from the fact that television—unlike all other media before or since—reaches children at a much earlier age and with a greater intensity. This enhanced potential for influencing the intellectual and emotional development of young viewers is simultaneously television's greatest promise and greatest disappointment. The history of these great expectations for television and the prospects for the future serve as the focus of this review of the developing child in a multimedia society.

Expectations

Television had its debut in North America in 1939 as an object of curiosity at a world's fair exhibition. During the half century since this official debut, television has contributed to major alterations in the life-styles and information environments of children. One of the first social commentators to offer a prediction on the impact of television was the essayist E. B. White, who previewed a demonstration of television in 1938. Writing in *Harper's Magazine* in that year, White noted:

> I believe television is going to be the test of the modern world, and in this new opportunity to see beyond the range of our vision, we shall discover either a new and unbearable disturbance of the general peace or a saving radiance in the sky. We shall stand or fall by television—of that I am quite sure. (White, 1938, cited in Boyer, 1991, p. 79)

And so it was that television, at its birth, gave rise to premonitions of conflict over its potential for benefit or harm.

This concern about the positive and negative influences of television has driven most of the research and public discussion concerning the development of this medium and the development of children over the past half century. The official starting date for television broadcasting in the United States is July 1, 1941, when the Federal Communications Commission (FCC) licensed and approved the full operation of the first commercial television stations. However, the development of television broadcasting was limited by World War II and full-scale broadcasting did not resume until 1946, when stations were once again required to broadcast a minimum of 12 hours of programming each week, with a gradual increase in broadcasting up to a minimum of 28 hours weekly by the end of the first 3 years of the broadcasting license (Andreasen, 1990; Comstock, 1989).

Despite the slow start to television broadcasting, this medium was quickly adopted and it diffused through the population at an accelerated pace. For example, in 1945 there were about 10,000 television sets in use, but that figure jumped to about 7 million sets 5 years later in 1950. By 1955, almost 65% of U.S. households had at least one television set, and by 1960 that figure had jumped to 90% of U.S.

households. Currently, 98% of households have a TV, with only 2% of households choosing not to purchase a television set.

Similarly, the amount of time spent watching television has increased over the years from about 4.5 hours per day in 1950 to 7.5 hours each day in the 1980s and 1990s. To give some reference for this magnitude of viewing, if you multiply 7.5 hours per day in the typical household by the number of households with television sets in use, you find that in 1 year Americans collectively spend about 30 million years of human experience watching television. This is a considerable amount of time to spend with television each year, and one might reasonably ask what effect this extensive viewing has on U.S. society.

To give a flavor of the range and depth of concern about television, one might reflect on the observations of a former chairman of the Federal Communications Commission, Newton Minow, who is best remembered for his "inaugural address" to the National Association of Broadcasters in 1961 in which he said:

> When television is good, nothing—not the theatre, not the magazines or newspapers—nothing is better. But when television is bad, nothing is worse. I invite you to sit down in front of your television set when your station goes on the air and stay there without a book, magazine, newspaper, profit-and-loss sheet, or rating book to distract you—and keep your eyes glued to that set until the station signs off. I can assure you that you will observe a vast wasteland. You will see a procession of game shows, violence, audience participation shows, formula comedies about totally unbelievable families, blood and thunder, mayhem, violence, sadism, murder, western bad men, western good men, private eyes, gangsters, more violence, and cartoons. And, endlessly, commercials—many screaming, cajoling, and offending.

Thirty years later, the now former chair of the FCC, speaking on the 30th anniversary of the "vast wasteland" speech, observed: "In 1961 I worried that my children would not benefit much from television, but in 1991, I worry that my grandchildren will actually be harmed by it" (Minow, 1991, p. 12).

The "vast wasteland" speech had a galvanizing effect on public discussion of the potential of television to influence young viewers for good or ill. Three decades later we are still attempting to sort out the costs and benefits of this medium of long-distance sight and sound. The controversies continue to rage about the most beneficial uses of television in all its forms and the difficulties of drawing the fine line between commercial profit and commercial exploitation. For example, concerns have surfaced around proposals to provide commercial television news services in schools, such as those promoted by Whittle Communications's Channel One (Murray, 1991; Pool, 1992). And yet, there are clearly great benefits to be derived from the effective use of television as an educational force in the lives of young viewers (Boyer, 1991; Palmer, 1988). So, what do we know about television's influence on the developing child and when did we know it?

Debates

The first official debates about television occurred in congressional hearings during the early 1950s (U.S. Congress, House Committee on Interstate and Foreign Commerce, 1952; U.S. Congress, Senate Committee of the Judiciary, Subcommittee to Investigate Juvenile Delinquency, 1955). These inaugural congressional investigations were focused on the impact of televised violence on children and youth and set the stage for subsequent commissions and committees. For example, the landmark reviews following the 1950s hearings include the National Commission on the Causes and Prevention of Violence (Baker & Ball, 1969), the Surgeon General's report on television violence (U.S. Surgeon General's Scientific Advisory Committee on Television and Social Behavior, 1972), the report on television and behavior from the National Institute of Mental Health (1982; Pearl, Bouthilet, & Lazar, 1982), and the American Psychological Association review of television and society (Huston et al., 1992). Each of these investigations began with basic questions about the impact of television on young viewers and each has added incrementally to our understanding of the processes by which children develop in a mediated society.

Questions about the impact of television on children and adults have occupied the time and talents of hundreds of social scientists and educators over the past 40 years. Consequently, there have been over 4,000 books, articles, reports, and papers published on this topic since the mid-1950s (Huston et al., 1992; Murray, 1980). The major concerns expressed about television have been focused on its impact on young viewers in relation to the influence of televised violence, the portrayal of the roles of men and women and various social and ethnic groups, and the influence of television viewing on school performance and general intellectual and emotional development in children.

Violence

As we noted earlier, one of the first concerns that surfaced in relation to the medium of television in the 1950s was a concern about the impact of televised violence on the behavior of young viewers. This was the principal focus of the congressional hearings in 1952 and 1955 and continued to be an issue in the violence commission in 1969, the Surgeon General's report in 1972, and in various other reports through 1992. The reasons for concern about violence, both then and now, include the fact that there has been a consistently high level of violence on television throughout much of its history  and that children are considered more vulnerable to these violent portrayals because they are in the early stages of developing behavior patterns, attitudes, and values about social interaction. However, this is not to deny that many reports and studies have addressed the impact of televised violence on adults as well as children for many of the same reasons. The earliest studies in this regard turned on the work of Albert Bandura who studied preschool children at Stanford University (Bandura, D. Ross, & S. Ross, 1961) and the work of Leonard Berkowitz at the University of Wisconsin, conducting studies on the impact of film violence on college students (Berkowitz, 1962). These early laboratory-based and relatively focused investigations gave rise to the conclusion that media violence could lead to some short-term changes in aggressive behavior and attitudes on the part of children and young adults.

Subsequent studies and reviews, such as the work of Aletha Huston and her colleagues (Friedrich-Cofer & Huston, 1986; Stein & Friedrich, 1972) expanded these studies and conclusions to take account of aggressive behavior occurring in more conventional or typical behavior settings. For example, one study conducted in the early 1970s (Stein & Friedrich, 1972) assessed the effects of viewing a diet of Batman and Superman cartoons on the aggressive behavior of preschoolers in the more natural setting of their classroom and playgrounds. One of the main conclusions from this study is that the youngsters who had watched the Batman and Superman cartoons were much more likely to get into minor confrontations in the classroom and on the playground, were more active in these settings, and played less well and less cooperatively with their peers. On the other hand, the youngsters who had watched the diet of *Mr. Rogers' Neighborhood* were more likely to play cooperatively, offer to help other children and teachers, share toys and equipment, and express concern about others' emotional well-being. One of the interesting features of this research is the suggestion that television can have either beneficial or harmful effects on viewers' behavior and that the nature of the effects depends upon the nature of the programming viewed. To be sure, there are many other factors that affect these relationships and there has been considerable debate about the nature of these influences and the extent of concern about televised violence (Comstock & Paik, 1991; Donnerstein, Linz, & Penrod, 1987; Freedman, 1984, 1986; Friedrich-Cofer & Huston, 1986; Huesmann & Eron, 1986; Huston et al., 1992; Murray, 1980; National Institute of Mental Health, 1982; U.S. Surgeon General's Scientific Advisory Committee on Television and Social Behavior, 1972). Nevertheless, it is clear that there is a considerable amount of violence on television and that this violence on the small screen may translate into changes of attitudes, values, or behavior on the part of heavy viewers. For example, studies by George Gerbner and his colleagues at the University of Pennsylvania (Gerbner & Signorielli, 1990) have shown that on average over the past 20 years, 1 hour of "prime-time" evening television programming contains 5 violent acts whereas 1 hour of Saturday morning children's programming contains an average of 20-25 violent acts. These figures and levels of violence have fluctuated somewhat over the past quarter of a century of detailed content analyses, but the average child watching an average amount of television will see about 20,000 murders and 80,000 assaults in his or her formative years. That's about 100,000 violent acts before a youngster becomes a teenager. Some of the violence will be seen on realistic programs and some will be seen on cartoons, but we know from various studies that all forms of violent programming may have possible harmful effects on viewers.

Three possible effects have been the focus of most concern about TV violence: Children may become less sensitive to the pain and suffering of others; youngsters may be more fearful of the world around them; and children may be more willing to behave in aggressive or harmful ways toward others. Although the effects of television violence are not simple and straightforward, meta-analyses and reviews of a large body of research (Huston et al., 1992; Wood, Wong, & Chachere, 1991) suggest that there are clearly reasons for concern and caution in relation to the impact of televised violence.

Roles

Content analyses of television programming over the past 20-30 years have consistently indicated that the portrayal of the roles of men and women and various social or ethnic groups bear little relationship to the life circumstances of these individuals beyond the small screen (Berry, 1988; Gerbner & Signorielli, 1990; Greenberg, 1980; M. Williams & Condry, 1989; Withey & Abeles, 1980). Although the portrayal of ethnic minorities and the roles of men and women have changed over the years as a result of increasing sensitivity to these issues on the part of both broadcasters and viewers, there remain clear limitations on opportunities for diverse role presentations for these groups. For example, following civil rights demonstrations during the 1960s, there were increases in the number of programs featuring Blacks in major roles on television. However, this trend began to reverse in the 1980s, when Blacks declined to about 8%, which is considerably below the percentage of Blacks in the U.S. population. So too, there were clear limitations on other ethnic groups. For example, Hispanics (3.5%), Asians (2.5%), and Native Americans (under 1%) (Berry, 1980; Greenberg, 1986).

In other areas, such as the portrayal of families on television, we know that there have been wide variations in the nature of families that dominate television at various periods in its history. One recent content analysis of over 900 television series broadcast between 1947 and 1992 suggest that there are some unusual peaks in particular types of families on televisions (Murray, 1992). For example, in the early days of television—from the late 1940s through the 1950s—the typical family consisted of one of two types: A mother and father with two or three children or husband and wife who were newlyweds just establishing their marriage and family relationships. However, in the late 1950s and throughout the 1960s, there was a sudden rise in the number of single-parent families portrayed on television. One might suspect that this was a response to a rising divorce rate in the United States and the consequent increase in single-parent families. In the U.S. population during the 1960s and 1970s, and continuing through today, most of the single-parent households are female headed. However, on television during the 1960s and 1970s, most of the single-parent households were male headed. Moreover, this overrepresentation of male-headed households continues through the 1980s and 1990s. The reasons for this odd circumstance are difficult to detect, but they seem to derive from an expedient formula in entertainment television. Nevertheless, it would be helpful to encourage broader representation of the diverse structures of families on television, because we know that young viewers are affected by the families they see on the small screen (Dorr, Kovaric, & Doubleday, 1990).

Clearly, it is important to think about the ways in which various social roles and groups are portrayed on television, because they can have an important influence in shaping children's views of the world. Consider, for example, the role of police officers on television and children's conceptions of police officers. On the small screen, most police officers are seen in highly active, violent situations: shootings, beatings, high-speed chases. If you ask children about their understanding of what police officers do, you will find that most young children readily report that police officers chase people and arrest them and shoot guns and drive fast cars. On the other hand, if you ask police officers on urban or rural police forces, you will find that most of their daily activities consist of filling out forms and writing reports. Indeed, many career veterans of police departments around the country report that they have rarely or never fired their guns at lawbreakers.

Education

One of the strongly held beliefs about television is the notion that it is simply designed for entertainment. And yet, when viewers are asked about how they use television—how often they view, what they view, and why they view—they frequently demonstrate that they use television for many purposes beyond mere entertainment. For example, studies of audience members in the context of "uses and gratifications" theory (Murray & Kippax, 1979) have shown that some viewers use television in a very thoughtful and directive manner. Individuals who report that they watch television to keep abreast of current events do, in fact, watch more news, documentaries, and current affairs programs. Conversely, those who watch large amounts of television often report that they use television to "escape the boredom of everyday life" or to relax and to be entertained and, indeed, watch a wide variety of television programs with no particular preferences evident in their viewing patterns.

With regard to the direct contributions of television to education and intellectual development in children, the pattern is somewhat mixed. We know that television is a window on the world; that programming can take viewers to places they might never see and offer experiences they might never feel or encounter in their daily life. With regard to children, we know that television is indeed a "special medium for a special audience" because it transcends the boundaries of time and space (Dorr, 1986). In addition, particular programs have been shown to have very special beneficial effects. One need only think of *Sesame Street* and *Mister Rogers' Neighborhood* to tap into a large body of research on the effectiveness of planned, carefully designed programming (Comstock & Paik, 1991; Dorr, 1986; Huston et al., 1992; Murray, 1980). On a more anecdotal level, it has been reported that programs such as *Reading Rainbow* have stimulated intense interest in the books featured on the programs, and an episode of *Happy Days* in which the Fonz acquired a library card prompted a rush on libraries (Charren & Sandler, 1983; Comstock, 1989; Huston et al., 1992).

On the other hand, television has been identified as a hindrance to education in the sense that television viewing is an activity that may "steal" time from other activities more directly related to success in school. For example, studies of the introduction of television in a small Canadian community have shown that television availability is associated with a decrease in reading ability or reading skills components (T. M. Williams, 1986). However, the evidence from other studies is somewhat mixed (Anderson & Collins, 1988; Bryant & Anderson, 1983). We do know that the outlook is not as bleak as Winn (1987) might believe, but it seems clear that we have not been particularly successful in using television to its full potential in the education of our youngest citizens (Boyer, 1991; Kunkel & Murray, 1991; Palmer, 1988). Moreover, we also know that television can be both entertaining and educational—a fact observed in studies of public broadcasting programs ranging from *Mister Rogers* to *Reading Rainbow* to *Sesame Street/Electric Company/Ghost Writer* but also observed in commercial television offerings such as a set of series developed by CBS in the mid-1970s: *USA of Archie, ISIS,* and *Fat Albert and the Cosby Kids*; along with the 30-year performance of a commercial/public swing program, *Captain Kangaroo.*

And yet, these educational programs represent only a small portion of the programs broadcast on our public and commercial television stations. True, cable television adds several channels and a different program mix, but this is still a relatively small and isolated attempt to use television for broad educational purposes. The history of television program development, as Turow (1981) noted, is one of economic enhancement at the expense of education. The more recent entry of a commercial news service for high school students developed by Whittle Communications is an example of one of the more problematic entrepreneurial activities (Murray, 1991; Pool, 1992). And yet, we know that the provision of news and current events through television programming designed for young viewers can lead to increase in awareness of important issues (Burkart, Rockman, & Ittelson, 1992). The policy question turns on whether noncommercial programming such as *CNN Newsroom* is a better alternative to the commercial programming of Channel One. And there are other policy-related concerns about the control—local versus national—of the content of current affairs information in the classroom.

Clearly, television can play a major role in the education of young viewers. Part of that role has been defined by a range of Public Broadcasting System television programs and some cable television channels. However, the commercial television networks have an important role to play in this process, and the Children's Television Act of 1990 has helped to define the nature of this role through the provision of broadly defined educational programming as a component of license renewal. As a nation, we can do more to enhance the educational uses of television.

Hopes

The expectations and debates about television's potential for benefit or harm have been great and heated but we have not achieved the goal of integration of television and other components of a multimedia society in the service of the developing child. Nevertheless, hope springs eternal and there are many changes on the horizon. For example, the 1992 decision by the FCC to allow telephone companies to compete with cable television systems in the delivery of television programming to the home—the "video dial tone" concept—portends a revolution in the range of services and greatly expanded opportunities for integration of voice, data, and video.

Other significant changes affecting the future of children's television include the Children's Television Act of 1990, which was born of frustration over the systematic failure of the FCC to regulate in the public interest (Kunkel & Murray, 1991; Kunkel & Watkins, 1987; Levin, 1980; Minow, 1991). The 1990 act reintroduced limits on the amount of advertising contained in each hour of children's television, encouraged commercial television stations to broadcast some educational programming (broadly defined) for children, and established the framework for a national endowment for the development of children's television programs. This is an important development in the struggle to convince both the television industry and the viewing public to take television seriously, but it is only the beginning.

What is most needed to ensure adequate support for the developing child in a multimedia society is a collaborative effort among researchers, educators, broadcasters, and public policy specialists (Boyer, 1991; Flagg, 1990; Huston et al., 1992; Palmer, 1988) to develop a national telecommunications plan that will ensure a broad range of television programs targeted to the needs of children at various ages and stages of development. These programs would differ in their scope and theme, but they would share the characteristics of thoughtful, purposeful programming. We need to develop more programming for children that is both entertaining and educational. In short, we need to take television seriously without being too serious.

References

Anderson, D. R., & Collins, P. A. (1988). *The impact on children's education: Television's influence on cognitive development.* Washington, DC: U.S. Department of Education.

Andreasen, M. S. (1990). Evolution in the family's use of television: Normative data from industry and academe. In J. Bryant (Ed.), *Television and the American family* (pp. 3-55). Hillsdale, NJ: Lawrence Erlbaum.

Baker, R. K., & Ball, S. J. (1969). *Mass media and violence: A staff report to the National Commission of the Causes and Prevention of Violence.* Washington, DC: U.S. Government Printing Office.

Bandura, A., Ross, D., & Ross, S. (1961). Transmission of aggression through imitation of aggression models. *Journal of Abnormal and Social Psychology, 63,* 575-582.

Berkowitz, L. (1962). *Aggression: A social psychological analysis.* New York: McGraw-Hill.
Berry, G. L. (1980). Television and Afro-Americans: Past legacy and present portrayals. In S. B. Withey & R. P. Abeles (Eds.), *Television and social behavior: Beyond violence and children* (pp. 231-248). Hillsdale, NJ: Lawrence Erlbaum.
Berry, G. L. (1988). Multicultural role portrayals on television as a social psychological issue. In S. Oskamp (Ed.), *Applied Social Psychology Annual: Vol. 8. Television as a social issue* (pp. 118-129). Newbury Park, CA: Sage.
Boyer, E. L. (1991). *Ready to learn: A mandate for the nation.* Princeton, NJ: Carnegie Foundation for the Advancement of Teaching.
Bryant, J., & Anderson, D. R. (Eds.). (1983). *Children's understanding of television: Research on attention and comprehension.* New York: Academic Press.
Burkart, A., Rockman, S., & Ittelson, J. (1992). *"Touch the world"—Observations on the use of CNN Newsroom in schools.* Chico, CA: California State University.
Charren, P., & Sandler, M. W. (1983). *Changing channels: Living (sensibly) with television.* Reading, MA: Addison-Wesley.
Comstock, G. (1989). *The evolution of American television.* Newbury Park, CA: Sage.
Comstock, G., & Paik, H. (1991). *Television and the American child.* San Diego, CA: Academic Press.
Donnerstein, E., Linz, D., & Penrod, S. (1987). *The question of pornography: Research findings and policy implications.* New York: Free Press.
Dorr, A. (1986). *Television and children: A special medium for a special audience.* Beverly Hills, CA: Sage.
Dorr, A., Kovaric, P., & Doubleday, C. (1990). Age and content influences on children's perceptions of the realism of television families. *Journal of Broadcasting and Electronic Media, 34,* 377-397.
Flagg, B. N. (1990). *Formative evaluation for educational technologies.* Hillsdale, NJ: Lawrence Erlbaum.
Freedman, J. L. (1984). Effect of television violence on aggressiveness. *Psychological Bulletin, 96*(2), 227-246.
Freedman, J. L. (1986). Television violence and aggression: A rejoinder. *Psychological Bulletin, 100,* 372-378.
Friedrich-Cofer, L., & Huston, A. C. (1986). Television violence and aggression: The debate continues. *Psychological Bulletin, 100,* 364-371.
Gerbner, G., & Signorielli, N. (1990). *Violence profile, 1967 through 1988-89: Enduring patterns.* Unpublished manuscript, University of Pennsylvania, Annenberg School of Communications.
Greenberg, B. S. (1980). Minorities and the mass media. In J. Bryant & D. Zillman (Eds.), *Perspectives on media effects* (pp. 165-188). Hillsdale, NJ: Lawrence Erlbaum.
Greenberg, B. S. (1986). Minorities and the mass media. In J. Bryant & D. Zillman (Eds.), *Perspectives on media effects* (pp. 165-188). Hillsdale, NJ: Lawrence Erlbaum.
Huesmann, L. R., & Eron, L. D. (Eds.). (1986). *Television and the aggressive child: A cross-national comparison.* Hillsdale, NJ: Lawrence Erlbaum.
Huston, A. C., Donnerstein, E., Fairchild, H., Feshbach, N. D., Katz, P. A., Murray, J. P., Rubinstein, E. A., Wilcox, B., & Zuckerman, D. (1992). *Big world, small screen: The role of television in American society.* Lincoln: University of Nebraska Press.
Kunkel, D., & Murray, J. P. (1991). Television, children, and social policy: Issues and resources for child advocates. *Journal of Clinical Child Psychology, 20*(1), 88-93.

Kunkel, D., & Watkins, B. A. (1987). Evolution of children's television regulatory policy. *Journal of Broadcasting and Electronic Media, 31*, 367-389.

Levin, H. J. (1980). *Fact and fancy in television regulation: An economic study of policy alternatives.* New York: Russell Sage Foundation.

Minow, N. N. (1961, May). *The "vast wasteland."* Address to the National Association of Broadcasters, Washington, DC.

Minow, N. N. (1991). *How vast wasteland now?* New York: Gannett Foundation Media Center, Columbia University.

Murray, J. P. (1980). *Television and youth: Twenty-five years of research and controversy.* Boys Town, NE: Boys Town Center for the Study of Youth Development. p6.

Murray, J. P. (1991, September/October). TV in the classroom: News and Nikes? *Extra*, p. 6.

Murray, J. P. (1992). *Families on television: A brief history, 1947-1992.* Unpublished manuscript, Kansas State University, Human Development and Family Studies.

Murray, J. P., & Kippax, S. (1979). From the early window to the late night show: International trends in the study of television's impact on children and adults. In L. Berkowitz (Ed.), *Advances in experimental social psychology* (Vol. 12, pp. 253-320). New York: Academic Press.

National Institute of Mental Health. (1982). *Television and behavior: Ten years of scientific progress and implications for the eighties: Vol. 1. Summary report.* Washington, DC: U.S. Government Printing Office.

Palmer, E. L. (1988). *Television and America's children: A crisis of neglect.* New York: Oxford University Press.

Pearl, D., Bouthilet, L., & Lazar, J. (Eds.). (1982). *Television and behavior: Ten years of scientific progress and implications for the eighties: Vol. 2. Technical reviews.* Washington, DC: U.S. Government Printing Office.

Pool, G. (1992, June). "What's with Whittle?" *Wilson Library Bulletin*, pp. 35-37, 147-148.

Stein, A. H., & Friedrich, L. K. (1972). Television content and younger children's behavior. In J. P. Murray, E. A. Rubinstein, & G. A. Comstock (Eds.), *Television and social behavior: Vol. 2. Television and social learning* (pp. 202-317). Washington, DC: U.S. Government Printing Office.

Turow, J. (1981). *Entertainment, education, and the hard sell: Three decades of network children's television.* New York: Praeger.

U.S. Congress, House Committee on Interstate and Foreign Commerce. (1952). *Investigation of Radio and Television Programs, Hearings and Report, 82nd Congress, 2nd session, June 3-December 5, 1952.* Washington, DC: U.S. Government Printing Office.

U.S. Congress, Senate Committee of Judiciary, Subcommittee to Investigate Juvenile Delinquency. (1955). *Juvenile Delinquency (Television Programs), Hearing, 84th Congress, 1st session, April 6-7, 1955.* Washington, DC: U.S. Government Printing Office.

U.S. Surgeon General's Scientific Advisory Committee on Television and Social Behavior. (1972). *Television and growing up: The impact of televised violence.* Washington, DC: U.S. Government Printing Office.

Williams, M., & Condry, J. (1989, April). *Living color: Minority portrayals and cross-racial interactions on television.* Paper presented at the meeting of the Society for Research in Child Development, Kansas City, MO.

Williams, T. M. (1986). *The impact of television: A natural experiment in three communities.* New York: Academic Press.

Winn, M. (1987). *Unplugging the plug-in drug.* New York: Penguin.

Withey, S. B., & Abeles, R. P. (Eds.). (1980). *Television and social behavior: Beyond violence and children.* Hillsdale, NJ: Lawrence Erlbaum.

Wood, W., Wong, F. Y., & Chachere, J. G. (1991). Effects of media violence on viewers' aggression in unconstrained social interaction. *Psychological Bulletin, 109*(3), 371-383.

2. Cognitive Developmental Influences on Children's Understanding of Television

CATHERINE N. DOUBLEDAY

KRISTIN L. DROEGE

Introduction

The decade between the 1972 U.S. Surgeon General's Report on Television and Social Behavior and its update (Pearl, Bouthilet, & Lazar, 1982) produced much of the initial research on how children's cognitive development modifies or influences their understanding of television. Underlying this empirical effort was a shift away from a focus on studies of televised violence and aggressive behavior to a broader range of possible viewer-television interactions (Rubinstein, 1983). Also contributing to this new perspective were beliefs that children do not understand what's on television in the same way adults do (Dorr, 1980, 1986; Noble, 1975) and that greater theoretical complexity in investigating questions of television's influence on children should be pursued (Pearl et al., 1982).

In the early years of research on children and television, a direct socialization model of television effects was utilized almost exclusively in empirical studies of television effects (Doubleday, Kovaric, & Dorr, in press). This model is built on the behaviorist and social learning principles that repeated associations among antecedent stimuli, specific responses, and contingent reinforcements or punishments account for learning from television. Another, cognitive mediation model began to be used in the 1970s. It emphasizes an active child constructing knowledge through transactions with television, making sense of information from television and the viewing environment, and evaluating such information and experience for meaning in terms of relevance to the self. A third, cognitive-socialization model came into some, more limited use in the 1980s. It assumes that principles represented in the other two models simultaneously account for children's use and understanding of television. Further, it posits that the child uses behavioral models and antecedent-behavior-consequence contingencies in making sense of and evaluating information and experience.

The latter two models assume that children's sense-making activities vis-à-vis television are carried out with the cognitive tools at hand. As the available cognitive tools change with age, developmental analyses of children's cognitions regarding television are essential for a complete understanding of children's experiences with television at different ages.

Cognitive Processes

Attention

The research of Daniel Anderson and his associates is primarily associated with a reconceptualization of the nature and function of children's attentional processes to content and form during television viewing. In a 1983 review of their work, Anderson and Lorch discuss findings that forced their reconsideration of visual attention to television as an active rather than a reactive process. In the reactive view, viewers are passively controlled by powerful characteristics of television, such as constant movement and change, that "lock" viewers into attending to the screen. In the active view, visual attention is seen as schema driven. Changes in visual orientation to television reflect the viewer's understanding of, expectations for, and questions about programming, as well as strategies for processing television in the context of other available activities.

In a recent study of 5- to 8-year-olds, Meadowcroft and Reeves (1989) addressed some of the limitations of existing developmental research on children's attention to television content, particularly its weak explanatory power because age is seldom defined theoretically. They asserted that age is typically a surrogate for unspecified variables, then use schema theory to predict and explain age-related differences in children's attention to television stories. Meadowcroft and Reeves (1989) concluded that story schema development does influence children's strategies for attending to and remembering stories on television. More highly developed story schemata were associated with efficient and flexible attention and increased memory of central story content. Their findings also showed that before the age of 7 years, children do not have well-developed story schema skills.

Visual attention may also be maintained across breaks in comprehension through a nonstrategic phenomenon called *attentional inertia* (Anderson, Alwitt, Lorch, & Levin, 1979; Anderson, Choi, & Lorch, 1987). Attentional inertia maintains "pauses" in visual orientation to television as well. Much needs to be answered about the nature of attentional inertia and its relation to comprehension, memory, and other attentional phenomena. One negative finding of Anderson et al. (1987) is of interest to the present discussion, however. In their study of 3- and 5-year-olds, no age differences were found in distractibility. The longer a look at TV was maintained, the greater was the probability that it would continue to be maintained by either age group.

There is more evidence of age trends in visual orientation to television. Dramatic increases in the percentage of time children visually attend to television occur from ages 0-5 years, leveling off during the school-age years after about age 10, and declining during adulthood (Alwitt, Anderson, Lorch, & Levin, 1980; Anderson, Lorch, Field, Collins, & Nathan, 1986; Anderson, Lorch, Field, & Sanders, 1981; Carew, 1980). In preschool and younger children, increases in attention reflect increasing comprehension of television programming as cognitive skills improve.

In the research literature, a considerable effort has been spent on determining which modality of a television program, audio or video, is monitored more by children to determine which information is attention worthy. This literature is summarized by Rolandelli, Wright, Huston, & Eakins (1991) as demonstrating a "visual superiority effect" for children who recognized visually presented information better than auditory information when shown different audio and video presentations or mismatched audio and visual television content. Studies also show that children sometimes comprehend certain types of information better when it is presented audiovisually, with congruent information in both channels, or visually rather than auditorily alone. Other investigations show comprehension is the same for audiovisual and audio-only programs. Rolandelli et al. (1991) conclude that most investigations comparing modalities have confounded sensory modality with mode of representation, abstractness, and complexity. Also auditory attention needs to be tested by a moment-by-moment measure of listening to television content rather than by visual orientation, as it has in the past.

Results of Rolandelli et al. (1991), using a new auditory measure with 5- and 7-year-olds, indicate that even for younger children, with inferior processing of auditory information compared to older children, attention and comprehension are better with narration. The auditory modality allows children, particularly younger children, to monitor the program for attention-worthy content. Younger children rely more on both modalities and their interdependence, whereas older children can process each modality more independently. Both groups rely more on the visual modality when narration is independent. Also, boys used the visual modality more than girls, and girls used the auditory modality more than boys.

Two of the few studies that directly address gender differences in attention to television were reported by Alvarez, Huston, Wright, & Kerkman (1988). In the first study of 5- and 7-year-olds, Alvarez et al. (1988) found differences in girls' and boys' attention to four animated programs, representing four combinations of high and low levels of action and violent content. Boys paid more attention than girls to the four cartoons, showing minimal attention differences across conditions. Girls, especially at 5 years of age, attended to low action rather than high action programs, regardless of violence level. In the second study, a secondary analysis of nine previous studies showed that boys attended significantly more than girls. There was not support for most content and form attributes accounting for these gender differences, except that violent content and animation may appeal more to boys than girls. Boys and girls did not differ in comprehension, however, leading to the proposition that girls may focus more on the verbal auditory content of television, and boys on its visual content.

Comprehension

Much of the early research on children's cognitive processing and comprehension of dramatic plots in television programming was carried out by Andrew Collins and his colleagues (Collins, 1983). He identified dramatic programs as a sequence of scenes subordinated to a plot or narrative, conveying information both relevant and irrelevant to the program that is explicitly or implicitly presented.

Program comprehension requires attention to and retention of explicit program information and inferences that "go beyond on-screen events" and capture their interrelations.

Patterns of retention and inferencing change with development such that children up to age 7 or 8 retain relatively little central content, but improve between 8 and 14 years. Recall of incidental content increases then decreases as an inverted U-shape function of age from preschool to late childhood to early adolescence. Further, children less that 8 or 9 years rarely or inaccurately infer missing content and cannot infer the relations between scenes in a program as well as older children (Collins, 1983; Dorr, 1986).

Accurate sequencing and integration of content also improves with age. Preschoolers tend to recall isolated events rather than focusing on plot. By the age of about 7, younger children have developed preferences for plotted programs and continuity rather than segmentation of content. At this age, children better recall such content, although the task can still be difficult for them (Dorr, 1986).

In addition to developmental differences in comprehension, program complexity and the viewer's background and experience influence how children comprehend television programming (Collins, 1983). John Wright and Aletha Huston (Huston & Wright, 1983; Wright & Huston, 1983) have been prolific in documenting program complexity by formal features and their effects on children's attention to and comprehension of television content. Generally, Huston and Wright and others have reported that although formal features influence all children's attention to television, developmental differences in their effects are not great. In terms of comprehension, formal features seem to function as an aid in children's selection of content to process and thereby also as an aid to comprehension. Younger children do comprehend television content better when the content is accompanied by salient features than when it is not. Older children's comprehension is less closely associated with feature salience, but developmental differences are overall relatively small.

Recent examples of research on the influence of children's background and experience on their comprehension of television are less numerous. Collins and Wellman (1982) summarize results of several studies to suggest that children demonstrate a "memory bias" that may reflect that they attend more closely to familiar content. Second graders who were middle or working class understood television characters and settings similar to their own background better than children from the opposite social class. This was not true of fifth and eighth graders, suggesting younger children's poorer comprehension of television may reflect their more limited familiarity with and schemata for roles, characters, and settings typical in television programs.

Other Cognitive Activities

In an interesting departure from other work on children's attention to and comprehension of television, Hawkins and Pingree (1986) propose an elaboration of the meaning of cognitive "activity" as it applies to children's use and understanding of television. They break down cognitive activities during viewing into a number of components used during processing television, based primarily on studies of children's comprehension of television. These activities include segmenting, focusing, reading formal features, using time, drawing inferences, drawing on other knowledge, evaluating information, making connections, and stimulation. Additionally, cognitive activity includes the amount of mental effort applied to processing.

Only a handful of relevant studies, at most, appear to exist in each of the more novel areas reviewed by Hawkins and Pingree (1986). To our knowledge, no more recent review of research using Hawkins and Pingree's conceptualization of cognitive activities and effort has been published. We are left with a tantalizing but incomplete look at age trends in a range of cognitive activities children bring to bear on their television viewing experience. The more complex view of children's cognitive processes vis-à-vis television in future research over the traditional focus on attention and comprehension per se seems desirable.

Sense-Making Activities

To this point, only developmental differences in the specific cognitive processes children use in television viewing have been discussed. Research on children and television has also focused on more global sense-making activities in which children engage while watching TV that may subsume a number of more specific cognitive processes. These activities suggest children transact with both the form and content particular to television in meaningful ways. As examples, we will consider the informative function of formal features, children's realism judgments about family content on television, and children's distinctions between program and commercial television content.

Informative Function of Formal Features

Huston and Wright (1983) reviewed functions of formal features that children may use to make sense of the auditory and visual images flowing from the television set. Use of these functions is thought to be more dependent on learning and experience than responses to the perceptual qualities of TV. Informative formal features include visual and auditory techniques such as fades and dissolves or musical themes at a program's end that structure content flow; forms such as animation or recurrent formats signifying or suggesting content; and modes of representation of content such as visual pictorial, visual symbolic, auditory verbal, and auditory nonverbal. Hawkins and Pingree (1986) suggest that informative formal features signify some of the meaning derived from television programming and require a cognitive activity that might be called "reading." Although Wright and Huston and their colleagues have demonstrated developmental differences in children's understanding of the informative nature of formal features, more research is needed on how children learn that formal features are potentially meaningful and then learn meaning for individual or combinations of features.

Realism Judgments

Dorr, Kovaric, and Doubleday (1990) studied developmental differences in the perceived social realism of families featured in television series. As part of this study, the substantial literature on children's reality judgments about television was reviewed. Between preschool and early elementary school, children learn that what they see on television is not likely to be real. Most television programs are portrayals of people, places, and events that only appear to be real (Dorr, 1983; Fernie, 1981; Kelly, 1981; Klapper, 1981).

Studies of age-related changes in children's perceptions about television's realism (i.e., its plausibility or representativeness) are not as conclusive. Some studies of 5- to 16-year-olds report weak developmental decreases in realism judgments about television (Brown, Austin, & Roberts, 1988; Fernie, 1981; Greenberg, Ku, & Li, 1989;

Pingree, 1978) and no developmental differences in realism judgments (Greenberg & Reeves, 1976; Hawkins, 1977; Klapper, 1981; Morison, Kelly, & Gardner, 1981). There was also a developmental increase found in very young children's reality perceptions of television content (Klapper, 1981). Presumably the different television content being judged across studies affected the pattern of results.

In their research, Dorr et al. (1990) attempted to go beyond existing work in representing the cognitive complexity of children's sense-making activities involved in realism judgments, in this case regarding television families. Children from a wide age range—6 to 16 years—judged the realism of television families based on content variations of family structure (more or less traditional) and content domain (family feelings, actions, demographics, and general realism). The study also controlled content domain in terms of which television families and which family characteristics children would consider when making realism judgments. Two other factors controlled for were children's familiarity with the content (family series) they rated and the realism criterion (probability in everyday life) used.

Findings suggested that children of different ages judged and compared categories of content differently. Also, children from 6 to 16 felt that roughly half of all real-life U.S. families are like those in the family series they watch most often. The most realistic content perceived was how the television families handled their emotions. If perceived realism mediates between television exposure and social effects, these findings suggest television families may be an important source of social learning for children and that children's realism judgments about social content on television warrant further study.

Distinguishing Program and Commercial Content

Children are exposed to television commercials from a relatively early age. Children's attention to and comprehension of commercial content has been extensively studied, particularly from about the mid-1970s to the mid-1980s. Ellen Wartella's (1980) review of children's responses to television advertising remains a comprehensive source of information about developmental changes in children's attention to and comprehension of television commercials.

From 2 years of age on, children are exposed to about 3 hours of television commercials each week. In naturalistic environments, attention to commercials is high at very early ages and then decreases among older children. Numerous commercial production factors affect attention (Wartella, 1980).

In 1974, the Federal Communications Commission (FCC) acknowledged in a report based on research studies and policy deliberations that young children have difficulties in distinguishing between programs and commercials (Wartella, 1980). The studies had shown somewhat contradictory findings about whether or not preschoolers and younger children make an attention shift to the television at the onset of a commercial, depending on the setting of the study, the order of the commercial in a cluster of commercials children were shown, and the observers used. Children older than 8 or 9 were reported to shift away from the television set or tune out at a commercial onset. Other kinds of evidence, such as recognition of commercial versus program characters and separators between commercials and programs, suggested 4- and 5-year-olds can perceive program and commercial differences (Wartella, 1980), and that by 6 to 8 years of age, children can differentiate commercials from programs more often than not (Dorr, 1986).

Wartella (1980) asserts that age is the major variable mediating children's cognitive processing of commercial content. There are generally few gender differences in recall of advertisements, except some slight evidence for gender differences in memory of sex-linked cues in commercials (e.g., girls remembering commercials with female race car drivers better than boys). Also, only modest ethnic differences in recall of commercials have been reported, and these may have been due to disproportionate representation of one ethnic group among the youngest age group studied. However, African-American children and those from lower social classes may accept advertising claims more readily than European-American, middle-class children.

In terms of age differences, younger children generally pay more attention to commercials and are more heavily affected by various production factors than older children. Younger relative to older children also have higher trust in advertising and lower recall and understanding of its messages. Dorr (1986), in a more recent review of the literature on children's understanding of commercials, provides some additional age trends. Somewhere between the ages of 7 and 9 children understand the persuasive intent of television advertising. Common persuasive techniques are not understood until near adolescence; by adolescence children have at their disposal more of the cognitive tools necessary to help them distinguish program and commercial content, evaluate commercial messages, and take charge of the influence commercials will have on their consumer behavior.

Summary

Given the various findings from the research literature on children's cognitive activities involving television, what can we expect children of different ages to bring to their television viewing experiences, cognitively speaking? Following are descriptions of children as they are typically grouped by age by those television researchers interested in cognitive developmental processes: preschoolers (2-5 years), young children (6-8 years), and older children (9-12 years).

Preschoolers

During the preschool years, children show dramatic increases in visual attention to television, driven presumably by increases in comprehension of television content and form, though not yet well-developed story schemata. Between 3 and 5 years there are no significant differences in children's distractibility from television. Comprehension studies show that preschoolers retain relatively little central content and gradually increase their recall of incidental content from dramatic television programs. Children in this age group rarely or inaccurately infer missing content and do not infer relations among scenes well. Preschoolers typically recall isolated events rather than plots and prefer magazine formats to plotted programs. Their representations of dramatic programs are incomplete and disorganized; they retain more stereotypical information and make recognition errors in the direction of greater stereotypicality than older children. A greater proportion of common knowledge scripts are also represented in preschoolers' spontaneously recalled plot events than for older children.

For preschoolers, comprehension is better when content is accompanied by salient formal features, and they can already assign meaning to some forms particular to television. Children of this age are learning what's on television is generally not real. Attention to commercial content is high for preschoolers when viewed in naturalistic environments. Preschoolers' attention typically shifts toward the television set at the onset of a commercial and 4- to 5-year-olds can usually perceive the difference between programs and commercials. At this young age, children are more heavily affected by various production factors, have higher trust in commercials, and lower recall and understanding of commercial messages than older children.

Younger Children

Children's attention to television continues to increase during this period as gains are made in comprehension skills. Five- to 7-year-olds' attention is better with narration due to their interdependence on audio and visual channels. Presumably the audio helps younger children monitor programming for attention-worthy content. Comprehension and retention of central content is still not great for this age group; recall of incidental content continues to increase. Inferences about missing content begin to improve as do inferences about the relationships among scenes. Story schemata are not well developed until age 7 or 8. Younger children like plotted programs and continuity not segmentation of content and have better recall of this content than preschoolers.

Younger children are similar to preschoolers in their increased comprehension of television content when it is accompanied by salient formal features. There is greater understanding of the meaning of some formal features among younger children than preschoolers. Judgments of the social realism of television may begin to decrease among younger children, depending on the content judged, familiarity with the content, and the realism criterion. Attention to commercials remains high in naturalistic settings with attention shifts generally to the television at the onset of advertisements. Six- to 8-year-olds can differentiate commercials from programs more often than not. They are still heavily influenced by various production factors, have higher trust, lower recall, and lower understanding of commercial messages than older children. By 7 to 9 years, though, younger children begin understanding the persuasive intent in television advertising.

Older Children

Attention to television begins to level off among this group after about 10 years of age and continues to decline into adulthood. Older children also evidence the capacity to process and monitor the audio and video channels more independently than preschoolers and younger children for attention-worthy content. Eight- to 14-year-olds show improvement in the comprehension and recall of central content and decreases in recall of incidental content. Older children's story schemata are better developed, and they do better at inferring missing content and relations between scenes than preschoolers and younger children. Older children have more complete and more organized representations of dramatic programs. Less stereotypical information is retained or evident in recognition errors, and common knowledge scripts are not as likely to be spontaneously recalled as plot events as they are for preschoolers and younger children.

Older children's comprehension of television content is less closely associated with feature salience, although overall developmental differences among the three age groups in this area is not great. Social realism judgments of content may continue to decrease for older children depending on factors of content judged, familiarity of content, and realism criterion used. Their attention to commercials starts to decrease in naturalistic environments, and they generally shift away from the television or tune out at the onset of a commercial. Children in this age group readily perceive differences between programs and commercials, are less affected by production factors, have lower trust, and better recall and understanding of commercial messages. Older children also understand persuasive intent, and near adolescence, common persuasive techniques.

Implications for Television Effects

Television viewing is not a one-way experience for children. Social effects of television viewing are not merely a result of the television content on the screen. Children bring various cognitive skills and abilities to the television viewing experience at different ages that will influence what they attend to, perceive, and understand of what they have viewed. In this way, a child's cognitive activities act as a filter and mediator between exposure to television content and its effects.

The previous sketches of young viewers suggest that children, especially preschoolers and young children, are indeed a "special audience" for the fascinating medium that is television (Dorr, 1986). Preschoolers and young children attend more to television than older children, comprehend less of truly central and more of incident content, and have difficulty making inferences about content. Knowledge of the informative meaning of formal features is not complete. These youngest viewers have difficulty representing television content and are likely to "fill in" their incomplete representations with stereotypes and familiar scripts taken from their more limited general knowledge of television and the world. They are more likely to believe in the reality or realism of television content on television. They are also less aware that some content is intended to sell them toys and breakfast cereal, rather than entertain or inform them. Older children do better than preschoolers and younger children in all of these areas, but they are still not processing and understanding what they view on television in the same way adults do.

It is this interesting discrepancy between adult and child viewers of television, in terms of how differently they process and understand television content, that creates implications for television's influence on children. Children's greater attention to television, and their less complete and more distorted understanding of what they view, suggest two possible outcomes. Children, particularly preschoolers and younger children, may miss some of what is good about television and be more vulnerable to the influence of what is not. Continued research on children's cognitive activities involving television and the application of these results by television producers, parents, and educators alike could enhance the more positive role of television in children's lives.

References

Alvarez, M., Huston, A., Wright, J., & Kerkman, D. (1988). Gender differences in visual attention to television form and content. *Journal of Applied Developmental Psychology, 9*, 459-475.

Alwitt, L., Anderson, D. R., Lorch, E., & Levin, S. (1980). Preschool children's visual attention to television. *Human Communication Research, 7*, 52-67.

Anderson, D. R., Alwitt, L., Lorch, E. P., & Levin, S. (1979). Watching children watch television. In G. Hale & M. Lewis (Eds.), *Attention and cognitive development* (pp. 331-361). New York: Academic Press.

Anderson, D. R., Choi, H. P., & Lorch, E. P. (1987). Attentional inertia reduces distractibility during young children's TV viewing. *Child Development, 58,* 798-806.

Anderson, D. R., & Lorch, E. (1983). Looking at television: Action or reaction? In J. Bryant & D. R. Anderson (Eds.), *Children's understanding of television: Research on attention and comprehension* (pp. 1-33). New York: Academic Press.

Anderson, D. R., Lorch, E., Field, D., Collins, P., & Nathan, J. (1986). Television viewing at home: Age trends in visual attention and time with TV. *Child Development, 57,* 1024-1033.

Anderson, D. R., Lorch, E., Field, D., & Sanders, J. (1981). The effects of TV program comprehensibility on preschool children's visual attention to television. *Child Development, 52,* 151-157.

Brown, B. M., Austin, E. W., & Roberts, D. F. (1988, May-June). *"Real families" versus "television families": Children's perceptions of realism in* The Cosby Show. Paper presented at the International Communication Association Convention, New Orleans.

Carew, J. (1980). Experience and the development of intelligence in young children at home and in day care. *Monographs of the Society for Research in Child Development, 45* (6-7, Serial No. 187).

Collins, W. A. (1983). Interpretation and inference in children's television viewing. In J. Bryant & D. R. Anderson (Eds.), *Children's understanding of television* (pp. 125-150). New York: Academic Press.

Collins, W. A., & Wellman, H. (1982). Social scripts and developmental patterns in comprehension of televised narratives. *Communication Research, 9,* 380-398.

Dorr, A. (1980). When I was a child, I thought as a child. In S. B. Withey & R. P. Abeles (Eds.), *Television and social behavior: Beyond violence and children* (pp. 191-230). Hillsdale, NJ: Lawrence Erlbaum.

Dorr, A. (1983). No shortcuts to judging reality. In J. Bryant & D. R. Anderson (Eds.), *Children's understanding of television: Research on attention and comprehension* (pp. 199-220). New York: Academic Press.

Dorr, A. (1986). *Television and children: A special medium for a special audience.* Beverly Hills, CA: Sage.

Dorr, A., Kovaric, P., & Doubleday, C. (1990). Age and content influences on children's perceptions of the realism of television families. *Journal of Broadcasting and Electronic Media, 34,* 377-397.

Doubleday, C., Kovaric, K., & Dorr, A. (in press). Theoretical models of television's role in learning about emotional expression and behavior. In A. Dorr (Ed.), *Emotions and television.* Hillsdale, NJ: Lawrence Erlbaum.

Fernie, D. E. (1981). Ordinary and extraordinary people: Children's understanding of television and real life models. In H. Kelly & H. Gardner (Eds.), *Viewing children through television* (pp. 47-58). San Francisco: Jossey-Bass.

Greenberg, B. S., Ku, L., & Li, H. (1989, June). *Young people and their orientation to the mass media: An international study* (Study No. 2: United States). Unpublished manuscript, Michigan State University, Department of Telecommunication, East Lansing.

Greenberg, B. S., & Reeves, B. (1976). Children and the perceived reality of television. *Journal of Social Issues, 32,* 86-97.

Hawkins, R. (1977). The dimensional structure of children's perceptions of television reality. *Communication Research, 4,* 299-320.

Hawkins, R., & Pingree, S. (1986). Activity in the effects of television and children. In J. Bryant & D. Zillman (Eds.), *Perspectives on media effects* (pp. 233-250). Hillsdale, NJ: Lawrence Erlbaum.

Huston, A., & Wright, J. (1983). Children's processing of television: The informative functions of formal features. In J. Bryant & D. R. Anderson (Eds.), *Children's understanding of television: Research on attention and comprehension* (pp. 35-68). New York: Academic Press.

Kelly, H. (1981). Reasoning about realities: Children's evaluations of television and books. In H. Kelly & H. Gardner (Eds.), *Viewing children through television* (pp. 59-72). San Francisco: Jossey-Bass.

Klapper, H. L. (1981). Children's perceptions of the realism of televised fiction: New wine in old bottles. In J. F. Esserman (Ed.), *Television advertising and children: Issues, research and findings* (pp. 55-82). New York: Child Research Service.

Meadowcroft, J., & Reeves, B. (1989). Influence of story schema development on children's attention to television. *Communication Research, 16,* 352-374.

Morison, P., Kelly, H., & Gardner, H. (1981). Reasoning about the realities on television: A developmental study. *Journal of Broadcasting and Electronic Media, 23,* 453-463.

Noble, G. (1975). *Children in front of the small screen.* Beverly Hills, CA: Sage.

Pearl, D., Bouthilet, L., & Lazar, J. (Eds.). (1982). *Television and behavior: Ten years of scientific progress and implications for the eighties* (Vols. 1 & 2). Washington, DC: U.S. Government Printing Office.

Pingree, S. (1978). The effects of nonsexist television commercials and perceptions of reality on children's attitudes about women. *Psychology of Women Quarterly, 2,* 262-277.

Rolandelli, D., Wright, J., Huston, A., & Eakins, D. (1991). Children's auditory and visual processing of narrated and nonnarrated television programming. *Journal of Experimental Child Psychology, 51,* 90-122.

Rubinstein, E. (1983). Television and behavior: Research conclusions of the 1982 NIMH report and their policy implications. *American Psychologist, 38,* 820-825.

U.S. Surgeon General's Scientific Advisory Committee on Television and Social Behavior. (1972). *Television and growing up: The impact of televised violence* (Report to the Surgeon General, U.S. Public Health Service). Washington, DC: U.S. Government Printing Office.

Wartella, E. (1980). Individual differences in children's responses to television advertising. In E. Palmer & A. Dorr (Eds.), *Children and the faces of television: Teaching, violence, selling* (pp. 307-322). New York: Academic Press.

Wright, J., & Huston, A. (1983). A matter of form: Potentials of television for young viewers. *American Psychologist, 38,* 835-843.

3. From Television Forms to Genre Schemata

Children's Perceptions of Television Reality

MARGUERITE FITCH

ALETHA C. HUSTON

JOHN C. WRIGHT

By now it is accepted that television is a medium in which meaning is conveyed by both its content and its form. The assertions of critics notwithstanding (Postman, 1979; Winn, 1977), it is also well established that children are active processors of the medium, using both content and form to interpret television's messages (Hawkins & Pingree, 1986; Huston & Wright, 1989). Early television research focused on content, particularly violence, stereotypes, and advertising. The next wave of research focused on the forms of television and their effects on attention, comprehension, and behavior. Typically, content and form have been analyzed in the laboratory as if they were independent aspects of television messages that had separate effects on viewers. It is clear, however, that viewers do not experience television in this way. Form and content are necessarily related and integrated. In fact, specific instructions must be given to viewers, especially children, to get them to focus on forms to the exclusion of content (Huston, Greer, Wright, Welch, & Ross, 1984). Thus, we have shifted from a theoretical approach in which we examined the cumulative effects of forms independently of content to a more

---

AUTHORS' NOTE: We are grateful to Denise Neapolitan for her comments on an earlier draft of this manuscript. The research reported was supported by the grant MH 44311 from the National Institute of Mental Health.

contextual approach that takes into account the whole television stimulus. We propose that certain formal features have come to be associated with certain types of content in ways that activate schemata for specific program genres. These genre schemata are how children organize the world of TV; they establish expectations concerning the processing demands required, the informative or entertainment value, and the reality status of programs. Perceived reality, in particular, has been hypothesized as an important mediator of television effects (Dorr, Kovaric, & Doubleday, 1989; Feshbach, 1972; Hawkins, 1977); thus, it has been a major focus for research.

Throughout this chapter we will examine support for the theory that children develop and use schemata about program genres to guide them in organizing and processing their television experience. We begin with a definition of television forms. Next we evaluate the research on forms, present an argument for reuniting form and content, and describe our conceptualization of children's schematic understanding of television. Finally, we turn to questions concerning the relationship between television forms and reality, and propose some directions for future research in this area.

What Are Television Forms?

The forms of television function as its syntax. Just as the syntax of a language conveys meaning through the structure and arrangement of words, which are the content of language, so television forms convey the meaning of television content by serving as markers of transitions in programs and signals of attention-worthy content. Television forms are specific visual and auditory production techniques, called *formal features*. Visual formal features include cuts, pans, zooms, dissolves, fades, wipes, and visual special effects, whereas auditory formal features include types of speech (adult, child, male, female), voice characterizations (peculiar voices, nonhuman characters), sound effects, music, and singing. On a molar level, forms also include program attributes such as action (rate of physical motion of characters through space), pace (rate of scene and character changes), and variability (number of different scenes and characters). Readers who are interested in the theoretical issues, details of studies, and interpretations of research on television forms should refer to our reviews (Huston & Wright, 1983, 1989; Wright & Huston, 1981).

Evaluation of Research on TV Forms

As we have reviewed our research on television forms, we have reconsidered some of our original conceptions about the independent influence of forms on attention, comprehension, and behavior. Form has been separated from content with mixed success. Moreover, the effects of television forms on comprehension and behavior cannot be consistently attributed to the attention given to perceptually salient features. In fact, comprehension appears to guide attention as much as it is a function of it (Anderson, Lorch, Field, & Sanders, 1981; Wright & Huston, 1981).

Consider the following evidence. In studies that crossed action with violence, attention was greater for high action than for high violence, but interactions between violent content and form (Huston-Stein, Fox, Greer, Watkins, & Whitaker, 1981) or violent content and toy cues (Potts, Huston, & Wright, 1986) accounted for greater effects on social behavior. In another study, visual attention was found to be greater for high violence than for low violence, and girls attended more to low action than high action (Alvarez, Huston, Wright, & Kerkman, 1988). Interactions with content were also found in a study on children's interpretation of instant replays (Rice, Huston, & Wright, 1986). By age 6 or 7, children began to interpret instant replays as television events rather than real-life events for baseball segments (i.e., sports), but not for segments showing phone calls (i.e., drama). Even third graders did not identify instant replays of phone calls unless they were accompanied by visual markers, though they consistently identified instant replays in baseball segments regardless of the presence of markers.

Indeed, we predicted interactions between form and content in our study of the effects of pace (high versus low) and continuity (story versus magazine format) on children's attention and comprehension (Wright et al., 1984). Attention and comprehension were greater for high-continuity, story formats than for low-continuity, magazine formats for both younger and older children. The only condition in which attention was greater to high-paced programs was for younger children who watched magazine formats. Older children's comprehension was equal for low-paced and story-format programs. Younger children's comprehension was aided by both low pace and story format, and was best for the combined condition. It was at this point that our research agenda began to shift from an emphasis on the independent influence of formal features to a consideration of schema theory as a framework for understanding children's processing of television.

Schema Theory as a Framework

Schema theory is based on the assumption that people use the regularities of their experience actively to construct knowledge and expectations about people, places, objects, and events. According to Fiske and Taylor (1984), a schema can be defined as "a cognitive structure that represents organized knowledge about a given concept or type of stimulus" (p. 140). A schema includes both the attributes of a concept and the relations among attributes. Schemata have been proposed as early organizers of children's knowledge about objects and spatial configurations (e.g., Mandler, 1983). Knowledge about social roles, groups, and events has been conceptualized as social schemata (e.g., Bem, 1981; Fiske & Taylor, 1984; Nelson, 1981). Schema theory has been used to explain how children understand the temporal and logical connections in television stories (Collins, 1982) and social portrayals on television (Collins, 1983).

We have found schema theory useful as a framework for conceptualizing how children organize the world of television. Through their many hours of viewing, children gradually learn to discriminate among different types of television programs and genres. One of the earliest discriminations they make is about the reality of the program. Does it show real people and events that actually happened, or does it show actors and stories that are scripted and rehearsed? How true to life is it? How believable are the portrayals of people and events?

We hypothesize that formal features serve as cues to the reality status of programs, and that children begin to classify television programs based on perceived reality. For example, very young children learn that animation signals that a program is not real, but they often believe that the rest of television is real. As their experience with the medium increases and they begin to associate particular forms with content in various programs, children develop schemata about television genres. A fundamental attribute of these genre schemata is reality. Thus, we propose that children organize the world of television into genres based on superordinate schemata about television reality. Next we turn to the topic of how these schemata about television reality develop and how they affect child viewers.

Perceptions of Television Reality

What Is Real on Television?

Many researchers agree that concepts of television reality are multidimensional (Dorr, 1983; Hawkins, 1977; Potter, 1988; Wright, Huston, Reitz, & Piemyat, 1992). At one level are questions concerning *factuality*: Are the people and events shown "real" outside the world of TV? That is, are these real people representing themselves or are they actors? Did the events actually happen in real life or were they scripted and rehearsed? Hawkins (1977) describes this dimension as a belief in television as a "magic window" on life. At another level are questions concerning *social realism*: Are the people, places and events similar to real life? Are they believable? Are they plausible? Related to social realism is utility: Can I learn something from the people, events or information shown that will be useful?

What Do Children Understand About Reality on TV?

Factuality

Children's concepts about reality begin in the preschool years with discriminations between the way objects appear and the way they really are (Flavell, 1986). Interviews with 2- to 3-year-olds suggest that they do not understand the representational nature of televised images. For example, when an egg broke on television, they attempted to clean it up (Jaglom & Gardner, 1981), and they said that a bowl of popcorn shown on television would spill if the TV were turned upside down (Flavell, Flavell, Green, & Korfmacher, 1990).

By age 4, children have mastered the distinction between real objects and televised images, and they begin to judge reality according to whether the images represent individuals and objects that are physically real outside the television world. For instance, they consider human actors "real," but cartoon characters "unreal" (Dorr, 1983; Jaglom & Gardner, 1981). Children understand that news is factual earlier than they understand that entertainment TV is fictional (Condry & Freund, 1988; Huston, Wright, Svoboda, Truglio, & Fitch, 1992; Wright, Huston, Truglio et al., 1992). Between the ages of 6 and 11, children's correct judgments about factuality increase (Condry & Freund, 1988; Dorr, 1983; Hawkins, 1977; Huston, Wright, Svoboda et al., 1992; Morison, Kelly, & Gardner, 1981; Wright, Huston, Reitz et al., 1992; Wright, Huston, Truglio et al., 1992). For instance, most 11-year-olds know that an actor who plays a police officer on TV is not a police officer in real life (Hawkins, 1977). By age 10 or so, children's factuality judgments are about as accurate as adults'. Thus, children's learning about factuality appears to have a cognitive basis and does not seem to be dependent on socialization or experience with television (Morison et al., 1981; Wright, Huston, Reitz et al., 1992).

Social Realism

Programs that are understood to be fictional may still be judged as socially realistic if they show people and events that appear similar to or useful for one's own life. Judgments about social realism appear to be more a function of motives for viewing (Huston, Wright, Svoboda et al., 1992; Potter, 1988) and television experience than they are of cognitive development. For example, beliefs that television is socially realistic are related to heavy viewing of entertainment programs such as cartoons, situation comedies, and violent action adventure programs (Dorr, Kovaric, & Doubleday, 1990; Greenberg & Reeves, 1976; Hawkins & Pingree, 1982; Huesmann, Lagerspetz, & Eron, 1984; Huston, Wright, Svoboda et al., 1992). Another investigation found that adolescents' beliefs in the realism of television portrayals of police was related to their viewing of police dramas (Elliot & Slater, 1980). Oddly enough, beliefs that TV is socially realistic are not consistently related to real-life experience (Elliot & Slater, 1980; Greenberg & Reeves, 1976; Rabin, Dorr, Kovaric, & Doubleday, 1991).

Developmental differences for social realism are less clear than for factuality. Though there is some evidence that judged realism declines with age (M. P. Winick & C. Winick, 1979), other studies have found no age differences (Dorr, 1983; Wright, Kunkel, Pinon, & Huston, 1989). It is more often true that age interacts with the content being judged. For example, the judgment of realism of violent programs (Greenberg & Reeves, 1976; Huesmann et al., 1984) decreased with age, whereas the judgment of realism of certain family comedies either increased with age (Dorr et al., 1990), or depended on the type of family structure portrayed (Dorr et al., 1989). Rabin and colleagues (1991) found that global realism of three family shows declined with age, but judgments about specific aspects of family life such as assets, homes, and the number and ethnicity of family members varied with the specific program being judged.

What Cues Are Used to Judge Reality?

To the extent that certain forms have come to be associated with certain types of content, formal features can signal the reality and genre of programs (Wright, Huston, Reitz et al., 1992). Live broadcasts are characterized by poor sound quality, disfluencies in speech due to lack of rehearsal, and the absence of background music and special effects (with the exception of instant replays, which are unique to sports programs). News and documentary programs feature narrators, sometimes as voice-overs during visual footage of the topic or event. After the space shuttle disaster, children identified the CNN logo, the lack of music, and the absence of close-ups of the astronauts' faces as cues that the televised explosion was real and not space fiction (Wright et al., 1989). By contrast, formal features in fictional television programs include close-ups of actors' faces, mood-setting music, studio-quality sound, and special effects. Situation comedies often have laugh tracks. Dramas feature adult voices and background music. Cartoons are animated, rapidly paced, and use many sound effects and peculiar voices.

Children's understanding of reality is based on judgments about the meanings of both content and form. During middle childhood, however, form replaces content as a cue for fact or fiction. Several studies have found that young children tend to name physically impossible events such as people flying as cues that a program is fictional, whereas older children increasingly named formal features (Dorr, 1983; Morison et al., 1981; Wright et al., 1989). Studies in our lab demonstrate that children's perceptions of TV reality can be successfully altered by manipulating formal features. Videotapes matched for content, but varying in formal features intended to denote real people and events were judged to be more factual and socially realistic than were the fictional tapes (Huston, Wright, Svoboda et al., 1992; Moghaddam, & Wright, 1992).

Judgments about social realism, on the other hand, are typically made on the basis of content. Even though a child may know that a program is scripted and rehearsed, the program may be judged as realistic if the characters and events are similar to those the child would likely encounter in real life. Studies confirm that judgments about social realism are tied closely to content (Dorr et al., 1989; Morison et al., 1981). Dorr (1983) also found that children mentioned genres and specific programs within genres as a basis for judging realism. News, sports, documentaries, and crime dramas were considered realistic, whereas cartoons were pretend.

Are Children More Influenced by TV If They Think It Is Real?

It is reasonable to expect that children will discount what they see in unrealistic television portrayals, and thus be less affected by it. Conversely, researchers have hypothesized and found with some consistency that television that is perceived as real has a greater effect than if is judged to be unreal. Experimental studies have found that "real" television violence stimulates greater aggression in adults (Berkowitz, 1984) and children (Feshbach, 1972; Sawin, 1981) than "fictional" violence. Children who saw commercials that portrayed women in nontraditional roles and were told that the commercials showed real people perceived the ads to be real and expressed less traditional attitudes toward women after viewing than subjects who saw traditional sex roles in commercials (Pingree, 1978). Donations of tokens to the Red Cross were higher from children who saw news footage of people who were victims of tornadoes and earthquakes than from those who saw footage from movies (Piemyat, 1992). In our lab, we have investigated the effects of perceived reality on social schemata, in particular the acquisition and elaboration of schemata about occupational roles. Recall our hypothesis expressed earlier in this chapter that children develop superordinate schemata for reality—TV fiction, TV fact, real world—or, more specifically for genres. Children may process and store social information from TV on the basis of these distinctions, that is, as "TV knowledge" or "real-world knowledge." Watkins (1988) found some support for this hypothesis: Children's stories as they might be shown on television were simpler, containing fewer elaborations and inferences about character actions, than stories that would be told in real life.

We designed two studies to examine the following questions: Do children separate TV and real-world knowledge for familiar occupations, and if so, how permeable are the boundaries between these knowledge sources? Do children acquire schemata for unfamiliar occupations from TV, and if so, do they rely more on factual than fictional programs?

To test the hypothesis that children form separate schemata for television and real life, we chose to ask about nurses and police officers because they are shown frequently on TV, observed by children in real life, and represent a balance of sex stereotypes (Wright, Huston, Truglio et al., 1992). Content analyses and commentaries from professionals in these occupations revealed consistent differences between TV portrayals and real-life roles. For example, nurses on TV are shown almost exclusively in hospitals, whereas in real life most nurses work in outpatient settings. Police officers on TV brandish guns frequently and are rarely shown on traffic duty, which is a major part of their jobs in real life. Second and fifth graders rated the factuality and social realism of television in general, rated reasons for viewing, and completed a checklist of programs they usually watched. In a two-by-two between-subjects design, they were asked to describe the job activities of nurses or police officers, on television or in real life. Next they were asked questions about the typicality of various job activities and their sources of knowledge about and aspirations for the assigned occupation.

Children of both ages clearly differentiated their schematic knowledge about the assigned occupation on TV and in real life. Most of their descriptions conformed to our hypotheses about expected directions based on the content analyses. That is, nurses and police officers on TV made more money, were more sex stereotyped and glamorous, and did not get hurt or sick as often as their real-life counterparts. Children believed nurses and police officers in real life worked harder and had more status and excitement in their jobs than as portrayed on TV.

Though children could separate TV information from real-life information about the occupations, perceived reality still influenced their real-world beliefs, particularly for older children. Fifth graders who believed that entertainment TV is factual and that portrayals of nurses and police officers on TV are socially realistic had more "TV-like" schemata for these jobs in real life. Children's schemata also predicted their aspirations to be nurses or police officers, especially for these jobs as they are shown on television. Moreover, aspirations were asserted most by heavy viewers of entertainment TV, who also perceived TV shows in general as factual (Wright, Huston, Truglio et al., 1992). Thus, it appears that though children form separate schemata for television and real life, these boundaries are not impermeable.

Our second study (Huston, Wright, Fitch, Wroblewski, & Piemyat, 1992) tested the hypothesis that children acquire schema information about occupations from TV and that they draw more of this information from factual than from fictional programs. To control for real-life sources of knowledge, we chose the occupations of caterer and film director because they are unfamiliar to children and balanced with respect to gender. As in the first study, second and fifth graders rated the factuality and social realism of TV in general, and completed a TV viewing checklist. In this within-subjects design, each child saw a drama and a documentary about a caterer or a film director. Stimuli were matched for occupational information portrayed, but used different formal features to convey factual or fictional status. Children's schemata about the occupational roles were measured by free response descriptions and ratings and recognition of typical job activities.

On two of these three measures, children drew more occupational information from the documentaries than from the dramas, though they cited elements from both programs more than content that was not shown at all. The reality manipulation was successful, as shown by the finding that children perceived the documentaries as more factual, socially realistic, and useful for learning than the dramas. As predicted, children who rated TV in general as unrealistic rated schema elements from the drama as less typical of real-life jobs than the documentary elements, and this difference was larger for fifth than for second graders (Huston, Wright, Fitch et al., 1992). Thus, children do acquire separate schemata for factual and fictional television, but even fictional TV can serve as a source of information about real-life occupations.

Concluding Remarks

In this chapter, we have proposed that children begin early to organize the world of TV. Reality status is a primary organizing principle. Initially, children probably believe all TV is real. At this point, their understanding of reality is primarily concerned with factuality—the relation of mediated TV content to the real world. This learning occurs as part of more general cognitive developmental changes involving representation, differentiating appearance from reality, and the like. Blanket assumptions about the reality of TV shift around age 3 or 4 when they learn that form cues, like animation, indicate that a program is not real. By age 5 or 6, they begin to identify co-occurring features of form and content that distinguish a grouping—usually a genre, sometimes a program. Once understanding of factuality is in place, evaluations of reality are based more on social realism—Is it true to life? Through middle childhood, children gradually develop concepts of program types based on more subtle form and content cues until more coherent genre schemata emerge (e.g., situation comedies, dramas, action adventure shows). These genre schemata in turn establish expectations about the processing demands required, the informative or entertainment value, and the reality status of programs.

Perceptions of television reality affect children's level of processing, comprehension, attitudes, and behavior. Children learn a lot about social reality from both factual and fictional television. When they have opportunities for real-world experience, they can differentiate, at least partly, the roles shown on TV from those in the real world. They also differentiate factual from fictional sources of information on TV. Our research suggests, however, that part of their schemata for real-world social roles is based on fiction as well as fact.

Future research should examine how individual differences in perceived reality interact with the television viewing context. There are good theoretical reasons to believe that children's differentiation between factual and fictional television is reduced under casual circumstances that require little involvement, like home viewing (Hawkins, 1977; Hawkins & Pingree, 1982). Given that children tend to model parents' use of the medium and program preferences (St. Peters, Fitch, Huston, Wright, & Eakins, 1991), research that simulates or actually examines home viewing conditions is an essential next step.

Finally, the "reality" viewers must judge is itself not static; new forms and genres challenge viewers to reevaluate reality criteria. A preliminary analysis of the formal features used in "reality programs" revealed that the distinction between fact and fiction in this genre is blurry (Neapolitan, 1992). Some programs use long segments of live footage with little music or voice-over, whereas others reenact crime scenes with dramatic music and special effects. At times, these reenactments are intercut with live footage. The popularity of "reality" programs is clear; viewers can watch a reenactment show every night of the week except Sunday. Given that they are two thirds the cost of a typical sitcom (Thomas & Litman, 1991), their proliferation is likely to continue. Clearly these new formats offer a continuing challenge for the further development of this line of research and for the comprehension of television by viewers of all ages.

References

Alvarez, M. M., Huston, A. C., Wright, J. C., & Kerkman, D. (1988). Gender differences in visual attention to television form and content. *Journal of Applied Developmental Psychology, 9,* 459-475.

Anderson, D. R., Lorch, E. P., Field, D. E., & Sanders, J. (1981). The effects of TV program comprehensibility on preschool children's visual attention to television. *Child Development, 52,* 151-157.

Bem, S. L. (1981). Gender schema theory: A cognitive account of sex-typing. *Psychological Review, 88,* 352-364.

Berkowitz, L. (1984). Some effects of thoughts on anti- and pro-social influences of media events: A cognitive neoassociation analysis. *Psychological Bulletin, 95,* 410-427.

Collins, W. A. (1982). Cognitive processing in television viewing. In D. Pearl, L. Bouthilet, & J. Lazar (Eds.), *Television and behavior: Ten years of scientific progress and implications for the eighties: Vol. 2. Technical Reviews* (pp. 9-23). Washington DC: National Institutes of Mental Health.

Collins, W. A. (1983). Social antecedents, cognitive processing, and comprehension of social portrayals on television. In E. T. Higgins, D. N. Ruble, & W. W. Hartup (Eds.), *Social cognition and social development* (pp. 110-133). Cambridge, UK: Cambridge University Press.

Condry, J. C., & Freund, S. (1989, April). *Discriminating real from make-believe: A developmental study.* Paper presented at the biennial meeting of the Society for Research in Child Development, Kansas City, MO.

Dorr, A. (1983). No shortcuts to judging reality. In J. Bryant & D. R. Anderson (Eds.), *Children's understanding of television: Research on attention and comprehension* (pp. 199-220). New York: Academic Press.

Dorr, A., Kovaric, P., & Doubleday, C. (1989, April). *Perceived realism of emotions, actions, and demographics in family series.* Paper presented at the biennial meeting of the Society for Research in Child Development, Kansas City, MO.

Dorr, A., Kovaric, P., & Doubleday, C. (1990). Age and content influences on children's perceptions of the realism of television families. *Journal of Broadcasting and Electronic Media, 34*, 377-397.

Elliot, W. R., & Slater, D. (1980). Exposure, experience and perceived TV reality for adolescents. *Journalism Quarterly, 57*, 409-414,431.

Feshbach, S. (1972). Reality and fantasy in filmed violence. In J. P. Murray, E. A. Rubinstein, & G. A. Comstock (Eds.), *Television and social behavior: Vol. 2. Television and social learning* (pp. 318-345). Washington, DC: U. S. Government Printing Office.

Fiske, S. T., & Taylor, S. E. (1984). *Social cognition*. Reading, MA: Addison-Wesley.

Flavell, J. (1986). The development of children's knowledge about the appearance-reality distinction. *American Psychologist, 41*, 418-425.

Flavell, J. H., Flavell, E. R., Green, F. L., & Korfmacher, J. E. (1990). Do young children think of television images as pictures or real objects? *Journal of Broadcasting and Electronic Media, 34*, 399-419.

Greenberg B. S., & Reeves, B. (1976). Children and the perceived reality of television. *Journal of Social Issues, 32*, 86-97.

Hawkins, R. P. (1977). The dimensional structure of children's perceptions of television reality. *Communication Research, 4*(3), 299-320.

Hawkins, R. P., & Pingree, S. (1982). Television's influence on social reality. In D. Pearl, L. Bouthilet, J. Lazar (Eds.), *Television and behavior: Ten years of scientific progress and implications for the eighties: Vol. 2. Technical reviews* (pp. 224-247). Washington, DC: U. S. Department of Health and Human Services.

Hawkins, R. P., & Pingree, S. (1986). Activity in the effects of television on children. In J. Bryant & D. Zillman (Eds.), *Perspectives on media effects* (pp. 233-250). Hillsdale, NJ: Lawrence Erlbaum.

Huesmann, L. R., Lagerspetz, K., & Eron, L. D. (1984). Intervening variables in the TV violence-aggression relation: Evidence from two countries. *Developmental Psychology, 20*, 746-775.

Huston, A. C., Greer, D., Wright, J. C., Welch, R., & Ross, R. (1984). Children's comprehension of televised formal features with masculine and feminine connotations. *Developmental Psychology, 20*(4), 707-716.

Huston, A. C., & Wright, J. C. (1983). Children's processing of television: The informative functions of formal features. In J. Bryant & D. R. Anderson (Eds.), *Children's understanding of TV: Research on attention and comprehension* (pp. 37-68). New York: Academic Press.

Huston, A. C., & Wright, J. C. (1989). The forms of television and the child viewer. In G. A. Comstock (Ed.), *Public Communication and Behavior* (Vol. 2, pp. 103-158). New York: Academic Press.

Huston, A. C., Wright, J. C., Fitch, M., Wroblewski, R., & Piemyat, S. (1992). *Effects of documentary and fictional television formats on children's acquisition of schemata for unfamiliar occupations*. Manuscript submitted for publication.

Huston, A. C., Wright, J. C., Svoboda, H. C., Truglio, R., & Fitch, M. (1992). *What children in middle childhood understand about the reality of news and fictional television*. Manuscript submitted for publication.

Huston-Stein, A., Fox, S., Greer, D., Watkins, B. A., & Whitaker, J. (1981). The effects of TV action and violence on children's social behavior. *Journal of Genetic Psychology, 138*, 183-191.

Jaglom, L. M., & Gardner, H. (1981). The preschool television viewer as anthropologist. In H. Kelly & H. Gardner (Eds.), *Viewing children through television* (pp. 9-30). San Francisco: Jossey-Bass.

Mandler, J. M. (1983). Representation. In J. H. Flavell & E. M. Markman (Eds.), P. H. Mussen (Series Ed.), *Handbook of child psychology: Vol. 3. Cognitive Development* (pp. 420-494). New York: John Wiley.

Moghaddam, M., & Wright, J. C. (1992). *Understanding television: The effects of fictional and factual portrayals on children's cognitive processing.* Paper presented at the annual meeting of the International Communication Association, Miami.

Morison, P., Kelly, H., & Gardner, H. (1981). Reasoning about the realities on television: A developmental study. *Journal of Broadcasting, 25*(3), 229-241.

Neapolitan, D. M. (1992). *A content analysis of "reality-based" programs.* Manuscript in progress, University of Kansas, Center for Research on the Influences of Television on Children.

Nelson, K. (1981). Social cognition in a script framework. In J. Flavell & L. Ross (Eds.), *Social cognitive development* (pp. 97-118). Cambridge, UK: Cambridge University Press.

Piemyat, S. (1992). *Children's emotional responses to real and fictional television and effects on their recall and prosocial behaviors.* Unpublished doctoral dissertation, University of Kansas.

Pingree, S. (1978). The effects of nonsexist television commercials and perceptions of reality on children's attitudes about women. *Psychology of Women Quarterly, 2*(3), 262-277.

Postman, N. (1979). *Teaching as a conserving activity.* New York: Delacourt.

Potter, W. J. (1988). Perceived reality in television effects research. *Journal of Broadcasting and Electronic Media, 32,* 23-41.

Potts, R., Huston, A. C., & Wright, J. C. (1986). The effects of television form and violent content on boys' attention and social behavior. *Journal of Experimental Child Psychology, 41,* 1-17.

Rabin, B. E., Dorr, A., Kovaric, P., & Doubleday, C. (1991). *Children's perceived realism of family television series.* Paper presented at the biennial meeting of the Society for Research in Child Development, Seattle, WA.

Rice, M. L., Huston, A. C., & Wright, J. C. (1986). Replays as repetitions: Young children's interpretation of television forms. *Journal of Applied Developmental Psychology, 7,* 61-76.

Sawin, D. (1981). The fantasy-reality distinction in TV violence. *Journal of Research in Personality, 15,* 323-330.

St. Peters, M., Fitch, M., Huston, A. C., Wright, J. C., & Eakins, D. J. (1991). Television and families: What do young children watch with their parents? *Child Development, 62*(6), 1409-1423.

Thomas, L., & Litman, B. R. (1991). Fox Broadcasting Company, why now? An economic study of the rise of the fourth broadcast "network." *Journal of Broadcasting and Electronic Media, 35*(2), 139-157.

Watkins, B. (1988). Children's representations of television and real life stories. *Communication Research, 15,* 159-184.

Winick, M. P., & Winick, C. (1979). *The television experience: What children see.* Beverly Hills, CA: Sage.

Winn, M. (1977). *The plug-in drug: Television, children, and the family.* New York: Viking.

Wright, J. C., & Huston, A. C. (1981). Children's understanding of the forms of television. In H. Kelly & H. Gardner (Eds.), *Viewing children through television* (pp. 73-88). San Francisco: Jossey-Bass.

Wright, J. C., Huston, A. C., Reitz, A. L., & Piemyat, S. (1992). *Young children's perceptions of television reality: Determinants and developmental differences.* Manuscript submitted for publication.

Wright, J. C., Huston, A. C., Ross, R P., Calvert, S. L., Rolandelli, D., Weeks, L. A., Raeissi, P., & Potts, R. (1984). Pace and continuity of television programs: Effects on children's attention and comprehension. *Developmental Psychology, 20,* 653-666.

Wright, J. C., Huston, A. C., Truglio, R., Fitch, M., Smith, E. D., & Piemyat, S. (1992). *Occupational portrayals on television: Children's role schemata, career aspirations, and perceptions of reality.* Manuscript submitted for publication.

Wright, J. C., Kunkel, D., Pinon, M., & Huston, A. C. (1989). Children's affective and cognitive reactions to televised coverage of the space shuttle disaster. *Journal of Communication, 39*(2), 27-45.

Carlsson-Paige & Levin, 1987-1988). In earlier times, television programs (such as *Sesame Street*) were developed before related commercial products; today, the product has increasingly come first.

In both host-selling and product-based programming, the program itself can be as potent (Bryant, 1985) or even more potent (Kunkel, 1984) than an explicit commercial in stimulating young children's desires for a product. Despite the enormous popularity of product-based programs such as *The Transformers* and *Teenage Mutant Ninja Turtles*, and the overwhelming market success of the featured toys, no published research currently exists on the psychological effects of these programs or of the toys themselves.

In addition to the effects of "program-length commercials" in selling toys, the featured toys themselves may have psychological effects that stem from their tie-in with television programs viewed by children. Because the toys featured in television programs are likely to be used by children in make-believe or imaginative play, and because imaginative play is an essential part of the growing process, we investigated the effects of these programs in this psychological domain.

Imagination can be defined as any form of representational activity that creates entities or events not found in the present or immediately preceding stimulus situation (Greenfield, Farrar, & Beagles-Roos, 1986). In terms of its significance for growth and development, imaginative play in the preschool period is, for example, positively related to creativity, reading, language comprehension, independence, and maturity in the elementary school years (Shmukler, 1983).

Television and Imagination

Given the significance of imaginative play in early childhood, there has been a great deal of concern about how television affects imagination in young viewers. Because television provides audiovisual images, one can hypothesize that television, rather than the child, will create the mental images that are the essence of imaginative play, thus supplanting the imaginal processes of the child. A number of studies have found television to have a negative effect on the imagination of children and adolescents (Greenfield & Beagles-Roos, 1988; Greenfield et al., 1986; Harrison & Williams, 1986; Meline, 1976; Meringoff et al., 1982; Peterson, Peterson, & Carroll, 1986; J. L. Singer & D. G. Singer, 1981, 1986); other studies have not (Murray,

4. The Program-Length Commercial

A Study of the Effects of Television/Toy Tie-Ins on Imaginative Play

PATRICIA MARKS GREENFIELD, EMILY

MABEL CHUNG, DEBORAH L

HOLLY KREIDER, MAURICE PAN

KRIS HOI

Television has become a major tool for marketing to child estimate is that children view more than 20,000 televis mercials annually (Adler et al., 1977). However, the use of t to market to children goes beyond commercials. Television themselves have become part of the marketing effort. For in host selling, the same characters that appear in a progran in adjacent commercials (Kunkel, 1988a).

The focus of the present research is a second, newer r using the TV program itself to market to children: prod programs. As part of the deregulation of the broadcast i the United States, in 1984 the Federal Communication Cc (FCC) lifted its prohibition against product-based progra it cynically termed "program-length commercials" (Kun Kunkel & Watkins, 1987). Since this repeal, the televisio advertisers, and toy manufacturers have joined forces tc flood of product-based cartoons aimed at children (B

SOURCE: "The Program-Length Commercial: A Study of the Effects of Tie-Ins on Imaginative Play" by P. M. Greenfield, E. Yut, M. Chung, D. La M. Pantoja, & K. Horsley, Winter 1990, *Psychology & Marketing*, 7(4), 237-
1990 by John Wiley & Sons, Inc. Reprinted with permission of John Wi

Kwiatek, & Clarke, 1982; Runco & Pezdek, 1984; J. L. Singer & D. G. Singer, 1976, 1981). Nevertheless, the majority of the research on television and imagination indicates a detrimental effect of the medium.

Possible Effects of Product-Based Programs and Program-Based Toys on the Development of Imagination

Critics of product-based programs such as Action for Children's Television and the American Academy of Pediatrics argue that these shows provide ready-made story lines for children to use in their make-believe play and therefore offer little motivation for them to think up their own creative ideas (Meyer, 1988). Studies comparing the effects of different media on imagination have shown that television not only elicits fewer creative responses but also elicits more recall-oriented responses than print or audiotape (Greenfield & Beagles-Roos, 1988; Greenfield et al., 1986; Kerns, 1981; Meline, 1976). Thus, past research indicates that it is the audiovisual medium, not the narrative form, that inhibits creative imagination.

Toys from product-based programs may also have an inhibitory effect on the imaginativeness of children's play because such toys could act as visual cues to the story lines and actions the children have just seen in the associated shows. Program-related toys could even serve as cues to recreate televised events seen in the more remote past. Work done by Hayes and Birnbaum (1980) suggests that preschool children tend to pay more attention to the visual aspects of television and ignore big chunks of the audio, thereby lending some support to this possibility.

In Piaget's (1962) scheme of representational development, delayed imitation is the earliest manifestation of imagination, appearing toward the end of the second year of life. With delayed imitation, the child mentally recreates an entity or action from a preceding situation. More creative forms of imaginal representation are added later to the child's repertoire. With development, there is also a movement toward symbolization that is increasingly independent of the immediate perceptual context (Fein, 1975; Ungerer, Zelazo, Kearsley, & O'Leary, 1981; Werner & Kaplan, 1963).

For all of these reasons, we expected product-based television and program-related toy products to stimulate the earlier, more imitative and context-dependent forms of imagination relative to the more creative and independent forms that develop later. This expectation was confirmed by the results of a pilot study. The same study also indicated that the combination of a product-based cartoon followed by cartoon-related toys might inhibit total imaginative output (i.e., imitative and creative imagination combined), in comparison with the same toys following a nonproduct-based cartoon.

Another possible outcome flows from Vygotsky's (1978) view that cultural tools stimulate cognitive development. A tool aids the developing child to carry out an emergent skill, thus preparing the way for later independent performance. Based on this view, televised narrative and thematically related toys may function as cultural tools that help the child to develop imaginative skills that can function independently at a later point in time.

Method

Design of the Study

To respond to the issues that have been raised, this study used an experimental pretest/posttest design with three randomly assigned groups. Based on Pulaski (1973), the pretest and posttest required the subjects to tell a story using one of two sets of toys: cartoon-related (Smurfs) or neutral (Trolls). In between the pretest and the post-test, subjects participated in one of two treatments: watching a cartoon (*Smurfs*) or engaging in a neutral activity (the game of connect-the-dots). Because an earlier study of children's imagination had already used radio in contrast to television (Greenfield & Beagles-Roos, 1988; Greenfield et al., 1986), it was decided to use a traditional children's game as the contrasting treatment in the present study.

The sequence of experiences in the three conditions can be summarized as follows:

Experimental Group—Smurf toys, Smurf cartoon, Smurf toys
Contrast Group 1—Smurf toys, dot game, Smurf toys
Contrast Group 2—Troll toys, Smurf cartoon, Troll toys.

Subjects

The subjects were 55 pairs of first- and second-grade children from an ethnically diverse public elementary school in Los Angeles.

All available pairs of children with sufficient language skills were used. Although grade level was not of direct interest for present purposes, it was added as an independent variable because of the importance of cognitive development to the growth of imagination.

The final sample consisted of 30 pairs of girls and 25 pairs of boys, 28 pairs of first graders and 27 pairs of second graders. Cell sizes for each combination of age and condition are shown in Table 4.2. (Table 4.2 is discussed more fully later.)

In terms of ethnicity, 12.8% of the children were classified as African American, 2.8% of the children were classified as Asian American, 11.9% as Hispanic, and 72.5% as White. A substantial minority of those classified as White were Iranian immigrants.

Materials

The toys were two sets of nonbendable toy figures 5 cm high. The Smurf set contained four identical Smurf figures without any props in hand. The Troll set also contained four identical figures resembling naked unisex children with long white hair. It was thought that the use of identical, unadorned figures in each set would maximize and equalize the opportunity for children to use their imaginations to transcend the stimuli in the case of each set of toys.

The product-related cartoon was a videotaped, 10-minute episode of *Smurfs Adventures* titled "Baby's Enchanted Didey." A VCR and television monitor were used to show the cartoon.

A worksheet for connect-the-dots contained a matrix of 100 dots equally spaced out in a 10 × 10 cm square area. Pencils or pens were provided by the experimenter to play the game.

A video camcorder with an auxiliary microphone was used to record pre- and posttest stories and the dot game.

A 7-item questionnaire was used to interview participants concerning their familiarity with the toys and the activity used in their condition.

Procedure

Pilot testing had determined that children were more relaxed and fluent when tested with another child, and so our unit of testing (and analysis) was the pair rather than the individual child. Pairs were formed randomly, but with the constraints that the children know each other and be of the same sex. In almost all cases, the former constraint was effected by pairing children within the same classroom. Because children usually play in same-sex groups, it was thought that they would feel more relaxed in same-sex than in mixed-sex dyads.

Testing began by presenting a set of four toys (either the Trolls or the Smurfs, depending on the condition) to each pair of children and asking them to tell a story using the toys. There was no time limit set for the stories.

After completing the pretest story, participants in the Experimental Group (cartoon plus cartoon-related toys) and Contrast Group 2 (cartoon plus neutral toys) viewed a 10-minute Smurf cartoon, whereas subjects in Contrast Group 1 (neutral activity [game] plus cartoon-related toys) played connect-the-dots, a paper-and-pencil game, for 10 minutes. Participants were taught how to play the game if they did not already know. However, they were not corrected if they subsequently broke the rules.

At the conclusion of the cartoon or the dot game, the participants were asked to tell another story using the same toys as in the pretest; this second story constituted the posttest.

At the end of the posttest, each child was interviewed alone to assess familiarity with the toys and activity used in his or her particular condition.

Conceptualization and Operationalization of Imagination

We began with the following conceptual definition of imagination that we had used in previous research (Greenfield & Beagles-Roos, 1988; Greenfield et al., 1987; Greenfield et al., 1986): Imagination is any form of representational activity that creates entities or events not found in the present or immediately preceding stimulus situation.

Although it was desirable to have a pretest, both as a baseline and to assess the impact of the program-related toys in and of themselves, it was not possible to assess the relationship of pretest stories to the immediately preceding stimulus situation, which varied from child to child and was not known to the experimenters. Therefore, we developed a general category of imaginative behavior, *transcendent imagination* (assessable on both pretest and posttest), with two subcategories, *creative imagination* and *imitative imagination* (assessable on posttest only).

Transcendent imagination was based on Pulaski's (1973) transcendence index: "the number of imaginary items supplied by the child, as opposed to what was already supplied in a given stimulus situation" (p. 85). Therefore, we assessed the extent to which the children's representations transcended the immediate stimulus situation, that is, the experimental toys. For example, if a child was playing with a Smurf toy and labeled it "Baby Smurf," this was not considered transcendent imagination. If, however, the Smurf was labeled as something else (e.g., "bunny rabbit"), it was coded as an instance of transcendent imagination. This is an instance of what researchers on the early development of symbolic play term "substitution symbols": using one object to substitute for or symbolize another (Ungerer et al., 1981). "Imaginary symbols" constitute verbally represented objects that have *no* object symbol or object referent in the present situation. The participants in our study often created imaginary symbols when they verbally created an entity that was not present, usually an object (e.g., "glasses") or place (e.g., "home"). In addition to "substitution symbols" and "imaginary symbols," children also received credit for transcendent imagination when they symbolically created actions, feelings, mental states, or character dialogue. On the pretest, all these instances were labeled *transcendent;* on the posttest, they would be divided into *creative* and *imitative* imagination.

To receive credit for *creative imagination,* the child had to transcend not only the immediate stimulus situation, as in transcendent imagination, but the immediately *preceding* situation as well. Creative imagination involved transcending the experimental treatment, either the Smurf cartoon or the dot game, depending upon experimental condition; therefore, it could be assessed only on the posttest. Thus, an instance of transcendent imagination was considered *creative* if it transcended not only the toys present in the immediate storytelling situation, but also went beyond events in the preceding cartoon or game. If, in contrast, a representation in the story was found in the earlier cartoon or game, it was considered *imitative imagination.* Thus, creative and imitative imagination, measured on the posttest only, constituted two mutually exclusive and all-inclusive categories of transcendent imagination.

Coding and Dependent Variables

Each pretest and posttest story was segmented into "propositions," usually the equivalent of a simple sentence or a single nonverbal action. Most propositions combined verbal and nonverbal information. Coding continued with the identification of toy- or story-related material, which was then coded into the following subcategories of transcendent imagination:

A *transcendent character* was any proper noun, identity, or role that used a toy or toys as a representation of something other than itself. For example, one pair of participants named two of the Smurfs after themselves. A character could also be an imaginary agent created through a verbal label not referring to a toy.

A *transcendent object or location* was any inanimate entity, usually an object or place labeled with a noun. "Jail," "boat," "forest," "mountain," and "bacon" were some examples used by our subjects.

A *transcendent physical activity* was any observable action, represented either through words or action. Walking, climbing, playing, drowning, flying, and going were some examples that appeared in the stories.

A *transcendent mental activity* was any unobservable deed performed by the mind (e.g., "think," "knew").

A *transcendent feeling or state* was any expression of emotion or condition of being. It included states of characters such as "bored" and "young," as well as states of inanimate entities such as "new" and "big" (applied to fire). (Most codings in this category were feelings and mental states, rather than physical states.)

Transcendent dialogue was coded when a participant spoke as a toy character, usually indicated through a change in voice.

As a summary measure for imaginative output, any proposition coded for any of the above transcendent elements was categorized as a *transcendent proposition.*

For purposes of data analysis, characters, physical activities, and objects/locations were considered opponents of *physical events;* these variables were grouped together in multiple analyses of variance. Similarly, mental activities, character dialogue, and feelings/states were considered components of *mental events,* which were also grouped together in separate multiple analyses of variance. On the posttest stories only, transcendent elements (characters, entities, physical activities, mental activities, and feelings/states) were divided into *creative* and *imitative*, depending on whether or not they had appeared in the preceding cartoon or videotaped dots game. Because of the essential creativity of language, it was hard to draw the line between dialogue that imitated the cartoon and creative dialogue. Therefore, transcendent dialogue was not subdivided into creative and imitative subcategories.

All data were coded from written transcripts of the videotaped data. After coding from a transcript, the videotape was viewed to correct any possible errors. Creativity coding, done only on the posttest, also took into account the preceding treatment condition; therefore, coders could not be blind to subjects' treatment condition.

In the case of the cartoon treatment, a transcript of the sequence of events and a list of featured entities in the Smurf cartoon were prepared in order to help assess whether transcendent elements in posttest stories were creative or imitative in relation to the preceding cartoon. For the dot game treatment, the videotape of the dot game of each pair was viewed to determine whether transcendent elements produced in posttest stories were creative or imitative in relation to what had transpired during the preceding game.

Detailed coding was based on the first 15 minutes of each story; almost all (94%) of the stories were 15 minutes or less. However, because the first pilot study had indicated that story length might be affected by the experimental conditions, the number of nonrepetitive propositions in the entire story was counted for all stories in their entirety; this variable was labeled *length.*

Reliability

Pilot data were used to develop coding categories, train coders, and assess intercoder reliability. For purposes of assessing reliability, the first of the four coders was considered the standard against which the other three were compared. The coders agreed upon segmenting propositions an average of 90.8% of the time. Given agreed-upon segmentation, content reliability was checked for all categories of transcendent, creative, and imitative imagination. Reliability for these categories averaged 94.7% agreement between coders. The various categories ranged from 83.9% agreement for dialogue to 100% agreement for imitative mental activity, imitative physical activity, and imitative entities.

Measures of Stimulus Familiarity

Data from the structured interviews were transformed into an 8-point scale of toy familiarity and a 4-point scale of cartoon or game familiarity. The individual scores of pair members were averaged to yield familiarity scores for each pair as a whole.

HYPOTHESES

H1: The imaginative stories of children who are shown an episode of a product-based cartoon and then given toys depicted in the cartoon will be less creative and more imitative than that of children who are shown the episode but given toys thematically unrelated to the program. (posttest prediction)

H2: The imaginative stories of children who are shown an episode of a product-based cartoon and then given toys depicted in the cartoon will be less creative and more imitative than that of children who use the same toys, but do not see a television program. (posttest prediction)

H3: Because of their past association with television shows, program-related toys alone (i.e., on the pretest) will stimulate a lesser quantity or quality of transcendent imagination. (pretest prediction)

Although not hypothesized in advance, the data analysis explored the following idea, based on Vygotsky's (1978) notion of the role of cultural tools in cognitive development: Product-based television and related toys could stimulate the creative imagination of younger children, helping them to move beyond delayed imitation, while inhibiting or supplanting the imagination of older children, already able to independently exercise their creative imagination.

Results

Pretest Imagination: Effect of Cartoon-Related Toys

To assess the effects of program-related toys per se on transcendent imagination, multivariate and univariate analyses of variance were carried out on pretest measures of transcendent imagination, using condition and grade as the independent variables. Contrary to H3, there were no significant main effects or interactions involving condition with respect to either individual imaginative components, overall quantity of transcendent imagination, or story length. In other words, scores on transcendent imagination were not substantially different whether a child told a story about Smurfs (cartoon-related toys) or about Trolls (neutral toys) on the pretest.

Although contrary to H3, the lack of significant differences between conditions on the pretest does establish that any group differences found on the posttest are a function of the differing experimental conditions and do not stem from sampling errors in group composition or systematic error as a function of the toy.

Pretest Imagination: Effect of Grade

Although no effect of condition appeared, the pretest analyses did reveal an age effect. A multivariate analysis of variance showed that there were significantly more *transcendent physical events* (transcendent characters, transcendent physical activities, and transcendent objects/places) created by second graders than by first graders (p=.021, Hotelling's multivariate test of significance). Although the multivariate tests were not significant for the effect of age on *transcendent mental events* (composed of transcendent mental activities, transcendent dialogue, and transcendent feelings/states), univariate tests of significance revealed that second graders created more mental activities ($F(1, 49)$=4.66, p=.036) and feelings than did first graders ($F(I, 49)$=4.50, p=.039). These developmental differences seemed to be mainly a function of the fact that the second graders produced stories that were, on the average, more than twice as long as those of first graders (means of 60 vs. 25 propositions). An analysis of variance indicated that the probability of this difference occurring by chance was .044 ($F(1, 49)$=4.28).

Posttest Imagination

The multiple analysis of variance for *creative physical events* (percentage creative characters, percentage creative physical activities, and percentage creative objects/locations) showed a significant effect for condition (p=.027, Hotelling's multivariate test), as well as a significant condition by grade effect (p=.008, Hotelling's multivariate test). (Percentage scores are based on the number of creative elements

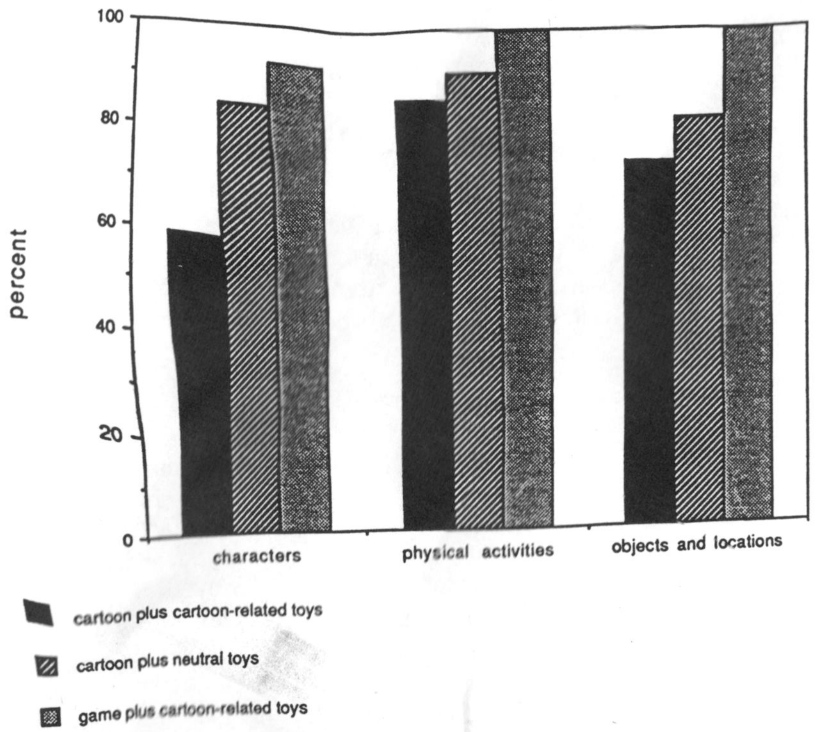

Figure 4.1. Percentage of Creative Elements in Imagined Physical Events Under Different Conditions

in a particular category divided by the total number of elements in that category.) The main effect is illustrated in Figure 4.1.

The graphs reveal a consistent pattern: The combination of product-based cartoon and cartoon-related toys results in the lowest proportions of creative imagination; the combination of cartoon plus neutral toys yields intermediate proportions of creative imagination; and the combination of game plus cartoon-related toys yields the highest proportions of creative imagination.

The univariate effects are significant for percentage of creatively imagined characters ($F(2, 42)=6.11$, $p=.005$) and percentage of creatively imagined objects and locations ($F(2, 42)=3.86$, $p=.029$); the univariate effect approaches significance for percentage of creatively imagined physical activities ($F(2, 42)=2.63$, $p=.084$). When toy famili-

Table 4.1 Percentage of Creative Elements in Imagined Physical Events Under Different Stimulus Conditions

	First Grade			*Second Grade*		
	Mean	*SD*	*N*[a]	*Mean*	*SD*	*N*[a]
Percentage creative characters						
Cartoon plus cartoon-related toys	30.00	42.82	7	85.36	23.68	8
Cartoon plus neutral toys	90.28	19.54	9	80.17	32.32	10
Game plus cartoon-related toys	100.00	0.00	6	87.50	35.36	8
Percentage creative physical activities						
Cartoon plus-cartoon-related toys	81.07	17.75	7	90.10	18.76	8
Cartoon plus neutral toys	97.89	3.65	9	85.98	28.71	10
Game plus cartoon-related toys	100.00	0.00	6	100.00	0.00	8
Percentage creative objects and locations						
Cartoon plus cartoon-related toys	78.57	19.25	7	69.75	35.15	8
Cartoon plus neutral toys	79.00	33.30	9	85.18	28.84	10
Game plus cartoon-related toys	100.00	0.00	6	100.00	0.00	8

NOTE: [a] Six pairs of first graders and one pair of second graders were lost to the analysis when they failed to produce even one element in a category, thus creating a zero denominator for the calculation of a percentage.

arity is statistically equated across conditions through analysis of covariance, the univariate effect for percentage creative physical activity also becomes statistically significant ($F(2, 41)=3.48, p=.040$). Post hoc *t*-tests found the percentage of creative characters in the Experimental Group (product-based cartoon plus cartoon-related toys) was significantly less than that in both the Contrast Groups ($t(32)=2.10$, $p=.022$; $t(27)=2.47$, $p=.010$, one-tailed tests). In addition, children produced a lower percentage of creative objects and locations when toys were combined with a thematically related program, than when the same toys were used in the absence of a TV program ($t(32)=1.92$, $p=.032$, one-tailed test). *This pattern of results confirms H1 and H2.*

The univariate analyses showed that the condition-by-age interaction is concentrated in the creative character variable ($F=6.59$, $p=.003$): The negative effect of product-based cartoon and program-related toys on the creation of imagined characters is extremely strong for first-grade children, but does not exist in the second grade (Table 4.1).

T-tests for differences between means indicated that for first-grade children, the combination of product-based cartoon and cartoon-based toy (Smurf toys, Smurf cartoon, Smurf toys) yielded

Table 4.2 Frequency of Elements in Transcendent Mental Events Under Different Stimulus Conditions

	First Grade			*Second Grade*		
	Mean	*SD*	*N*	*Mean*	*SD*	*N*
Mental activities						
Cartoon plus cartoon-related toys	0.78	1.39	9	2.22	1.99	9
Cartoon plus neutral toys	0.67	1.12	9	1.40	1.78	10
Game plus cartoon-related toys	0.30	0.68	10	2.38	2.72	8
Feelings or states						
Cartoon plus cartoon-related toys	4.44	9.13	9	5.11	7.46	9
Cartoon plus neutral toys	4.67	3.54	9	8.80	7.33	10
Game plus cartoon-related toys	1.80	1.81	10	15.63	18.54	8
Dialogue						
Cartoon plus cartoon-related toys	16.67	30.94	9	10.11	19.61	9
Cartoon plus neutral toys	9.00	17.13	9	35.00	35.67	10
Game plus cartoon-related toys	8.50	17.58	10	22.50	28.50	8

a significantly lower percentage of creative characters than game plus cartoon-based toy (Smurf toys, dot game, Smurf toys) ($t=3.98$, $p=.0025$, one-tailed test) or than cartoon plus neutral toys (Troll toys, Smurf cartoon, Troll toys) ($t=3.77$, $p=.0045$, one-tailed test).

To place these effects in context, it is important to note that condition had no effect on story output (length). The effects were specific to qualitative measures of imagination, particularly creative (vs. imitative) imagination. Although increased age brought increased imaginative production, the proportion of creative and noncreative output did not generally change between first and second grade.

For *mental events* (mental activities, character dialogue, and feelings/states), the multivariate analysis could not use percentage of creative elements because imagined mental activities and feelings were almost always creative, imagined mental activities were infrequent, and a coding distinction between creative and imitative dialogue could not be made.

Instead of percentage creativity scores, therefore, our multivariate analysis of variance used posttest frequencies of transcendent mental activities, feelings, and dialogue as the dependent variables for creative mental events. Hotelling's multivariate tests revealed a significant condition-by-grade interaction ($p=.033$), in the context of a significant main effect for grade ($p=.034$) (Table 4.2).

Although the creation of mental events increases between first and second grade, the effect of condition changes. For the first graders, the cartoon (with both thematic and neutral toys) is a positive stimulus for the creation of mental events; for second graders, in contrast, it tends to have an inhibiting effect. This pattern is strongest for feelings/states (Table 4.2). Although none of the univariate effects was significant, Table 4.2 indicates that the interaction works slightly differently for character dialogue: The combination of thematically related toys plus cartoon leads to the highest production of character dialogue for first graders, whereas this same combination leads to the lowest production of character dialogue for second graders. These results tend to confirm H1 and H2 for second graders only (although the pattern is most visible for dialogue and feelings/states, as Table 4.2 shows). The results also support the idea that television, particularly when combined with thematically related toys, functions as a cultural tool that aids the imaginative development of younger children.

Effects of Stimulus Familiarity

Whereas Smurf toys were not significantly more familiar than Troll toys, the Smurfs cartoon was significantly more familiar than the game of connect-the-dots ($F(2, 47)=14.89$, $p=.000$). However, there were almost no significant correlations of treatment (program or game) familiarity with any measure of creative imagination, either within individual conditions or across the whole sample. The only exception was a significant negative correlation of –.29 (one-tailed probability of .022) for the total sample between familiarity of treatment and percentage of creative characters. To see whether familiarity could account for the effect of condition on creative characters, a univariate analysis of covariance was carried out, this time using cartoon or game familiarity as a covariate. The interaction of condition and grade remained highly significant ($F(2, 41)=6.66$, $p=.003$) although the main effect of condition entered the borderline area ($F=3.11$, $p=.055$).

Although there were no significant differences in familiarity between Smurfs and Trolls, there was a significant positive correlation of .48 ($p=.037$, two-tailed test) between the familiarity of the Trolls (in the Troll condition) and number of transcendent mental activities on the posttest. Therefore, the mental events multiple analysis of variance was run again with toy familiarity as a covariate; the Hotelling's multivariate test remained significant (p=.045).

From these results, we can conclude that overall the experimental effects on creativity are not an artifact of differential familiarity of the stimuli in the different conditions.

Discussion

As predicted (H1 and H2), the combination of product-based television and thematically related toys is clearly most inhibiting to creative imagination, and conversely, most stimulating to imitative imagination. No predictions were made concerning the relative effects of television alone (cartoon plus neutral toy) versus program-based toys alone (game plus cartoon-related toys) on imagination. However, Figure 4.1 indicates that television alone is consistently more inhibiting to the imagination than are toys alone, although the differences are not statistically significant.

Conversely, a neutral activity with a TV-related toy consistently stimulates more creative responses than television plus a neutral toy. The following excerpt from a pair of children who played connect-the-dots and then told a story about the Smurfs may explain why. Their story does not reflect the preceding game, but instead reflects marked experiences (Bruner & Lucariello, 1989) in the life of Los Angeles children:

> Sometimes everybody visits in different houses. Sometimes they have a party at the house. Sometimes they, they go out and they buy some new clothes. Sometimes they go out and buy, um, bicycles to ride the, to ride, uh, to go faster to get a guy that stole their things. Sometimes they go fishing and they go bike riding at the ocean.

The contrast between this example and the more imitative stories told following the Smurfs cartoon suggests that images of characters and actions from a TV program partially supplant creative imaginal elements generated by the child's own experience. Although the cartoon in our study was prosocial in thematic content, the implication of the results is that antisocial TV models, such as violent behavior, will also be incorporated in children's imaginative play.

Thus, our results complement previous studies showing that television elicits more recall-oriented and fewer creative responses than other media (Greenfield & Beagles-Roos, 1988; Greenfield et al., 1987; Greenfield et al., 1986; Kerns, 1981; Meline, 1976). Although imitation is valued over creativity in some subsistence cultures (e.g., Greenfield, Brazelton, & Childs, 1989), television differs in providing models created by institutions that are more remote than the child's family and face-to-face social group.

The difference made by one year of age was unexpected. However, when one considers the nature of cognitive development in this age range, the developmental differences become understandable. According to Piagetian theory, as children become concrete operational (a development that consolidates around second grade), there is a general increase in the ability to conceptualize transformational connections between successive states. This development could yield longer narratives with more complex connections by the second graders. At the same time, increasing metacognitive awareness (i.e., the ability to symbolically represent mental states) could manifest itself in the observed age-related increase in the symbolic creation of mental events.

One difficulty with the study lies in the definition of creative and imitative imagination. Only elements repeated from the immediately preceding stimuli could be coded as imitative, the experimenters having no way of measuring what each individual child's experiences consisted of preceding the experiment. So, although the subjects were coded as having highly creative responses across all conditions (see Figure 4.1, for example), the true originality of their responses was probably lower. In addition to personal experience, some children's stories coded as creative came from other media sources. For example, one pair of participants used the Smurfs to reenact *Charlie and the Chocolate Factory*, and another built their story around *Teenage Mutant Ninja Turtles*. These informal observations indicate that it is probably more accurate to say that television and program-related toys change the *source* of imagination, rather than its creativity or quantity.

At the same time, these examples show the children's willingness to transcend the Smurf-like properties of the toys to create characters from other films—thus illustrating that television or film has far greater power than toys to influence the content of children's imagination. Indeed, when they are separated in time from a thematically related television show (pretest measures), program-based toys do not seem to have any discernible effect on imagination; H3 thus failed to be confirmed. However, when program-based toys are temporally linked to the show, they do seem to act as a damper on creative imagination (posttest measures). Thus, the difference between Smurfs and Trolls did not affect transcendent mental events on the pretest; but the combination of toy-based program and thematically related toy was for the older children a detriment to the creation of transcendent mental events on the posttest.

Although the absence of condition effects on the pretest may argue against long-term effects of TV-based toys, the fact that children in the United States watch about 3 hours of television a day means that the influence may well take place as an extended series of ongoing short-term effects.

In line with Salomon's (1979) conceptualization of the supplanting effects of media, we found that television (especially combined with thematically related toys) stimulated the transcendent imagination of mental events for the younger child not yet able to do it on his or her own, whereas it dampened the transcendent imagination of mental events for the older child with more advanced cognitive skills. Therefore, we would predict that television would stimulate the creative imagination of physical events for an even younger child, not yet able to imaginatively create physical events on his or her own. The findings and predictions are very consonant with the Vygotskian emphasis on the role of cultural tools in cognitive development (Vygotsky, 1978). Our results suggest that television, as well as TV-based toys, are potent cultural tools for developing the symbolic representation of mental events.

Implications for Using Toy-Based Programs and Program-Related Toys to Market to Children

In terms of imagination, product-based television is not in and of itself any different from other forms of television. Nor are program-related toys any different in their impact on imagination than other comparable toys. However, the fact that the *combination* of program-related toys and toy-based programs ultimately has a negative impact on creative imagination could be an argument for the elimination of both the product-based programs and the program-based toys. What would be useful are alternative sources for funding children's television that do not rely on selling toys to a young audience. This development would move children's television in the United States toward the elimination of both product-based television programs and program-based toys.

References

Adler, R., Friedlander, B., Lesser, G., Meringoff, L., Robertson, T., Rossiter, J., & Ward, S. (1977). *Research on the effects of television advertising on children.* Washington, DC: U.S. Government Printing Office.

Boyer, P. J. (1986, February 3). Toy-based tv: Effects on children debated. *New York Times,* pp. A1, C22.

Bruner, J. S., & Lucariello, J. (1989). Monologue as narrative recreation of the world. In K. Nelson (Ed.), *Narratives from the crib* (pp. 73-97). Cambridge, MA: Harvard University Press.

Bryant, J. (1985, October 28). Testimony at hearings before the U.S. House of Representatives' Subcommittee on Telecommunications. Consumer Protection, and Finance (Serial No. 99-66), 7A-88.

Carlsson-Paige, N., & Levin, D. E. (1987, December/1988, January). Young children and war play. *Educational Leadership,* pp. 80-84.

Fein, G. G. (1975). A transformational analysis of pretending. *Developmental Psychology, 11,* 291-296.

Greenfield, P. M., & Beagles-Roos, J. (1988). Radio vs. television: Their cognitive impact on children of different socioeconomic and ethnic groups. *Journal of Communication, 38*(2), 71-92.

Greenfield, P. M., Brazelton, T. B., & Childs, C. (1989). From birth to maturity in Zinacantan: Ontogenesis in cultural context. In V. Bricker & G. Gossen (Eds.), *Ethnographic encounters in Southern Mesoamerica: Celebratory essays in honor of Evon Z. Vogt* (pp. 177-216). Albany, NY: Institute of Mesoamerican Studies, State University of New York.

Greenfield, P. M., Bruzzone, L., Koyamatsu, K., Satuloff, W., Nixon, K., Brodie, M., & Kingsdale, D. (1987). What is rock music doing to the minds of our youth? A first experimental look at the effects of rock music lyrics and music videos. *Journal of Early Adolescence, 7,* 315-329.

Greenfield, P. M., Farrar, D., & Beagles-Roos, J. (1986). Is the medium the message? An experimental comparison of the effects of radio and television on imagination. *Journal of Applied Developmental Psychology, 7,* 201-218.

Harrison, L. F., & Williams, T. M. (1986). Television and cognitive development. In T. M. Williams (Ed.), *The impact of television* (pp. 87-142). Orlando, FL: Academic Press.

Hayes, D. S., & Birnbaum, D. W. (1980). Pre-schoolers' retention of televised events: Is a picture worth a thousand words? *Developmental Psychology, 16,* 410-416.

Kerns, T. Y. (1981, February). Television: A bisensory bombardment that stifles children's creativity. *Phi Delta Kappan,* pp. 456-457.

Kunkel, D. (1984). *Children's understanding of television advertising: The impact of host-selling.* Unpublished doctoral dissertation, University of Southern California, Annenberg School.

Kunkel, D. (1988a). Children and host-selling television commercials. *Communication Research, 15,* 71-92.

Kunkel, D. (1988b). From a raised eyebrow to a turned back: The FCC and children's product-related programming. *Journal of Communication, 38*(4), 90-108.

Kunkel, D., & Watkins, B. (1987). Evolution of children's television regulatory policy. *Journal of Broadcasting and Electronic Media, 31,* 367-389.

Meline, C. W. (1976). Does the medium matter? *Journal of Communication, 26*(3), 81-89.

Meringoff, L. K., Vibbert, M. Char, C. A., Fernie, D. E., Banker, G. S., & Gardner, H. (1982). How is children's learning from television distinctive?: Exploiting the medium methodologically. In J. Bryant & D. R. Anderson (Eds.), *Children's understanding of television: Research on attention and comprehension* (pp. 151-179). New York: Academic Press.

Meyer, M. (1988). Tackling the tie-in triangle. *Video, 12,* 61-62.

Murray, J. P., Kwiatek, K., & Clarke, P. (1982, April). *Television and fantasy: Children's viewing and storytelling.* Paper presented at the meeting of the International Communication Association, Boston.

Peterson, C. C., Peterson, J. L., & Carroll, J. (1986). Television viewing and imaginative problem solving during preadolescence. *Journal of Genetic Psychology, 147*(1), 61-67.

Piaget, J. (1962). *Play, dreams and imitation in childhood.* New York: Norton.

Pulaski, M. A. (1973). Toys and imaginative play. In J. L. Singer (Ed.), *The child's world of make-believe: Experimental studies of imaginative play* (pp. 74-103). New York: Academic Press.

Runco, M. A., & Pezdek, K. (1984). The effect of television and radio on children's creativity. *Human Communication Research, 11,* 109-120.

Salomon, G. (1979). *Interaction of media, cognition, and learning.* San Francisco: Jossey-Bass.

Shmukler, D. (1983). Preschool imaginative play predisposition and its relationship to subsequent third grade assessment. *Imagination, Cognition and Personality,* 2(3), 231-241.

Singer, J. L., & Singer, D. G. (1981). *Television, imagination, and aggression: A study of preschoolers.* Hillsdale, NJ: Lawrence Erlbaum.

Singer, J. L., & Singer, D. G. (1986). Family experiences and television viewing as predictors of children's imagination, restlessness, and aggression. *Journal of Social Issues,* 42(3), 107-124.

Ungerer, J. A., Zelazo, P. R., Kearsley, R. B., & O'Leary, K. (1981). Developmental changes in the representation of objects in symbolic play from 18 to 34 months of age. *Child Development, 52,* 186-195.

Vygotsky, L. S. (1978). *Mind in society.* Cambridge, MA: Harvard University Press.

Werner, H., & Kaplan, B. (1963). *Symbol formation.* New York: John Wiley.

5. Creativity of Children in a Television World

DOROTHY G. SINGER

Introduction

In the remote Amazonian rain forest village of Gorotire, Brazil, a satellite dish brings He-Man and the Flintstones to the naked Kaiapo Indian children. No longer do the families gather at night to meet and to talk, to pass on information or to tell stories. The villagers call television the "big ghost." Beptopup, the oldest medicine man, says, "The night is the time the old people teach the young people. Television has stolen the night" (Simons, 1989, p. 36). If television has stolen the night away from the Kaiapo Indians, it has stolen the day and night away from most U.S. children. The average U.S. family watches approximately 28 hours of television a week; school-aged children watch 30-31 hours of TV weekly—more time spent in any other activity except sleep. Can such heavy doses of television affect the imagination and creative output of our children?

Parents, educators, and mental health workers are concerned about television's effects on the cognitive development of children, and especially their imaginative and creative capacities. It is important to make a distinction between imagination and creativity. Imagination may be a precursor of creativity in that a child skillful in imagery and fantasy spinning possesses the essential ingredients necessary for the creative spirit. Whereas imagination requires the ability to form symbols of missing objects, persons, and places in one's mind, and to deal with similes, metaphors, and abstract thought, creativity is usually identified by two criteria (Barron, 1969): (a) originality—new or unusual elements must be involved, and (b) adaptation to reality outcomes must be meaningful to others rather than random or idiosyncratic. Thus, we think of creativity as the ability to generate new ideas or to think about things in original and different ways. Intelligence may complement creativity, but it is not necessarily related to it (Barron, 1969).

Current Definitions of Creativity

Sternberg and Lubart (1991a; 1991b) suggest that creativity is not inborn, but nurtured and even developed through schooling. According to what they call an "investment theory," the authors state that the greatest creative contributions are generally made in areas that are undervalued. Their notion of investment is drawn from the financial realm where one "buys low and sells high." An individual who can generate and advance a new idea in art or science may eventually be regarded as highly creative, whereas a person who produces work that is already in vogue or similar to that of others may be viewed as merely competent.

According to Sternberg and Lubart, there are six areas involved in creativity: (a) *intelligence,* or the ability to define and redefine problems, and to think insightfully; (b) *knowledge* of a specific field; (c) *intellectual styles,* or the way abilities are used—specifically a "legislative" proclivity, formulating problems and creating new systems of rules and new ways of seeing things; (d) *personality,* or tolerance of ambiguity; willingness to grow, persevere, and take risks; (e) *motivation,* or intrinsic desire to excel; and (f) *environmental context,* or setting that sparks ideas, encourages follow-up of ideas, and rewards ideas and their fruits.

Teresa Amabile (1983) argues that creativity is not a personality trait or general ability but is a "behavior resulting from particular constellations of personal characteristics, cognitive abilities, and social environments" (p. 358). Her belief is that the social-psychological issues have generally been ignored by those who have studied creativity. Amabile's conceptions of creativity includes (a) *domain-relevant skills,* that is, knowledge about a specific domain and technical skills; (b) *creativity-relevant skills,* that is, appropriate cognitive style, conducive work style; and (c) *task motivation,* that is, appropriate attitudes, intrinsic motivation, ability to minimize extrinsic constraints. Amabile further believes that creativity follows a continuum from lower levels of "garden variety" creativity found in everyday life to the more important and significant contributions to the arts, literature, and science. In all cases, however, creativity refers to "productions of responses or works that are reliably assessed as creative by appropriate judges" (Amabile, 1983, p. 362). All three components of Amabile's framework for conceptualizing creativity contain elements that include cognitive abilities, personality characteristics, and social factors that contribute to different stages of the creative process.

Creativity Research

Research by Harrington, J. Block, and J. H. Block (1983) supports the idea that early indications of creativity are maintained over a span of years. Using the California Child Q-Set instrument, children who were imaginative and sensitive to task constraints at ages 4 and 5 were evaluated for creativity at age 11 and found to be rated as creative by their teachers. Traits of curiosity, ego resilience, and self-confidence were continuous across time and may have been the result of environmental factors. This supports the position of Amabile (1983) and Sternberg and Lubart (1991a, 1991b) that social and environmental conditions contribute to creativity. In addition, Harrington and colleagues (1983) make the point that parents who provided their children with environments conducive to divergent thinking and intellectual playfulness in early childhood appear to continue to do so 6 or 7 years later.

There is some evidence that imaginary companions of childhood may have a bearing on adolescent creativity. Schaefer (1969) found that among his sample of 800 high school students, those who produced creative works in literary genres reported a greater incidence of imaginary companions than did matched less creative controls. The criteria for assessing creative achievement included two standardized tests of creative thinking as well as teachers' evaluations. In another study, Cangelosi and Schaefer (1991) followed the progress of 10 exceptionally creative high school girls ages 16 and 17 who had shared a number of common characteristics such as similarities in familial and educational histories, leisure activities, fantasy experiences, and self-concept. They also looked at such contributing extrinsic factors as role models of creative behavior, outstanding teachers, awards for creative achievement, and noncontrolling parents. Cangelosi and Schaefer located the 10 subjects

25 years later when they were 41 and 42 years old. Participants completed the various tests tapping their creativity. Results indicate that six pursued talents in writing, two in fine arts, one became a physician. Only one, who was in chronic pain, did not fulfill her creative interests, but recently did submit a story to a national magazine. Consistent with the Lifetime Creativity Scales of Richards, Kinney, Benet, and Merzel (1988), 9 of the 10 subjects indicated that they were engaged in outcomes based on real-life activities that involved originality or innovativeness and were relevant to persons other than the creator.

Schaefer (1969) found imaginary companions among children who showed more imaginativeness in their spontaneous play in nursery school, were more positive emotionally during such play, had more cooperative behavior with adults, and had somewhat more extended language usage. What is of significance here is the finding that children with imaginary companions watched less television.

Heath (1982) found that children who enacted a variety of story themes developed a sense of narrative and were often successful at school-based literacy tasks. Through symbolic play, children tell stories, suspend reality, ascribe fictional features to everyday objects, and as a result, the "organization of children's decontextualized play should be related to their literate behavior" (Pellegrini, 1985, p. 82). Children engaged in social pretend play use explicit and elaborated language to interpret their play vignettes, to resolve conflicts, to clarify meanings, to compromise and adapt. These particular benefits of play would appear to be necessary ingredients for creative growth. In addition, children who play try on different roles, are flexible, can delay gratification, and learn to be empathic. The paracosms or private societies or worlds that children invent such as the "ant" people of the Tolstoy brothers or the "kingdoms" of the Brontë siblings were the foundations for the later creative literary genius of Leo Tolstoy and Charlotte and Emily Brontë. We question whether television, like social pretend play, can lead to creativity.

Creativity and the Media

Neil Postman (1985) believes that many children's programs, such as *Sesame Street* and *The Electric Company*, undermine the traditional idea of what schooling represents. According to Postman, these programs encourage children to love school only if school is like *Sesame Street;* and

> whereas a classroom is a place of social interaction, the space in front of a television is a private preserve. Whereas in a classroom one may ask a teacher questions, one can ask nothing of a television screen. Whereas school is centered on the development of language, television demands attention to images. (p. 143)

If we review the definitions of creativity, certainly the environmental context, as described, would exclude the medium of television as a stimulus to creativity. According to Sternberg and Lubart (1991b), creativity is best nourished by a teacher urging the student to follow up on an original idea, giving the student rewards and encouraging the student to define problems and pose questions. Television could do this if programs were designed to be interactive, but currently the main goal of commercial television is entertainment.

D. Salomon (1981) suggests that if children were directed to watch television for its content, they would indeed benefit from some of the information imparted by the medium. Using the measure AIME—for amount of invested mental effort—Salomon found that children who were directed to give their full attention to material presented on TV did better on posttests related to the particular programming than children who were not given instructions to direct their full attention to material being presented on TV.

Curious about television's effect on creativity, Stern (1973) used Guilford's tests to measure the creativity of 250 mentally gifted fourth, fifth, and sixth graders. They were divided into seven groups—six of which watched specific categories of television exclusively. The control group had no instructions. Subjects were posttested on an alternate form of the Guilford test 3 weeks later. Children who had watched cartoons had the greatest decrease in creativity scores. Although Stern reports that the decrease was not significant, he states that the trend was important in terms of the long-range effects of indiscriminate viewing among children.

When children are engaged in play, there is ample opportunity for creativity to develop. Does television interfere with such play? Examining the impact of toy-based television programs and program-related toys on 110 first- and second-grade children, Greenfield, Yut, Chung, and Land (1990) found that either watching toy-based cartoons alone or playing with cartoon-related toys alone can lead to imaginative play that included creative characters, physical activities, objects, and locations. However, these researchers also found that for aspects of imagination at a more advanced cognitive level, the cartoon combined with cartoon-related toys stimulated the imaginative process of the first graders, but inhibited the imaginative process of the second graders.

Attitudes towards imagination and giftedness can be shaped by parents. Abelman (1987) found, for example, that parents of gifted children were more likely to speak to their children about television and explain the mechanics of it as a mediatory device. These parents were also more likely to see television as influencing their children's thought processes. In contrast, other parents were inclined to see television as having behavioral effects. They tended to remove children from the source rather than carry out explanation or mediation. A lack of parental mediation seems to affect the way children process and comprehend television. When there is an active stance toward the medium, more information can be gleaned from it (Desmond, J. L. Singer, D. G. Singer, Calam, & Colimore, 1985).

Sharon Gadberry (1980) was interested in what happens to first graders' leisure time, IQ, and cognitive style when parents restrict their television viewing. Children age 6 years were blindly assigned to restricted or unrestricted television viewing groups. The restricted parents not only halved their children's television viewing rates, but interacted 20 minutes a day with their children for a 6-week period. Unrestricted parents provided similar interactions but no limits were set on viewing. Results indicated that during leisure time, reading was chosen more often by both groups, but that the restricted group exceeded the unrestricted group in reflectivity as measured by the Matching Familiar Figures test. The ability to search for visual details, thus, was enhanced in children who spent less time watching television. According to Gadberry, the television format externally limits processing time "by virtue of motion and typically rapid scene changes" (p. 55). The creative process involves the ability to reflect, to be flexible, to see things in new ways. The slower-paced educational programs may promote a reflective style, according to Gadberry. Her study found that viewing of such noncommercial programs as *Sesame Street* and *The Electric Company* was positively related to latency scores on the Matching Familiar Figures test. Hall, Esty, and Fisch (1990) found that fifth-grade children who watched *Square One TV*, an educational program, made significant gains in problem-solving behavior from pretest to posttest compared to children in the control group.

Reading, as Gadberry (1980) found, can have an influence on a child's constellation of skills that comprise IQ. The increased reading in the leisure time of the restricted television viewing children in her study led to higher scores on Picture Completion Performance, a test requiring an ability to find missing details on commonplace objects. It may be that the verbal scanning needed in reading, where configurations must be encoded, is enhanced by continuous practice in reading and carries over to a test where details must be noted. Peirce (1983), for example, found in a study with 100 fifth, seventh, eighth, and ninth graders that creativity and writing ability were positively associated with the number of books read, with parental involvement (through television rules and discussion), and with television viewing. The amount of television viewed and creativity were negatively related. The ability to write creative stories about an imagined situation was the dependent variable.

Similarly, Watkins (1988) analyzed the completed stories of third graders, fifth graders, and eighth graders. There were two periods for test administration so that each child wrote one story from a real-life perspective and one from a television perspective. In addition, data were collected to determine the television shows viewed, television viewing habits, perceptions about television effects, and parent attitudes towards viewing and enforcement of restrictions. Results indicated that real-life stories were more elaborate and complex for low television viewers. However, by eighth grade, television stories were considerably more complex than real-life stories for high viewers. Higher viewers at all three age levels represented real events in a less complex, less invested manner than did low viewers. These high-viewing children provided less detail, with fewer insights into what characters were thinking and feeling, and showed greater emphasis on superficial descriptions based on observable actions at the expense of unobservables. The more television the young children viewed, the more similar their real-life stories were to television. Watkins believed that for older children, televised events and characters appear to take on lives of their own that seemed more interesting and elaborate than real-life characters. Heavy television viewing may indeed interfere with a child's ability to grasp the "subtleties of social cognition" (Watkins, 1988, p. 181).

The creative abilities of the high television viewers appeared to have suffered when they were asked to generate original ideas within a real-life setting.

In a rare kind of experiment, Williams (1986) was able to examine the effects of television on the creativity of fourth and seventh graders. Williams compared three communities in Canada, Notel (a town with poor TV reception and few regular TV viewers); Unitel (one TV channel was available); and Multitel (several channels were available). Two creativity tasks were used, Alternative Uses and Pattern Meaning. The former, a test of divergent thinking, asks for novel applications for such common objects as a button, a shoe, chair; the latter, a measure of ideational fluency, requires the identification of things that ambiguous drawings might represent. There is no limit on the number of answers. Comparing different samples of the same grades in the three communities before Notel had limited access to television and after it had more access to television, scores on the Alternative Uses task had declined. Children in Notel had initially scored better than those in Unitel and Multitel, but after television arrived, the scores for the three communities were similar. In the longitudinal sample, when compared at two points in time, scores for the Notel children decidedly decreased, whereas those for the other communities did not.

Results of the Patterns Meanings task did not demonstrate any significant differences. There was no evidence, however, that television enhanced spatial abilities. The relationship, for example, between block design performance for children in Notel after television was introduced was negatively related to television viewing. Hoffmann and Flook (1980) were also interested in this issue. Could television play a role in facilitating shape recognition among young children? Children aged 4 viewed a television program dealing with simple shapes while a control group participated in regular classroom activities. Results indicated that the TV program was ineffective as an aid in developing concrete operational thought.

A Comparison of Print, Radio and Television, and Creativity

It is important to understand how much of the visual and auditory components of television contribute to a child's understanding of the medium. In a review of the literature, Rolandelli (1989) concludes that the visual superiority effect of television is confounded with comprehensibility of the auditory-verbal component. The auditory formal features alert children to what is comprehensible and worthy of their attention. The language of television can even help children follow a program without constant visual attention. Certainly in our research we found this to be true. Children who watched *Mr. Rogers' Neighborhood* often did not watch the program with undivided attention, but because of Fred Rogers's slow, clear way of speaking, they were able to comprehend the sense of the program (J. L. Singer & D. G. Singer, 1981).

A study by Meringoff, Vibbert, Kelly, and Char (1981) examined the effects of radio, television, and picture book presentations of the same story on visual imagery. Children were requested to draw pictures about the story. The radio version stimulated more imaginative drawings, but in terms of *quality,* children who were in the television and picture book groups did better. These children depicted more characters from unusual perspectives and drew more unusual details. In an earlier study of imagination (Forsythe, 1970), children who were taught by radio and television tended to copy the television renditions in drawings, whereas they were stimulated by radio to use their own imagination.

Not only were drawings more imaginative after radio exposure as the above studies indicated, but as Beagles-Roos and Gat (1983) found, using 48 subjects in Grades 1 through 4, recognition of expressive language in forced choice questions was facilitated by a radio story. A radio story also increased the children's use of knowledge unrelated to the story. The television version enhanced references based on actions and augmented picture sequencing. Thus, radio stimulated verbal content, whereas television stimulated the use of action.

Runco and Pezdek (1984) were also interested in the effects of television and radio in children's creativity. Their subjects were 32 third graders and 32 sixth graders. Two stories were used in this study, each presented in a television and radio condition. Immediately after the presentation, children were administered the Just Suppose test requiring them to generate ideas in response to a hypothetical situation. The protocols were scored for fluency, flexibility, and originality, measures of creativity. No differences were found between the two media in terms of consequent ideational fluency, flexibility, or originality. These findings contradict those of Meline (1976) and Greenfield, Farrer, and Beagles-Roos (1986). One reason may be that experimental measures were different in this study compared to the two cited. Runco and Pezdek (1984) believe that the task in the Greenfield et al. study was a *convergent* thinking task, whereas their task was one of *divergent* thinking, which is more consistent with the definition of creativity and is commonly used to estimate creative potential. The authors concluded that creativity measured by standardized tests of ideational fluency, flexibility, and originality are not affected differently by short-term exposure to television versus radio. The authors also suggest that their study lends support to the trait theory of creativity.

Greenfield et al. (1986) continued their work comparing the effects of radio and television on the imagination of first- through fourth-grade children and responded to Runco and Pezdek's (1984) argument, citing differences in the design of the two studies. Runco and Pezdek used a between-subjects design, whereas Greenfield et al. used a within-subjects design. Greenfield et al. also criticized Runco and Pezdek's procedure, arguing that it did not elicit enough creative material in either medium to make any difference. Greenfield et al. (1986) confirmed their hypotheses that radio is more stimulating to imaginal processes than is television. They also noted that having a radio story as one's first stimulus enhanced the imaginative response to the subsequent television story, whereas having a television story as the first stimulus depressed the imaginative response to the subsequent radio story.

Greenfield and Beagles-Roos (1988) were interested to see if there might be differences in imagination between ethnic or social class groups as a result of television viewing. If television actually depresses imagination, then heavier viewing groups such as working-class and black children might exhibit less imagination overall and might respond less to the stimulation of radio. A sample of 192 children containing three equal subsamples of middle and working-class children, black and white, and younger (first and second grade) and older (third and fourth grade) participated in the study. In an elaborate design, children were exposed to two radio and television versions of two incomplete stories. Children were then asked to complete the story. The results indicate that radio led to significantly greater creation of new story material for the measures of imaginative events, specific characters, vague characters, and imaginative words. Radio induced significantly more original completions than television for white but not for black children, whose low level of imaginative response did not differ for the two media. Action was more memorable in the audiovisual (television) format for all children whereas dialogue was more memorable in the audio (radio) format. As in the Greenfield et al. (1986) study, the radio version, if presented first, enhanced both imagination and memory, but these diminished when the television version preceded the radio version.

The main results of the studies that find radio conducive to expressive imagination and creativity of play are in accord with G. Salomon's (1979) assumptions that aural renditions enhance verbal comprehension. Hayes, Kelly, and Mandel (1986) evaluated the effectiveness of radio and television for conveying narrative information. They used two samples, 44 children between 3 and 6 years of age, and 44 adults. After presentation of the story, subjects (half at each age level viewed the story on television or listened to the story on a tape recorder encased in an old-fashioned radio) were asked to retell the story. Results indicate that children included a significantly greater proportion of events of high rather than of medium centrality when stories were presented via radio rather than television. The radio versions promoted significantly more dialogue by the children, but the dialogue was not always associated with events judged to be of highest importance. Children in the radio group included more sound effects in their synopses whereas children in the television condition described more visual-action sequences. Results of the study suggest that although children's retention of story language is greater with radio than with television, "this enhanced recall of verbal or auditory features is not based on retention of the most important story elements" (Hayes et al., 1986, p. 346).

A television program can perhaps enhance creativity if visuals are accompanied by verbal narrative or dialogue. This enables children to interpret and comprehend the material with greater ease, and then they can incorporate such material into original stories or drawings using television as a stimulus.

Interactive Television and Creativity

With the advent of the optical video disc, educators have been experimenting with prototypes to determine whether this interaction technology can enhance children's cognitive development and stimulate more creative learning styles. One prototype, Palenque, an optical disc, has been described by Wilson (1987). It is targeted for 8- to 14-year-olds and their families as a less traditional method of teaching. It allows for flexibility (a requirement for creativity) and fosters incidental learning. In Great Britain, the use of video discs and video recorders has been introduced for classroom use for students aged 3 to 11 (Choat & Griffin, 1988). Thus far, there has been no report on its impact. The Alpha interactive microcomputer system for teaching reading, writing, and communication skills to hearing-impaired children has been evaluated by Prinz, Pemberton, and Nelson (1985) to determine its efficacy in improving communication skills. Subjects aged 3 years 2 months to 14 years 3 months made significant advances on measures of general communication and referential communication. Although creativity was not assessed in this study, the students learned to "write" their text answers on the TV screen by pressing words on their keyboards to match an acting sequence on television. This ability to encode the actions was mastered by the students both for animated pictured-action sequences and sign language sentence animations. The use of the microsystem emphasized exploratory learning (necessary for creativity) rather than typical programmed instruction.

The notion of "exploratory learning" has been cited by Houston (1985) along with the following benefits of the microcomputer: Children can (a) learn about properties, directions, location in space; (b) have experiences they cannot normally have through simulation; (c) overcome certain physical barriers or mechanical barriers (e. g., writing); (d) learn graphic designs, color drawings; and (e) control pace of lesson. In addition, the microcomputer (a) is an excellent motivator; (b) allows for problem solving; (c) requires children to engage in decision making; (d) being a machine of infinite patience, does not tire of child's repetitive questions or of the child who cannot get the right answer; (e) presents materials in different ways and thus gives children wider experiences; (f) holds the attention of the child longer than most teaching tools; and (g) allows children to work cooperatively with one another, and this interaction stimulates the development of language skills.

If children can be inspired to become more original, creative problem solvers, teachers can also benefit from the new technologies. Fredin (1983) explored the effects of an interactive cable television systems on the dynamic interpersonal communication and diversity of new ideas within work groups. This was a field experiment designed to test the effectiveness of disseminating new teaching ideas. The 504 teachers who participated were from 41 elementary schools. Results revealed that the diversity of new ideas brought about by the interactive communication system was regulated by intermediation. Systems depend on and interact with intermediation. The author contends that intermediation can actively enhance or suppress the diversity of new ideas.

An example of teacher and student participation is presented by Rescigno (1988). A "smart classroom" was developed for a seventh-grade science class that integrated personal computers, interactive laser disc video programs, closed circuit television, VHS programs, satellite downlinks, local area networking, and phone modems. In this high-technology atmosphere, 192 students, including students from the gifted and talented program, special education program, and limited English proficient programs, were enrolled. Results indicate that students worked at their own pace and thereby maximized achievement. Students gained confidence in themselves and were eager to accept new challenges.

Conclusions

The evidence for negative effects of television on the creativity of children appears to be stronger than for positive effects. There are some cautions, however. Many of the studies cited are correlational; different age groups are used in the various studies, and numbers of subjects are generally small. The literature strongly suggests that because television is a visual modality, verbal skills—specifically expressive language—is enhanced more from aural or print exposure. Nevertheless, mediation on the part of parents can help children process television programming more effectively. Educational programming for young children appears to be more conducive to creativity and imagination. This may be a result of the slow pacing and the closer collaboration of the auditory and visual modalities. The newer technologies hold some promises for motivating children to learn, to become more exploratory in their stance towards problem solving, and to achieve.

References

Abelman, R. (1987). Child giftedness and its role in the parental mediation of television viewing. *Roeper Review, 9*(4), 217-220, 240.

Amabile, T. M. (1983). The social psychology of creativity: A componential conceptualization. *Journal of Personality and Social Psychology, 45*(2), 357-376.

Barron, F. (1969). *Creative person and creative process.* New York: Holt, Rinehart & Winston.

Beagles-Roos, J., & Gat, I. (1983). Specific impact of radio and television in children's story comprehension. *Journal of Education Psychology, 75*(1), 128-137.

Cangelosi, D. M., & Schaefer, C. E. (1991). A twenty-five year follow-up study of ten exceptionally creative adolescent girls. *Psychological Reports, 68,* 307-311.

Choat, E., & Griffin, H. (1988). Modular video with children aged 3 to 11. *British Journal of Educational Technology, 19*(2), 123-130.

Desmond, R., Singer, J. L., Singer, D. G., Calam, R., & Colimore, K. (1985). Family mediation patterns and television viewing: Young children's use and grasp of the medium. *Human Communication Research, 11,* 461-480.

Forsythe, R. O. (1970). *Instructional radio: A position paper* (ERIC Clearinghouse on Educational Media and Technology No. ED 044 9033). Stanford, CA: Stanford University.

Fredin, E. S. (1983). The context of communication, and their effect on ideas. *Communication Research, 10*(4), 553-581.

Gadberry, S. (1980). Effects of restricting first graders' TV-viewing on leisure time use, IQ change, and cognitive style. *Journal of Applied Developmental Psychology, 1*(1), 45-57.

Greenfield, P., & Beagles-Roos, J. (1988). Radio vs. television: Their cognitive impact on children of different socioeconomic and ethnic groups. *Journal of Communication, 38*(2), 71-72.

Greenfield, P., Farrer, D., & Beagles-Roos, J. (1986). Is the medium the message? An experimental comparison of the effects of radio and television on imagination. *Journal of Applied Developmental Psychology, 7,* 201-218.

Greenfield, P., Yut, E., Chung, M., & Land, D. (1990). The program-length commercial: A study of the effects of television/toy tie-ins on imagination play. *Psychology and Marketing, 7*(4), 237-255.

Hall, E. R., Esty, E. T., & Fisch, S. M. (1990). Television and children's problem-solving behavior: A synopsis of an evaluation of the effects of *Square One TV. Journal of Mathematical Behavior, 9*(2), 161-174.

Harrington, D. M., Block, J., & Block, J. H. (1983). Predicting creativity in preadolescence from divergent thinking in early childhood. *Journal of Personality and Social Psychology, 45*(3), 609-623.

Hayes, D. S., Kelly, S. B., & Mandel, M. (1986). Media differences in children's story synopses: Radio and television contrasted. *Journal of Educational Psychology, 78*(5), 341-346.

Heath, S. B. (1982). What no bedtime story means. Narrative skills at home and school. *Language in Society, 11*, 49-76.

Hoffmann, R. J., & Flook, M. A. (1980). An experimental investigation of the role of television in facilitating shape recognition. *Journal of Genetic Psychology, 136*, 305-306.

Houston, E. (1985). *Making child development relevant for all ages.* Paper presented at the Annual Conference of the National Association for the Education of Young Children, New Orleans.

Meline, C. (1976). Does the medium matter. *Journal of Communication, 26*, 81-89.

Meringoff, L. R., Vibbert, M., Kelly, H., & Char, C. (1981, April). *How shall we take your story: With or without picture?* Paper presented at the meeting of the Society for Research in Child Development, Boston.

Peirce, K. (1983). Relation between time spent viewing television and children's writing skills. *Journal Quarterly, 60*, 445-448.

Pellegrini, A. D. (1985). Relations between preschool children's symbolic play and literate behavior. In L. Galda & A. D. Pellegrini (Eds.), *Play, language, and stories: The development of children's literate behavior* (Chapter 5, pp. 79-97). Norwood, NJ: Ablex.

Postman, N. (1985). *Amusing ourselves to death.* New York: Viking.

Prinz, P., Pemberton, E., & Nelson, K. E. (1985). The Alpha interactive microcomputer system for teaching reading, writing, and communication skills to hearing-impaired children. *American Annals of the Deaf, 130*(5), 444-461.

Rescigno, R. C. (1988). *Practical implementation of educational technology. The GTE/GTEL smart-classroom: The Hueneme School District Experience.* Paper presented at the US/USSR Joint Conference on Computers, Education, and Children, Moscow, USSR.

Richards, R., Kinney, D. K., Benet, M., & Merzel, A. P. C. (1988). Assessing everyday creativity: Characteristics of the Lifetime Creativity Scales and validation with three large samples. *Journal of Personality and Social Psychology, 54*(3), 476-485.

Rolandelli, D. R. (1989). Children and television: The visual superiority effect reconsidered. *Journal of Broadcasting and Electronic Media, 33*(1), 69-81.

Runco, M. A., & Pezdek, K. (1984). The effect of television and radio in children's creativity. *Human Communication Research, 11*(1), 109-120.

Salomon, D. (1981). Introducing AIME: The assessment of children's mental involvement with television. In H. Kelly & H. Gardner (Eds.), *Viewing children through television* (pp. 89-102). San Francisco: Jossey-Bass.

Salomon, G. (1979). *Interaction of media, cognition, and learning.* San Francisco: Jossey-Bass.

Schaefer, C. E. (1969). Imaginary companions and creative adolescents. *Developmental Psychology, 1*, 747-749.

Simons, M. (1989, February 26). The Amazon's savvy Indians. *New York Times Magazine*, p. 36.

Singer, J. L., & Singer, D. G. (1981). *Television, imagination, and aggression: A study of preschoolers.* Hillsdale, NJ: Lawrence Erlbaum.

Stern, S. L. (1973). Television and creativity: The effects of viewing certain categories of commercial television broadcasting on the divergent thinking abilities of intellectually gifted elementary students. *Dissertation Abstracts International, 34,* 3176A. (University Microfilms, No. 73-31, 675)

Sternberg, R. L., & Lubart, T. L. (1991a). An investment theory of creativity and its development. *Human Development,* 34, 1-31.

Sternberg, R. L, & Lubart, T. L. (1991b). Creating creative minds. *Phi Delta Kappan,* 72(8), 608-614.

Watkins, B. (1988). Children's representations of television and real-life stories. *Communication Research,* 15(2), 159-184.

Williams, T. M. (1986). *The impact of television: A natural experiment in three communities.* New York: Academic Press.

Wilson, K. S. (1987). *The Palenque optical disc prototype: Design of multimedia experiences for education and entertainment in a nontraditional learning center.* Paper presented at the annual meeting of the American Educational Research Association, Washington, DC.

6. Children and Media in Media Education

JAMES A. ANDERSON

MILTON E. PLOGHOFT

Media in education have developed within two distinct areas. The first has to do with teaching *with* media: The application of film, video, sound, and graphics to the standard speech and textbook of the classroom. These applications range from the rather simple audiovisual methods of overheads and slides to the much more complex systems of distance learning that may involve satellite linkage and full-spectrum interaction. The preponderance of the writing about media and education has been directed toward the uses of media to more effectively teach the subject matter that has traditionally occupied the time and energies of the teachers in our schools.

The second area of media in education is media education itself or teaching *about* the media. Such education has three rather distinct foci that distinguish the purposes and approaches of separate areas of instruction: (a) the modes and methods of production, a focus associated with the teaching of journalism, film, and video production as well as graphics, and since the early 1980s, computer programming and applications; (b) the nature and character of media industries, generally appearing in management, marketing, and occasionally sociology; and (c) the critical analysis of media texts.

Production curriculum rarely makes its entrance in the United States prior to middle school, although computer applications and some programming instruction are becoming more frequent. The teaching of journalism and video production is not uncommon in high schools and is typically offered in some form at the college level. The focus on the structure, conduct, and performance of the media as an industry, however, is almost entirely a college-level emphasis. On the other hand, the critical analysis of media texts bridges the entire curriculum from the rarefied heights of doctoral deconstructionism to studies in popular culture to the high school analysis of news and political campaigns to the education of the very young concerning the meaning and messages of television.

Theoretical Foundations of Media Education

We are concerned, in this chapter, with this third focus of the second area of media in education, and particularly to its applications in the elementary and middle school. Here, in practice, the concern is almost exclusively with television and is fueled by the many hours children spend with this medium and accelerated by social activist alarms.

Seven separate theoretical paths have characterized the historical development of media education at this level, according to Piette (1992). He lists these paths as stimulus-response, agenda setting, cultivation theory, uses and gratifications, cultural studies, critical analysis, and semiology. The paths of these theories diverge on two points, what philosophers (Roth, 1987) call "meaning realism" and what social scientists (Bauer, 1963; Biocca, 1988) call the "active audience." *Meaning realism* is the doctrine of content as a meaning delivery system in which the determinants of "right" interpretation are contained entirely in the content itself. Content has a literal and proper meaning for all the competent to decode. The *active audience* principle deals with the contribution of the auditor (audience member) to the formula of content-auditor-effect. Audiences become more active as they gain agency in this formula (agency given by the theoretical perspective).

Piette's categories of media education theories can be arranged on these two axes. The upper left-hand corner with full meaning realism and a completely disempowered audience would be occupied by agenda setting and S-R theories. Semiology (or structural semiotics), cultivation analysis, and much of critical theory move across to the "high meaning realism, active audience" position by holding that categorical audiences (audiences typed by psychographics and demographics) decode content differently but in ways true to their categories. The bottom left-hand corner is occupied by cultural approaches that elevate ideology rather than content as the mode of interpretation but also disempower all but the elite of the audience. Finally the lower right is held by what in the 1960s and 1970s was loosely identified as a "uses and gratifications" approach. This tradition has most recently migrated upward toward notions of categorical audiences in response to pressure from an enlightened cultural approach originating from a British-Australian-Canadian coalition (Masterman, 1985) and from a social action approach that has been mostly based in the United States (e.g., Anderson & Meyer, 1988).

Objectives of Media Education

The theory of these last two approaches has provided the basis of the most successful media education efforts in Canada (Duncan, 1988), Australia (Canavan, 1975), and Britain (Bazalgette, 1989). Anderson (1992) laid out the characteristic objectives of media education curriculum derived from this theory. His analysis is adapted within the following explanation.

Media education objectives begin with those skills needed to identify and understand the media as methods of social construction and discourse, as well as one's own motives and practices for attending to the several media one uses. These analyses lead to an understanding of the methods we apply to accommodate our practices of use, the media themselves, and their symbolic material in everyday life. This understanding involves the skills of comprehending language and symbol, icon and image, signal and sound discriminately, equally to act as a competent member of our society, to manage the effects of content, and to increase our pleasure from it.

Media education is intended to make it possible to thoroughly engage the meanings and intents of mediated content to go beyond surface meanings and to permit the analysis of the discourse as well as the visual and aural images in order to specify the working elements of each within the realm of the social action in progress.

In the engagement of content, media education fosters the observation of details and their sequence and relationships in a purposeful manner to arrive at an understanding of the ideological structures, themes, values, claims, and evidence, and their warrants, as well as narrative elements such as motivations, plot lines, characters, and characterizations. Media education provides for a reflective evaluation of fact and opinion, logical and affective appeals, imaginative and creative exposition, and imaging. It looks to develop an understanding of the perspectivity present in all media messages that is inherent in the medium, in the semiotic characteristics of the methods selected to produce the content, and in the qualities of the message genre.

Last, individuals trained in programs of media education will be equipped to assign value or worth to the content and their interpretation of it for some purpose. Such individuals should be able to integrate the message into and test it against other information bases. They will enter into an understanding of the role of the semiotic in the action of knowledge and desire. They will be able to make inferences and draw appropriate conclusions and see the ethical implications for the lives they live.

Classroom Practices

In the classroom, media education programs generally pursue two sets of activities. The first is the deconstruction or analysis of existing mediated content. This activity generally focuses on some industry-defined unit of content such as a television program, magazine advertisement, or newspaper article and applies some analytical framework to it. The British Film Institute's Primary Program, for example, uses the frame of "category [medium and genre], language, agency (who made it?), technology, audience, and representation" (Bazalgette, 1989, p. 8) as the basis of analysis of any selected unit. This sort of activity is immediately recognizable as traditional criticism, although the empowering of multiple interpretations that are typically encouraged by media education curricula may not be.

The second set of activities involves the production of mediated content, usually once again within industry-defined categories (a commercial, a news program, a magazine article). Unlike journalism or telecommunications curricula, however, the purpose here is not to gain competence in production methods but to learn about the encoding of messages through these methods.

Practical Outcomes

Schools interested in providing media education in their classrooms now have a number of models to follow most notably from the British Film Institute (Bazalgette, 1989, Bowker, 1991) and the Ontario Ministry of Education (1989) as well as the several projects reported in Brown (1991) and in Dorr and Brannon (1992). There is little question that children can gain knowledge about the media and about analytical technique in dealing with media texts through any of these programs. There have been questions raised along the way, however, as to the practical necessity for such curricula as measured by "improvement" in the actual media practices.

Anderson and Meyer (1988) have claimed children are knowledgeable agents in the use of media in their own right, and these arguments are echoed by Buckingham (1992). It would appear that the model of the child as unwitting victim that drives much of media education is indeed naive. Nonetheless, there is at least one study that showed positive practical outcomes for media education. Long (1989) studied the decision-making practices of children who had participated in a media education program based on a "critical thinking model" with similar children who had not. Using two roughly matched samples from the same school district and practical decision scenarios (buying a common product, picking a restaurant), he found that the media-educated children had more complex decision-making processes and used more information sources and sources of apparent higher quality than did children not enrolled in media education classes.

Media education is not the only program challenged by the "so what" question of practical outcomes. The special significance of the questioning arises from its direct counterposition to the social concerns about children and television that motivate much of the interest in media education in the first place. If media education programs do not make a difference in media practices or if children are suitably equipped without direct instruction, then such programs are highly vulnerable to any change in the support climate.

The Cycle of Interest and Decline

In fact, the history of media education, which is as old as the media themselves, is one of repeated cycles of interest and decline (Anderson, 1980). These cycles in U.S. education can be quickly and roughly noted by a cursory examination of the articles on the subject of television listed in *The Education Index* over the past 40 years. For the 3-year period 1947-1950, less than two pages of *The Education Index* were required to list the articles that dealt with all aspects of television and education. During the 2-year period 1953-1955, five pages were required to carry the listing of such articles, and by the 1971-1972 period, the listing of articles dealing with television and education for a single year filled more than five pages. Then a decline set in. From 1978-1985, listings of articles dealing with all aspects of education and television averaged less than a page per year. Presently, of course, we are once again on an upswing. In 1990-1991, such listings took up 3½ pages as perhaps we move back to the level of interest of the early 1970s.

The testimony by Piette and others at the just completed German-American conference on media education suggests that many of the recent players in media education are unaware of its extended history and of its characteristic failure to sustain its presence particularly in U.S. classrooms but elsewhere as well. Members of that conference issued a call for a "complex understanding" of this history.

Some Recent History

We will not accomplish that complex understanding in this short chapter, but we can point out some salient aspects. The comprehensive study of media education that was carried out by Brown (1991) provides an appropriate starting point for considering the status of media education today. He concluded that "the ground swell of exploration and experimentation in the 1970s grew into a proliferation of [media education] projects by the early 1980s in the United States" (p. 320). He further observed that, as the "initial intrigue and enthusiasm" subsided and funding priorities shifted, many projects were "left in limbo," especially the massive projects that had been supported by the U.S. Office of Education. (Boston University, the Far West Laboratory, Southwest Educational Development Laboratory, and WNET/13).

With the exception of the WNET/13 project, the federally funded projects were most active during the period 1978-1981, hardly of sufficient duration to provide for broad dissemination of information to schools that may have been interested in critical viewing skills. Although funds provided were considerable ($400,000 to Boston University and $410,000 to the Far West Laboratory), they were insignificant when compared with other federally funded curriculum projects in the 1960s and 1970s. For example, career education initiatives in the early 1970s were carried out through state educational agencies with more than $3 million in federal funds allotted to Ohio alone.

It is not then surprising that the 21 major critical viewing skills projects in the United States have left relatively few imprints on the curriculum. Brown's (1991) survey of projects according to type of sponsorship revealed no then-current funding of any such project by a state department of education or federal agency.

The undertaking of the Ministry of Church and Education in Norway affords an interesting contrast. Dahl (1981) reported on developments in media education in the 9 year compulsory school in which earlier preoccupations with hardware have yielded to a concern for the broader role of the mass media in the social and cultural development of a nation. In 1974-1975, comprehensive media education was available as an optional subject to children ages 13 to 19. Since then media education has become a main subject at the university level and is offered as a 1-year course for teachers. In 1980, 50% of Norway's secondary schools were offering a mass media course.

This example from a nation where there is a centralized control of education and where the roles of church and schools appear to be well articulated serves to remind us of the complexities involved in bringing about change in the decentralized U.S. system where strong consensus is slow to develop and sustainability depends upon true institutionalization of any initiative.

What has happened to media education in those school districts where the programs were locally developed and locally supported? The history of the five projects designed and initiated by the present authors (Syracuse, NY; Norfolk VA; Las Vegas NV; Idaho Falls, ID; and Eugene, OR) is perhaps instructive. Of these five projects, two remain active in some form.

The Idaho Falls Project, which was initiated in 1977, has had a continuing influence there. According to Craig Ashton, project director and now an elementary school principal, the study of bias in television commercials and the use of entertainment content to teach literary analysis have been continued in the curriculum at selected schools and by certain teachers. Fifth-grade pupils study their own uses of television, employing individual diaries of viewing to provide an empirical basis for the activity.

In Eugene, Oregon's District 4J, Channel 1, the commercial-based news service, is being used at the high school level, according to curriculum director Martha Harris, who was earlier on the district's television teacher. At the elementary level where the original project had sought to integrate critical viewing skills into "regular" curriculum areas, individual schools and classrooms treat critical viewing skills through various approaches. Eugene's District 4J is very decentralized, using site-based decision making. There are, therefore, significant differences in classroom presence of media education.

The Failure to Sustain

The experience of the Idaho and Oregon projects—sustained school by school or classroom by classroom—appears to be the typical history of media education implementations. In 1992, some 23 years after our earliest pilot activity in Belpre, Ohio, we conclude that media education has not yet been accepted into the mainstream of curriculum at either the elementary or secondary levels of U. S. schools. There is some utility in examining why. Our analysis would suggest at least three interacting conditions: inadequate models of media in society, the positioning of media education within the curriculum, and lack of infrastructure. We offer a short analysis of each in the headings that follow.

Inadequate Models

Small-scale studies of the views of parents regarding the inclusion of media education in the elementary school curriculum have consistently shown that there is strong support for such programs (Ploghoft, 1985). At the same time, there is strong evidence that parents do not consider the media to be a practical threat to their children (Anderson & Meyer, 1988; Buckingham, 1992).

Media education programs are often presented as a set of coping skills or interventionist instruction to inoculate children against the dangers of media. As has been noted, the implicit concern is dismissible based on the practical experience parents and children alike have with the media.

The protectionistic foundation of much of media education in the United States appears to be insufficient to sustain teacher interest and curriculum development. The more successful programs all present a critical thinking foundation that connects media education to a common conceptual base that literary theory, critical analysis, and the scientific method all share. Unfortunately, the connection appears not to have been made within the education establishment. In 1984, three widely read professional journals, *Social Education, Educational Leadership,* and the *Journal of Reading* each published articles that dealt with teaching critical thinking. In none of these articles was the content of television programming recognized as grist for the mills of the young minds that were being prepared to be critical. The entertainment programming of television, the commercial messages aimed at young customers, and the news as well apparently continue to be perceived as content that neither deserves or requires viewing with an analytic and discriminating attitude that calls for critical thinking at its best. Clearly, the goals and objectives of media education ought not to differ from those of other highly respected curriculum components that are designed to enable our youth to be independent problem solvers and decision makers in a democratic society.

Positioning

Education may be thought of in five parts: essential, canonical, foundational, social, and custodial. Very briefly, essential education deals with the basic skills of literacy and numeracy; canonical presents the cultural truths, texts, and themes of a society; foundational studies are those that lead to the next instructional level and finally to some exit position in society; social has to do with relational skills, developing the ability to enter into coordinated collective action; and custodial encompasses a host of "right living" learning by which education demonstrates good trusteeship of students' lives.

In the competitive arena of time and money, each discipline seeks to present itself as being as high in this hierarchy as it can. Despite its efforts to seize the high ground by naming itself variously critical receivership skills, media literacy, or cultural studies, media education typically remains at the lowest rung within the custodial domain.

It is situated here by its own protectionist models and the strong loyalty to traditional subject matter that has characterized the attitudes of educators and parents alike since the close of the 19th century. This situation has been most evident in the secondary schools where the curriculum has been driven by the entrance requirements of colleges and the current measure of quality is the performance of college-bound students on the American College Test. The priorities of the high school curriculum inevitably drive the programs of the elementary schools, hence critical viewing skills have encountered a stone wall of apathy. Other curriculum innovations such as career education have experienced a similar fate.

Positioned in this manner, media education becomes an easy target for budget cuts or curricular efficiencies. It also can offer no more than soft-bodied resistance to the constant time squeeze of the more solid, traditional content areas. The crowded curricula of elementary schools leaves little room for consideration of new programs. The most sensible entree would seem to be through the integration of new elements into existing curriculum fields such as social studies, language arts, consumer economics, and contemporary problems. However, the curriculum continues to be delivered through textbooks that are written by specialists who apparently lack interdisciplinary interest and linkages.

Lack of Infrastructure

Given the decentralized administration of U.S. schools, the persistence of curriculum depends on a number of separate but related elements. Inertia, as we have seen, is certainly one of these, but so too are continuing programs in teacher education and the market availability of textbooks and supporting curricular materials and technology.

Of these, only the market availability of supporting technology has come squarely behind media education. Video production and playback equipment costs have dropped to where these technologies are familiar household appliances. In the 11 years since its appearance, microcomputer costs have declined 300% to the point of being common classroom tools.

Unfortunately, textbooks and curricular applications that can bring this technology into education in a meaningful way remain sadly lacking. Media education, as an instructional concern, has received most serious attention and study by the community of communication scholars. An interactive bridge has not yet been established that would link the work of communication scholars to the special curriculum area groups that act as gatekeepers for the textbooks and the curriculum materials that are championed by state departments of education and by local school systems across the nation.

For example, the 1991 Association for Supervision and Curriculum Development publication, *Renewing the Social Studies Curriculum,* makes no mention of the ubiquitous medium of television as a source of social, political, and economic information or as a medium that presents special challenges to the critical decision-making abilities of the citizens in a democracy. It could well be assumed that the attention that has been devoted since the 1960s to the development of critical thinking, problem-solving skills, and the processes of rational inquiry in the social studies would have recognized the role of television in the lives of most Americans, young and old alike. But that has not been the case. An examination of the social studies textbooks that are widely used at elementary and secondary school levels reveals an almost complete absence of any provision for the development of the critical analytical skills of media education.

Language arts textbook materials are equally lacking in consideration of media education. Three major publishers, Houghton Mifflin (Haley-James & Steivig, 1990), Macmillan (Thoburn, 1987), and Laidlaw (Ney, Hars, Lapp, Meerson, & Armstaad, 1983), have put language arts texts on the market that reveal no awareness of the massive use of television by young people and the implications for language development that such use holds.

It should not be surprising that the textbooks written for use in teacher education programs have also neglected to attend to the educational implications of television. Considine (1990) notes that teacher education in general, "tends to ignore concepts such as visual literacy, critical viewing skills, and media education despite the fact that the concepts are now more than twenty years old" (p. 30). Dorr and Brannon (1992) conclude their analysis of teacher education in media with the comment: "Few receive much training in the social, political, ethical and economic aspects of American media and technology" (p. 18).

Requirements for Success

John Pungente, S.J., of the Jesuit Communication Project[1] has offered the following nine requirements for the successful implementation of media education based on his personal visits to projects in some 23 countries (personal communication, November 1991).

1. Media education, like other innovative programs, must be a grass roots movement and teachers need to take a major initiative in lobbying for this program.
2. Educational authorities must give clear support to such programs by mandating the teaching of media studies within the curriculum, establishing guidelines and resources, and making certain that curricula are developed and that materials are available.
3. Faculties of education must hire staff capable of training future teachers in this area. There should also be academic support from tertiary institutions in the writing of curricula and in sustained consultation.
4. In-service training at the school district level must be an integral part of program implementation.
5. School districts need consultants who have expertise in media education and who will establish communications networks.
6. Suitable textbooks and support materials relevant to the country/area must be available.
7. A support organization must be established for the purposes of workshops, conferences, dissemination of newsletters, and the development of curriculum units. Such a professional organization must cut across school boards and districts to involve a cross section of people interested in media education.
8. There must be appropriate evaluation instruments suitable for media studies.
9. Because media education involves such a diversity of skills and expertise, there must be a collaboration between teachers, parents, researchers, and media professionals.

Concluding Remarks

Worldwide, media education is undergoing a revival. Within the past 5 years, there have been international conferences in Sweden, Switzerland, France, Great Britain, Canada, and Germany. Effective programs have been put in place in Norway, Great Britain, Ontario, and in Catholic education in Australia. The United States, as the world's largest producer of popular culture, is still missing from this list despite the individual efforts of people like Aimee Dorr in teacher education, Kathleen Tyner in curriculum development, Karen Webster in public television, and Lyn Lacey in elementary education. In truth, much of Pungente's plan for success remains unfulfilled. The need, however, remains, as Dorr and Brannon (1992) so clearly state:

American children need education about the important and influential media and technology in their world of today, about how to use any medium or technology well for everyday life activities, about how to adapt to change and about how to become skilled users of whatever medium or technology may become an important part of the world tomorrow. (p. 22)

Note

1. John Pungente, S.J., Jesuit Communication Project, Mary Street, Suite 500, Canada M4Y 1PG.

References

Anderson, J. A. (1980). The theoretical lineages of critical viewing curricula. *Journal of Communication, 30,* 64-71.

Anderson, J. A. (1992). *Media education: A response.* Testimony given at the Media Competency: A Challenge to School and Education Conference, Gutersloh, Germany.

Anderson, J. A., & Meyer, T. P. (1988). *Mediated communication: A social action perspective.* Newbury Park, CA: Sage.

Association for Supervision and Curriculum Development. (1991). *Renewing the social studies curriculum.* Alexandria, VA: Author.

Bauer, R. A. (1963). The initiative of the audience. *Journal of Advertising Research, 3,* 2-7.

Bazalgette, C. (Ed.). (1989). *Primary media education: A curriculum statement.* London: British Film Institute.

Biocca, F. A. (1988). Opposing conceptions of the audience: The active and passive hemispheres of mass communication theory. In J. A. Anderson (Ed.), *Communication yearbook 11* (pp. 51-80). Newbury Park, CA: Sage.

Bowker, J. (Ed.). (1991). *Secondary media education: A curriculum statement.* London: British Film Institute.

Brown, J. A. (1991). *Television "critical viewing skills" education: Major media literacy projects in the United States and selected countries.* Hillsdale, NJ: Lawrence Erlbaum.

Buckingham, D. (1992). *Media literacy and the regulation of children's viewing.* Paper presented at the Standards in Screen Entertainment Third International Conference, London.

Canavan, K. B. (1975). *Mass media education.* Sidney: Catholic Information Office.

Considine, D. M. (1990). Media literacy: Can we get there from here? *Educational Technology, 30,* 27-32.

Dahl, T. (1981). *Media education in Norway.* Oslo: Ministry of Church and Education.

Dorr, A., & Brannon, C. (1992). *Media education in American schools at the end of the twentieth century.* Paper presented at the Media Competency: A Challenge to School and Education Conference, Gutersloh, Germany.

Duncan, B. (1988). *Mass media and popular culture.* New York: Harcourt Brace.

Haley-James, S., & Steivig, J. (1990). *English.* New York: Houghton Mifflin.

Long, J. F. (1989) *Critical viewing and decision strategies.* Unpublished doctoral dissertation, University of Utah, Salt Lake City.

Masterman, L. (1985). *Teaching the media.* London: Comedia.

Ney, J. W., Hars, W., Lapp, D., Meerson, M. L., & Armstaad Jr., M. (1983). *Language 8.* River Forest, IL: Laidlaw.

Ontario Ministry of Education. (1989). *Media literacy resource guide.* Toronto: Government of Ontario Publications.

Piette, J. (1992). *Teaching critical viewing skills from theory to practice to theory.* Paper presented at the Media Competency: A Challenge to School and Education Conference, Gutersloh, Germany.

Ploghoft, M. E. (1985). *A survey of parent views of their schools.* Athens: Center for Higher Education, Ohio University.

Roth, P. A. (1987). *Meaning and method in the social sciences.* Ithaca, NY: Cornell University Press.

Thoburn, T. (1987). *Macmillan English.* New York: Macmillan.

7. The Medium of Television and the School Curriculum

Turning Research Into Classroom Practice

GORDON L. BERRY

School-aged children in the United States live in a vast and ever-expanding multimedia environment. This environment means that they are part of a communications experience that is able to open the cultures of the world to them with the push of a button or the turn of a knob. One electronic communicator that is a leader in providing an information base for a large number of academic (cognitive) and attitudinal (affective) learning experiences for children is the medium of television.

Ready or not and like it or not, television is a major part of the culture of the country, and it is also a highly attractive medium to children. The tremendous use, and all too often misuse of television by children indicate its firm roots in our society, and its pervasive visual and auditory information provides another type of nonschool learning experience for the young viewer. Lloyd Morrisett (1982-1983) summarized television and its instructional qualities in the following way:

> Television is everywhere in our lives, widening our world and shaping our outlook. Television is America's home entertainer and instant informer, a living room salesman, a babysitter, time waster, and mass marketer of culture. Familiar as we are with television, we consistently overlook one of the functions it performs relentlessly, day in and day out: education. Television is America's neglected teacher. (p. 1)

AUTHOR'S NOTE: The author wishes to acknowledge the assistance of Crystal Cianfrini in the development of this chapter.

I subscribe here to the assumption of Morrisett that "Television is America's neglected teacher." Moving his concept further, however, my general assumptions are that television plays a major role in the life of children because it is a highly attractive medium, and it is also a type of electronic teacher that can provide through its visual and auditory content instructional information from which young viewers can and do learn.

Television in the School Curriculum

It would be natural for any classroom teacher who is considering using television in the classroom to have some concerns about it. After all, the research literature is full of such issues as: (a) children learning aggressive behavior from television; (b) children spending too much time looking at television; (c) children being negatively influenced by advertising; and (d) a host of other professional and parental concerns.

Our concern for children, especially those in preschool and the elementary grades, stems from the developmental notions that television program content involves character portrayals, ideas, and attractive models that can assist children in their social learning and other socialization activities. At the same time, my interpretation of the research in all of the areas of concern suggests, as Rudyard Kipling did in one of his famous poems, "We cannot look too good, nor talk too wise," about television and its effects on children. The reason for my caution is that there are a great many subtle and overt television messages that are frequently too complex for even researchers to truly understand what psychosocial impact they are having on one child as opposed to another (Berry, 1988). There is little doubt that television for some children offers value-oriented messages and attractive portrayals of role models that are admired, believed, and potentially imitated.

The major focus of this chapter is on the issues related to introducing television into the curriculum of the classroom. Curriculum within the context of this paper includes all of the planned learning experiences and activities for the learners under the school's guidance, direction, and supervision. Such a definition implies that the classroom teacher, as well as his or her institution, is involved in the preplanning of the curriculum using the theories, conditions of learning, and human development factors that are at the core of curriculum development. It is also assumed that any introduction of a new activity into the curriculum, such as the utilization of television, has met the curricular guidelines for making decisions about what is to be taught.

Every teacher knows it is important that parents understand what is going on in the school in general and the classroom in particular. It is crucial, therefore, that parents be brought into the planning and information loop in terms of the teacher's plans for using television in the curriculum. Helping parents to be a part of this teaching and learning process is not much different from assisting them in understanding new math, reading, and science programs. The essential key is that teachers and the other school professionals must inform parents early of their plans and seek parental input into the process. Early parental involvement is especially necessary when one is planning the use of the television in the classroom because parents will have to become active in providing access to the television set for their children and even learn to assist and guide the child's viewing behavior.

Television as a Teacher and the Child as a Learner

Program content from commercial television and videotape now offers for the young learner a new set of instructional experiences that were not possible before the advent of the medium. That is to say, television provides a new way of communicating information to the child. Television also permits many variations in the teaching and learning process, but its effective use in the school curriculum should be based upon those fundamental psychological principles that apply to all successful learning activities.

Television as a medium of entertainment and information can and frequently does require, especially of young children, active cognitive and affective processing in order for them to understand the content and formal features of selected programs. Wright and Huston (1984) highlight this mental activity concept by pointing out that selecting central content from incidental content, sequencing and temporally integrating events, inferring condition and events not shown, and the motives and feelings of characters all require a child to draw upon his or her world and television knowledge. These two researchers continue by noting that part of what a child uses to understand and learn from television is its formal features, which include such aspects as action, pace, visual techniques, and verbal and nonverbal auditory events. These formal features are not the same as content, according to these researchers, but it could be stated that there is a strong interrelationship between the two factors because the formal features are the mechanisms that young children use to make the content have meaning. Without focusing directly on formal features, Pezdek (1985) does support the notion that there is a learning activity that a child engages in while watching television by suggesting a need to conceptualize the viewing behavior of children as a series of information-processing stages; we perceive information, *attend* to it, *encode* it, *retain* it in memory, and later *retrieve* the information from memory.

If teachers are to capitalize on the positive uses of television in the classroom, they cannot approach their planning in a piecemeal or haphazard manner. The process of using television effectively can only be accomplished through a systematic approach that (a) establishes clear goals and objectives for using television in the classroom curriculum; (b) develops a plan that fully integrates television, videocassettes, and other media tools into the teaching and learning activities; (c) ensures that the pupils are properly prepared with critical television viewing skills so that they can understand the content, special features, and unique attributes of the medium; and (d) creates a plan for evaluating the effectiveness of using television in the classroom. Rapaczynski, D. Singer, and J. Singer (1982), recognizing that kindergarten to second-grade children might be particularly in need of critical viewing skills, developed a curriculum that included such topics as commercials, the portrayal of violence on television, stereotypes about sex and race, and the comprehension of sequence or "magical" effects in a television show.

Preparing Students to Be Visually Literate

The television set that is available in 98% of all U.S. homes and manages to occupy a great deal of children's time is not, taken alone, a villain. After all, it is only a box full of electronics. Our problem with television today is that neither parents nor children use it wisely, and professional communicators who make the decisions as to the nature of its content do not challenge them enough with quality content. It is therefore worth stating again that television properly used in the home and classroom can be an excellent medium for entertainment, information, and the subsequent learning that comes from both areas. As Greenfield (1984) stated: "Television and the new electronic media, if used wisely, have great potential for learning and development. They give children different mental skills from those developed by reading and writing" (p. 2).

Teachers can assist children to become wise television viewers by introducing into their instructional activities those skills that will prepare the learner to be visually literate. A visually literate person is able to discriminate and interpret both the natural and manufactured visual stimuli that the person encounters in his or her environment (King, Tudrick, Post, Strickland, & Petty, 1981).

Program Examples of Television in the Classroom

Teachers across the nation have been taking advantage of students' motivations to watch television by putting it to work in several areas in the classroom. However, the literature documents the difficulty of using live or over-the-air broadcasts in the classroom, due to factors such as timing, lesson planning, and an inability to screen programs for appropriateness (Mielke, 1988). As videotaping has become simple and inexpensive, many teachers choose to tape television shows in advance or use such tapes already available in their schools' media libraries to get around these drawbacks. In fact, some studies show that television programs are used much more extensively and more often by teachers if they are videotaped first (Cropp, 1990; Gayeski, 1989; Mielke, 1988).

Unlike some of the more recent electronic devices, television and the video recorder as potential teaching tools are generally common and available for all of the children in a particular classroom. There are, to be sure, families who have different rules governing the use of television, but few children will be without one.

The next section will cover in outline fashion some of the specific ways in which television can or has been integrated into the school curriculum. Although the areas identified are treated as separate subjects, it is important to remember that television content, like other curricular information, can be handled in a manner where two or three different studies are integrated within one lesson plan.

Finally, the curricular suggestions are not grade specific, because they only serve as a point of departure for ideas that teachers can adapt to their respective age groups.

1. TV and video have been incorporated into a curriculum design for the Virginia public schools to teach existing classroom lessons as well as to teach students how to be competent, critical users of both the programming shown and the media equipment itself (Orlando & Farrelly, 1987). A selection of suggested exercises are included in the literature. In fifth grade, students are taught how to use video cameras and video recorders (VCRs). In eighth grade, students study the difference between primary and secondary sources by viewing segments of *60 Minutes,* followed by student library research on the topic(s) covered on the tape. In ninth grade, students compare the presentation of one news story across a variety of media to see which media highlight which types of information and why. By 12th grade, students learn about the strengths and weaknesses of the various media by analyzing advertising strategies used in television, print, and other forms of communication.
2. A paper presented at the Annual Conference on Newspapers in Education and Literacy (Shapley, 1991) describes a media literacy project in which high school students can be taught how to critically use TV and print. They are taught the needs and priorities of the different media, and how each can shape the reality of the stories it runs.
3. In Canada, TVOntario was enlisted to produce programming related to the science curriculum, to add to its already broad collection of science programs (Gillis, Glegg, Larkin, & Ojo, 1991). In one report evaluating a teacher-training model using this science programming, a total of 36 schools and 44 teachers in four school districts used TVOntario's programming over 3 years. The students were of four curriculum levels: primary, junior, intermediate, and senior. Student activities ranged from viewing experiments and then replicating them to participating via television in activities they might not have experienced otherwise, like whale watching. The program resulted in increased use of TV in the curriculum over the course of the 3-year project. The teachers in the study attribute this increase to "a

greater awareness of available programs, a greater familiarity with the content of the programs, and more opportunity to preview" (Gillis et al., 1991). Although some of the teachers went beyond the parameters of the study and used extra TV and film programs (e.g., National Geographic, National Film Board), most teachers expressed satisfaction with TVOntario's programming. Several teachers became so comfortable with the media and convinced of their effectiveness that they reported using them in areas other than science, such as English and language arts.

4. One study described the possible social studies curriculum uses of educational programming produced by the Children's Television Workshop (CTW), such as *3-2-1 Contact*, *Sesame Street*, and *Square One TV* (Mielke, 1988). The target audience for these programs ranges in age from approximately 2 years to 12 years. The materials available from CTW were found to be properly in line with the educational imperatives for grades K-6, as set out by the National Council for the Social Studies (NCSS). Examples were cited in the study that applied particular episodes of the programs to critical areas of learning in social studies, such as a *3-2-1 Contact* clip using a time-lapse animation sequence to illustrate continental drift, and a theme week from the same show on various environmental and economic aspects of the tropics.
5. Of particular interest to social science educators is LEARNING LINK, a service developed by WNET in New York (Bodwell, 1988). This system meshes TV, the VCR, and the computer in order to share information with and among educators about how to link classroom lessons with appropriate programming. Some of these programs are produced on public television, and some supplementary programs come from commercial television.
6. A class of Missouri high school juniors and seniors responded quite favorably to a six-part videotape series on contemporary poets and their poetry: "The Power of the Word," hosted by Bill Moyers. The subjects in this series are living, writing poets of various ethnic backgrounds. They are introduced and interviewed, then they read selections from their work. Excerpts from the students' written reactions to the tape indicate a high level of interest and involvement with the subject matter.
7. A group of Navajo high school students known to be at risk were involved in a program designed to bring about "critical

awareness" and empowerment in their English class (Squires & Inlander, 1990). The students' language codes and concerns were elucidated using dialogue between students and teachers, then these codes and concerns were used to guide the curriculum. The students were encouraged to develop a videotape of their own that served as an impetus for discussion of story, style, and taping procedures. The project resulted in increases in communication skills, media literacy, personal and social growth, and critical thinking in a group.

8. A program designed to stimulate writing among students from K-12 encouraged them to use TV's style of scripting as a framework within which to organize their own news and fiction stories (Raper, 1987). Children were first exposed to the notion that TV contributes to poor writing skills, then to the concepts of storyboards via instruction and activities. Eventually, they read scripts from professional TV shows, news, and commercials, and then wrote their own.

These brief examples of approaches for using television in selected areas of the curriculum are rather basic and straightforward. They were intended to serve only as a springboard for the creative teacher who can see ways to positively exploit and expand subject matter through the use of television. Not only can teachers expand information, television is also a medium that can be used by them to reinforce in the child less familiar areas of the curriculum, foster problem-solving skills, and enhance a variety of thinking styles. According to Rowe (1985), television content can be an excellent tool for teaching divergent thinking and the discipline needed for critical thinking. Rowe's position is that as some children become actively involved in television, they think freely and at a higher cognitive level because they feel comfortable with it.

Finally, teachers should not feel alone in their efforts to find materials that will help them exploit the positive uses of television. There are free and inexpensive materials available to assist them in their programmatic efforts to integrate television into the classroom curriculum. A classroom teacher can find networks, governmental units, and nonprofit groups who have prepared materials that can be related to this instructional program.

Children, Television, and the Curriculum: Challenge to Teachers in a Period of Reform

An appropriate way to begin some final thoughts is to state in summary fashion that the teacher who is planning to use television and other media in the classroom is one who: (a) understands the role of television in our culture; (b) understands the potential of television as a teacher and its special characteristics in the teaching/learning process; (c) understands how to prepare the pupils in the classroom to become visually literate and critical television viewers; (d) understands some of the guidelines for making assignments and how to handle discussions related to television; and (e) understands that parents have to be kept informed as to plans to use television in the curriculum.

The research related to television and children tells us that it is a powerfully attractive medium that is firmly rooted into our culture. Although it is clear that schools today have enough burdens thrust upon them by society, I have suggested throughout this chapter that educators should begin to utilize this medium in the classroom, and to assist our children to become wise television consumers and visually literate adults. Children of today live in a multimedia, information-based technical world in which the television set is but the tip of the iceberg. Schools must not fail to prepare children to utilize this technically based medium with complicated social messages. Frank Withrow's (1990) quote from Edward R. Morrow places television in perspective: "This instrument can teach, it can illuminate; yes it can even inspire. But it can do so only to the extent that humans are determined to use it to those ends, otherwise it is merely lights and wires in a box" (p. 3). Clearly, it has been this fear that television is more than just "lights and wires in a box" that has caused some educational reformers to overlook its role as a systemic part of our culture and powerful teacher of our children.

The words attributed to Edward R. Morrow identify the challenge for the classroom teacher and all of us concerned with the education of children who are growing and developing in an information-oriented and multimedia world. That challenge is for all educators to learn both the positive and negative potentials of television, and to be rigorous in their application of it in the teaching/learning process inside and outside of the classroom. This rigor implies that each educator will fully appreciate the role of this medium as a potential vehicle for continuing with education's important task of developing critical thinking in children. The challenge for educators who decide to use television in the classroom is also to select content that will sharpen and reinforce intellectual, social, and multicultural skills in children.

Television should not be used as a passive pictorial quick fix for learning about complicated issues related to the human condition. The challenge to the classroom teacher is to assist the children in their charge to become visually literate so that they can read and analyze television in the same way they do books. If we as teachers, researchers, parents, and reformers can meet the challenges of the problems and promises of this important medium, we will be able to capitalize on its many educational, informational, and entertainment strengths, as well as develop a group of future adults who can also understand its weaknesses.

References

Berry, G. L. (1988). Multicultural role portrayals on television as a socio-psychological issue. In S. Oskamp (Ed.), *Television as a social issue* (pp. 118-129). Newbury Park, CA: Sage.

Bodwell, D. F. (1988). A perspective on public broadcasting and education. *Social Education, 52*(5), 354-357.

Cropp, D. (1990). Are media needs being met for the beginning teacher? *Journal of Educational Technology Systems, 18*(3), 215-234.

Gayeski, D. M. (1989). Why information technologies fail. *Educational Technology, 29*(2), 9-17.

Gillis, L., Glegg, L., Larkin, J., & Ojo, M. (1991). *The summative evaluation of the science quality education project (SQEP)* (Evaluation and project research report No. 9-1990-91). Toronto: Ontario Educational Communications Authority.

Greenfield, P. (1984). *Mind and media, the effects of television, video games, and computers.* Cambridge, MA: Harvard University Press.

King, K. L., Tudrick, J. A., Post, G. L., Strickland, J. D., & Petty, B. A. (1981). *A systematic approach to instructional media competency, orientation, operation, action.* Dubuque, Iowa: Kendall Hunt.

Mielke, K. W. (1988). Television in the social studies classroom. *Social Education, 52*(5), 362-365.

Morrisett, L. N. (1982-1983). *Television: America's neglected teacher.* New York: John and Mary R. Markle Foundation. (Reprinted from Annual Report)

Orlando, L. S., & Farrelly, D. (1987, October). *Captain Video introduces power, process, and production: Media to enhance learning, K-12.* Paper presented at the annual conference of the Virginia Educational Media Association, Roanoke, VA.

Pezdek, K. (1985). Is watching TV passive, uncreative, or additive? Debunking some myths. *Television and Families, 8*(2), 41-46.

Rapaczynski, W., Singer, D., & Singer, J. (1982). Teaching television: A curriculum for young children. *Journal of Communication, 32*(2), 46-54.

Raper, L. F. (1987). *Techniques from television to stimulate classroom writing* (ERIC Document Reproduction Service No. ED 284-299).

Rowe, M. (1985). Educating children in the television age. *Television and Families, 8*(2), 24-26.

Shapley, B. (1991, May). *Integrating mass media instruction: "Connecting" NIE and TV programs for the 21st century.* Paper presented at the Annual Conference on Newspapers in Education and Literacy, New Orleans.

Squires, N., & Inlander, R. (1990). A Freireian-inspired video curriculum for at-risk high-school students. *English Journal, 79*(2), 49-56.

Withrow, F. B. (1980, March). *Critical television viewing skills.* Paper presented at the National Workshop on Television and Youth, Washington, DC.

Wright, J. C., & Huston, A. C. (1984). The potentials of television for young viewers. In J. M. Murray & G. Salomon (Eds.), *The future of children's television* (pp. 65-80). Boys Town, NE: Boys Town and The John and Mary R. Markle Foundation.

PART II

Television and the Development of a Child's Worldview

Television offers children an opportunity to embark on a social-cultural journey that reaches beyond the family and neighborhood with which they are familiar. Through this audiovisual experience, children not only gain a perspective of how they are perceived, but also develop perceptions about how others think, feel, and behave. Hence, television contributes to the development of a child's worldview.

The chapters in Part II are intended to provide an understanding of what children learn about themselves and others from the interdependent relationship that has emerged between this medium and our youth. The contributors come from diverse academic backgrounds and hence offer the reader an opportunity to experience a stimulating variation in how the scholarship is presented. The chapters range from think pieces to traditional empirical content, but the common thread that exists among the contributors is that television does have a significant role in shaping the worldview of children.

Part II begins with a chapter by George Comstock delineating a historical perspective on the role television has played in U.S. society, particularly in regards to the influence this medium has had on the socialization of our youth. He talks about television providing "the imagery and the impressions which become part of the social fabric."

Bradley S. Greenberg and Jeffrey E. Brand focus their research efforts on what would be considered more typical children's television fare, evaluating the cultural content of Saturday morning television programming on the three major commercial broadcast networks. These researchers were interested in providing the reader with some understanding as to what children learn about the diverse races and cultures of the United States from the programs and commercials to which they are exposed each Saturday morning.

In a review co-authored by Edward L. Palmer, K. Taylor Smith, and Kim S. Strawser, the point is made that television provides an opportunity for the children of the world "to catch a glimpse of one another." A concern raised by these contributors is whether these glimpses reflect the multicultural perspective that truly exemplifies the world in which we exist.

Finally, Richard L. Allen shares with readers his theoretical propositions as to what is involved in a child's development of a worldview. Emerging from a sound empirical basis, he specifically traces the development of an African-American child's belief system, acknowledging that his worldview development theory could be easily adapted, with minor modifications, to other cultures within our nation. The media, in particular television, are cited as an important factor in how African-American children learn about themselves and others.

8. The Medium and the Society

The Role of Television in American Life

GEORGE COMSTOCK

The only item to rival television in consumer excitement in the years after World War II was the auto, newly arrived from Detroit plants converted from the war effort. Sightseers flocked to dealerships and prospective buyers joined waiting lists. Television similarly quickened the acquisitive pulse. Introduced in the late 1940s and early 1950s, the medium immediately captured the public's enduring fancy with onlookers clustering around the windows of appliance outlets where it was displayed in operation. In communities where it was introduced immediately, it took a mere 4 years before three fourths of households had sets. Where it was introduced later, after people had a better understanding of what they would be getting, the rate of adoption was about twice as rapid.

The public liked what they saw. As soon as television became available in a community, soaring set purchase ensured an increasing market for additional programming. In 1946, there were 10,000 sets in use with 11 hours of programming in the evenings provided by two networks with a few outlets. Four years later, the number had increased more than 1,000-fold to 10.5 million with 90 hours broadcast weekly by about 100 stations representing four networks, the American Broadcasting Company (ABC), Columbia Broadcasting System (CBS), and National Broadcasting Company (NBC) that remain preeminent, and the soon-to-falter DuMont Television Network (DTN). By 1970, the number of sets in use was 93 million. One or more were in 96% of U.S. households. Today that figure exceeds 98%. Television can be fairly said to be ubiquitous in the United States.

Looking back from the beginning of the 1970s, the well-known sociologist and media analyst Leo Bogart (1972) described the preceding years in *The Age of Television*. He concluded that the medium had significant and wide-ranging effects, particularly on other media and on leisure. Later as more evidence became available from the behavioral and social sciences, others (Comstock, 1989, 1991a, 1991b) would add everyday behavior, politics, and the role of the media and particularly entertainment in daily life, to the list.

Television as a social-cultural force in fact presents a nest of paradoxes. In the short run, its influence is typically minute. No single program or segment of programming makes much of a difference. The reason is that most of programming is redundant, so that what is experienced—whether entertainment, sports, or news—does not differ much from what has been experienced already. Yet, there will be embedded in this sameness recurring effects, such as on the behavior of children. These will be repeated day after day, and in the case of children, may contribute to the development of traits that will remain evident in adult life. This redundancy is nevertheless regularly interrupted by displays that capture the attention of some segment of the public—small, large, and sometimes seemingly entire—to an extraordinary degree: the particularly popular serial or powerful program, the calamitous or preeminent event, the confrontation in sports that decides a championship. These become the focus of millions, and for them the currency of social interaction through conversation. These events often persist in memory as nostalgic evocations or symbols of historic occurrences or human tragedy. In these instances, the influence of the medium resides not in affecting how people behave but in what they think about. The medium becomes a social-cultural force not because people are what they see, but because what they see and talk about are important parts of their experience of U.S. life. These effects are confined to the mind and social exchange. There also is the potential for regular viewing in the long run to cultivate the values and beliefs represented by the characters, situations, themes, and topics emphasized recurrently, and thus give shape to the worldview on which behavior is based, as well as for the unusually compelling portrayal to affect immediate behavior among teenagers and adults as well as children, sometimes in nontrivial ways.

The medium should be seen in context—one of ideology, technological development, and historical evolution. The first is responsible for the shaping of television. The second accounts for the significant differences between the television of today and that of the two decades of network hegemony, the 1960s and 1970s. The third signifies the remarkable continuity in the character of television that has marked the adoption of the innovations that have changed it.

The ideology was expressed in nonpaternalism, which led to two prominent features, competition and entertainment (Comstock, 1980, 1989). This three-part paradigm derives from broadcasting, but applies equally well to the present landscape of cable, pay services, satellites, and in-home recording and playback.

The U.S. system of broadcasting was established for radio by the Federal Communications Act of 1934. Chaotic crowding of the limited spectrum space was expected if some form of regulation were not imposed. The act established the Federal Communications Commission (FCC) to license stations and otherwise oversee national electronic communications. The airwaves were defined as public property, and in exchange for their use, licensees are required by the act to serve the "public interest, convenience, and necessity."

The system exemplifies the values of free enterprise. No concept of what "public interest, convenience, and necessity" might mean guided the arrangement. Instead, the philosophy that would govern programming became defined by the marketplace. This is in sharp contrast to the development of broadcasting in many other societies, where philosophy has guided structure. In Great Britain, for example, the British Broadcasting Corporation (BBC) was founded as a public corporation independent of the government but dependent for revenues on government-authorized license fees imposed on set owners to serve a vision of service to the nation. Even today, with the proliferation of both BBC and independent, advertiser-supported channels, all are assigned broad goals to strive for and specific audiences to serve.

The two defining consequences are competition and entertainment. In broadcasting, audiences that are bigger or demographically more attractive are more profitable because advertisers will pay more to reach them. The result is the quick discard of programs that are not optimally popular in a business where information about success or failure can be almost immediate, as indicated by the nomenclature for major market ratings and shares ("overnights"). For cable channels where advertising is not the principal source of revenue, popularity still determines viability because operators will discard those not optimally contributing to income. Inevitably, then, entertainment—as a programming category and a creed governing sports and news—becomes the dominant factor because it is more certain to attract viewers.

Paradoxically, this dominance persists when cable, pay services, satellites, and in-home recording and playback make possible almost infinite diversity. The explanation lies partly in media economics, partly in audience psychology, and partly in cultural sociology. However, before pursuing these topics the stage should be set by the story of how television has become what it is.

Three Ages

So far in fact there have been three ages of U.S. television, each with its distinct character: (a) the late 1940s through the 1950s, (b) the 1960s and 1970s, and (c) the 1980s to the present.

The first, marked by expansion, saw the medium assume its essential shape and role. Diffusion was almost complete by the end of the 1950s, with 86% of households (44 million) having one or more sets and 510 privately owned commercial stations in operation. A brief flirtation with original, live drama—*Kraft Television Theater, Philco Television Playhouse, Playhouse 90, Revlon Theater, Robert Montgomery Presents, Studio One, U.S. Steel Hour*—produced in New York, in which television was the nucleus for Oscar-winning movies and hit Broadway plays, gave way to series filmed in Hollywood. The shift was not merely one of mode (live versus filmed), length (60 minutes versus 30), or format (original story versus series episode); it marked the demise of the attempt to present compelling, often controversial stories striving for human and social significance in favor of programming more consonant with the economic foundations of the medium (Boddy, 1991). The series exchanged bold invention for the reiterative arranging of characters, themes, and settings constituted in advance. They were easier and quicker to produce; as the nomenclature implies, they were suited to assembly line production; and filming made advance inventory feasible. Advertisers were now assured that their commercials were not likely to fall adjacent to the disturbing or disagreeable.

Finally, the networks adopted in place of program sponsorship the contemporary practice of selling commercial time piecemeal on programs tailored to their specifications. The ostensible reason was the halting of the renowned advertiser meddling (Barnouw, 1982; Boddy, 1991) in program content. Probably more important was the foreclosing of sponsor decisions contrary to network goals such as support for a program not optimal in ratings, image, or lead-in to the next offering. With the importance of the overall schedule in attracting and holding viewers becoming increasingly apparent, the move gave the networks the power to shape it as they wished. It also vastly increased the market for network advertising by opening it to those not able to underwrite whole programs, and additionally gave the networks a share of an unexpected but growing source of revenue, syndication or "program resales." By the end of the decade, network television was entrenched as a purveyor of popular programming to mass audiences.

The second time period, distinguished by comparative stability, saw the three major networks extend and consolidate their hegemony. At the beginning of the 1960s, almost 90% of households had sets; by the end of the 1970s, the figure was approaching 100%. Cable, available since the days of radio to relay broadcast signals to remote locations, by the end of the 1970s was subscribed to by only 20% of households, and by the mid-1960s fully one fifth of communities could receive only the outlets of the three networks. By the midpoint of the two decades, more than 9 out of 10 commercial stations were affiliated with the networks and their prime-time audience share was even more exaggerated.

Technological developments increased the medium's appeal and thereby strengthened the prevailing pattern. Set costs declined; screens became bigger and reception clearer. Portable sets became lighter and trimmer, and households with two or more sets increased from 7% to 50%. The networks converted to color in the mid-1960s, and households with color sets increased from fewer than 1% in 1960 to about 80% by the end of the 1970s.

Public television was founded by Congress in 1967, with the three-tier system that still persists—the Corporation for Public Broadcasting (CPB) as the national policymaker; the Public Broadcasting System (PBS) as the amalgam of stations for program dissemination; and as major sources of financial support, government, private foundations, and viewers. By the end of the era, there were about 250 public stations in operation, a 700% increase over the 35 educational stations in existence at the end of the 1950s. In contrast, there were by this time more than 725 commercial stations, and their ratio between VHF (Very High Frequency) and the harder to receive UHF (Ultra High Frequency) was 70/30 compared to a far less favorable 40/60 for the public stations. Public television offered an alternative but hardly a challenge, as its audience share for the past 2½ decades has consistently fallen below 5%. These two decades saw network television seemingly unassailable.

The third time period was the setting for substantial changes. Network hegemony, but not preeminence, was ended. Programming sources became more varied—independents, superstations, pay-per-view, basic and premium cable, videocassette recorders (VCRs). Technological developments that had begun to accumulate by the end of the 1970s were largely responsible, but the term evolution was more applicable than revolution (Comstock, 1989).

By the beginning of the 1990s, a majority of households were receiving television by cable. The respecification of spectrum limitations led to an enormous increase in the number of commercial stations from about 700 in 1970 to about 1300, with most coming into being during the 1980s. As a result, only slightly more than half (55%) of stations remained affiliated with one of the three major networks. In the mid-1960s, 40% of households could receive four or fewer channels. That figure is now approaching zero. About 80% can receive 11 or more, with about one fourth receiving 30 or more. Network prime-time audience shares declined throughout the 1980s, and have fallen below 70%. The VCR has captured the public's heart. In about 5% of households in 1983, today more than two thirds have one or more.

Much that was prophesied nonetheless has not come to pass (Comstock, 1991a). The wired city and wired nation, with most households linked by cable in an electronic network delivering private and public services such as security, education, civic information, banking, and investment is far in the future. Cultural cable channels with highbrow schedules have gone into bankruptcy, and other specialized channels—"narrowcasting," in the jargon—for health, finance, children, travel, erotica, and the like, in general have found they need to widen their appeal to succeed. Children's cable programming free of commercials was short-lived, as commercials increase total revenues. The electronic newspaper, with information displayed on the screen or printed out in the home to the specifications of the receiver, has failed repeatedly in market tests. Original programming for cable, and especially drama, has not had a major role.

Cable adds to or diverts the household income expended on the media, and for many—more than a third of households—it has not been seen as justifying the added expense or the jettisoning of other media. Production costs are high, and the small audiences that original programming, highbrow offerings, and narrowcast concepts attract do not lead to revenues that make them viable.

Television in U.S. society has the role of satisfying popular tastes with entertainment, sports, and news. People seek other gratifications elsewhere. When television offers alternatives, there are comparatively few to put it to such uses partly because those who seek them, although large in number, are a modest segment of the mass audience and partly because only a few among them would consider the medium an appropriate means to such ends.

Thus, television today, although in many ways very different from what it was in its first two decades, is also fundamentally very much the same. What is different is that people have a vastly larger array of choices from which to choose. The satisfactions, although small in the large scheme, are considerable—24-hour news and weather, sports not popular enough for broadcasting, old films, new movies, television drama and comedy from other eras, recycled documentaries. What is the same are the broad contours of the enterprise.

Broadcasting remains the source of most people's viewing. Its prime-time share exceeds 80%. The share of the three major networks has decreased even as that of the independents, including the stations that have become part of the nascent Fox Network, has increased. Even so, at slightly below 70%, the three networks remain predominant, and in the matter of what people see, this is markedly enhanced by the reliance of many of these independents (as well as affiliates when they are not being fed a signal by the network) on reruns of programs originally produced to network specifications. Much of what is viewed by cable subscribers are broadcast channels, although they may be relayed by satellite from distant cities as are the superstations TBS (Atlanta), WGN (Chicago), and WOR (New York) that in effect have become national outlets. The prime-time audience shares of basic and premium cable, although growing slowly, are smaller than that of the independents. Even the VCR, which exceeds cable in household diffusion and has been adopted at a rate almost as rapid as that for television itself, has not had a great impact on national viewing patterns (Dorr & Kunkel, 1990). The most noteworthy effect has been to increase markedly the viewing of movies, including those branded with a warning advisory, by young persons (Greenberg & Heeter, 1987). Otherwise, use is divided between recording for later replay and viewing prerecorded tapes, with the latter becoming increasingly dominant as persons not attracted by the former acquire VCRs for access to the increasingly inexpensive and wide array of software. However, half or more of what is recorded is never replayed, and the likelihood of replay decreases sharply with the passage of time (Comstock, 1991a). Except among the young persons in the typical household, movies are rented only about once every 3 weeks (Dorr & Kunkel, 1990); a week often passes without any VCR use (Wartella, Heintz, Aidman, & Mazzarella, 1990); some viewing of prerecorded tapes represents time that would not be spent on ordinary television; and the total time spent in VCR usage typically is a small proportion of time spent on television (Comstock, 1991a). The VCR is psychologically catalogued by people as belonging to media where great selectivity is usually exercised, such as books, theater movies, and recorded music (Cohen, Levy, & Golden, 1988), but it has not changed the way people use television or the amount of ordinary television that is consumed (Levy, 1989). Thus, television remains constant to its founding paradigm despite the potential offered by technological innovations.

Allocation of Time

Television has had as large an impact on the allocation of time as any modern consumer item (Robinson, 1977, 1990). In turn, the time spent on television has had significant implications for other media and for other activities.

Television has increased time spent on the mass media by an average of about 1 hour per day (Comstock, 1991b). It stands by far first in leisure time in the United States, and is third in total expenditure of time behind work or school and sleep (Condry, 1989). Much of the time spent on television was drawn from other media (Bogart, 1972; Robinson, 1977), with radio listening, magazine reading, and movie going all declining upon the introduction of the medium. Other activities that were somewhat curtailed included the pursuit of hobbies, conversations with friends, religious observations, house cleaning, minor leisure travel, and by a very few minutes, sleep.

Comic book sales declined. Movie theaters began to close. Hugely popular general circulation magazines with heterogeneous audiences like that attracted by television went out of business—*Collier's, The American, The Saturday Evening Post, Look,* and *Life.* The first two represent functional displacement—a newer medium cutting into the audience of an established one because it serves similar functions, personal or social, in a superior manner, whether measured by lower cost, greater convenience, or enhanced pleasure and reward. The third represents economic undercutting—the newer medium attracted the advertising revenues that formerly had gone to the national magazines.

The medium in fact has the potential for highly variable influences on leisure activities of all kinds—it can promote them by drawing the public's attention, finance them by fees for television rights (as has been the case with many sports). One result was a new national holiday created by television, Super Bowl. It also can substitute for or compete with other activities. Thus, early weekly boxing shows drove local live boxing into relative poverty and obscurity; early major league telecasts turned fans away from minor league baseball, with attendance falling from 42 million in 1949 to only about 10 million two decades later; and the National Football League blanks out local coverage unless there is a sellout—an arrangement imposed by Congress in the only fans' rights legislation ever enacted.

The A. C. Nielsen Company estimates average household consumption during the fall and winter at about 55 hours per week (Comstock, 1991b). By age, this translates into about 28 hours for children 2 to 11, about 23½ hours for teenagers, about 29 hours for men, and about 34 hours for women 35 to 54, and considerably more—9 hours more for males and 8 for females—for those older, with younger adults viewing about 1½ hours less. The amount of viewing in the United States has always been inversely associated with socioeconomic status, with education having a larger role than income, so taste is certainly a factor, but the role of time available is so great that the age groups that are higher in exposure also are those more likely to be at home—children, women, older adults.

Television viewing has been said to be characterized by "content indifference," "low involvement," and "monitoring" (Comstock,

1991b). The commodity typically consumed is the medium, not the program. Estimated hours of viewing thus include much else and do not represent attention to the screen, but because this "discontinuous, often interrupted, and frequently nonexclusive activity for which a measure in hours and minutes serves only as the outer boundary of possible attention" (Comstock, Chaffee, Katzman, McCombs, Roberts, 1978, pp. 146-147) is what people are engaged in when they record themselves as viewing in audience measurement, they represent what viewing is taken to mean in our society by the viewers themselves and have the validity of folk definition.

Public Events and Occurrences

Television has become synonymous with the portrayal of public events and occurrences. It has become in the public eye the symbol of news. It has achieved this status principally by three endeavors of the major networks—the regular nightly newscasts, the protracted focus on the out of the ordinary, and the coverage of presidential campaigns.

Today, about two thirds of Americans tell pollsters they get most of their news from television (Comstock et al., 1978; Roper Organization, 1987). This attests to the high esteem in which the public holds the medium, but it vastly overrepresents television as the daily source of news. Careful analyses (Lichty, 1989; Robinson & Levy, 1986) indicate that about twice as many people are likely to see some part of a newspaper than any portion of a network evening news program over a 2-week period, and that fewer than 5% and perhaps as few as 1% will tune in every day during a week.

The explanation is almost certainly that television connotes "news" because it covers the big events nationally and internationally in a memorable way. Television is typically less rapid than radio because of its more restricted schedule, but for major events—disasters, riots, warfare—it quickly becomes the source to which much of the public turns. It enjoys a reputation for credibility and fairness because film implies validity, news personnel are chosen for their authoritative and trustworthy manner and can be judged by any viewer, and the style of presentation strives for aloof observation.

In the case of unusual events and occurrences, television becomes a means for vicarious involvement. These instances range across the tragic, the historic, and the ceremonial. Sometimes, they are unexpected, as in the case of presidential assassinations, the crushing of the prodemocracy movement in China's Tianamen Square, and the collapse of the Soviet Union. When they are expected, as in the case of royal weddings and the Super Bowl, they may become the occasion for social gatherings reminiscent of the excitement television was able to generate in its early years.

Television has become the framework for presidential campaigns. The medium has contributed to their lengthening by giving attention to the most minor of contests for delegates and public attention, made national events of state and regional contests, participated in the narrowing of the field by drawing attention to front-runners to the comparative exclusion of others, and become a major means by which the electoral decision making about leadership is placed on the nation's agenda. Television news coverage and paid-for spots are central to campaign strategy, the latter often becoming the subject of the former because of their presumed importance. Televised debates are now an established institution in which no candidate dare refuse to participate. Conventions produce few surprises, only partly because delegates mostly chosen in primaries are pledged. Other reasons are that the hundreds of journalists arrayed by television tabulate every outcome in advance and the conventions themselves have become orchestrated by the parties to make a favorable impression on viewers. Network television in turn has abandoned gavel-to-gavel coverage in favor of packaging the highlights—a more succinctly entertaining portrayal of politics.

Thus, television supplies the imagery and the impressions that become part of the social fabric. These become the subject matter for our thoughts and feelings. Given the daily emphases of the news, television justifies, legitimizes, and celebrates the society's institutions.

Socialization

The influence of television on children and teenagers is not limited to time allocation. It enters into socialization in three interrelated ways—as a portrayer of behavior that may be emulated, as the provider of impressions that may serve as the basis of action, and as the means by which entertainment and consumption become established early for many as part of the substance of everyday life.

Television shapes behavior by providing examples (Bandura, 1986). These examples are particularly likely to have some influence when the behavior in question is portrayed as effective, normative, or pertinent; that is, as helping to achieve a goal, as what people ordinarily do, or as especially applicable to the circumstances of a viewer (Comstock, 1991b). Violence is only the most studied example. The empirical pattern, accumulating for three decades, has resisted every challenge (Hearold, 1986; Kang, 1990; Paik, 1991). Experiments demonstrate causation within their limited and artificial boundaries—young persons of all ages behave in a more antisocial manner after exposure to a violent portrayal. Surveys document that violence viewing and greater aggressive or antisocial behavior are associated in everyday life. This pattern favors the conclusion that violent programming encourages socially undesirable behavior. Analogous effects occur for other categories of behavior, including those falling under the rubric "prosocial," such as generosity, helping, and interethnic cooperation. Television is a catalogue of modes of behavior; whether they affect what viewers do depends on their being taken as rewarding, acceptable, and applicable. In the case of violence, most of the evidence represents interpersonal aggression and minor incursions, but that which exists for seriously harmful or criminal behavior suggests that they are similarly affected (Comstock, 1991b; Cook, Kendzierski, & Thomas, 1983; Paik, 1991) so that effects are not necessarily trivial.

Another means by which television figures in socialization is by the "cultivation" of beliefs through the way in which the world is repeatedly depicted by the medium (Gerbner, Gross, Morgan, & Signorielli, 1980, 1984; Hawkins & Pingree, 1980, 1982; Hawkins, Pingree, & Adler, 1987; Morgan, 1988). For example, there is some evidence that the greater the amount of television violence seen, the greater the likelihood that the world will be perceived as "mean and risky" (Hughes, 1980). If such an effect occurs it is primarily for cognitive beliefs, or pessimism about social relations, rather than feelings of personal endangerment or fearfulness (Comstock, 1991b; Tyler & Cook, 1984). Similar claims have been made about other topics, such as gender roles. The process conceivably is one in which the emphases of programs tend to make people somewhat more homogeneous in outlook, a long-standing hypothesis in regard to television (Bogart, 1972). Whatever the long-term effects of consistencies across-program, those programs that depart from the ordinary, such as powerful movies about those differing in ethnicity or presentations counter to gender stereotypes, can have an immediate impact on beliefs and attitudes, although again principally about how the world works and what others might do rather than the self (Comstock, 1991b; Johnston & Ettema, 1982).

Regular viewing typically begins between 2½ and 3 years (Comstock, 1991b) at about 1½ hours a day, a figure that will rise to about 4 hours by age 12 before the decline during the teenage years. Because the direction that television would take was unremittingly resolved in favor of those who saw it primarily as a purveyor of goods and secondarily as a disseminator of culture and information (Boddy, 1991), children are expected to pay for the programming they view through their exposure to commercials. Below the age of 8 years, most do not comprehend the self-interested persuasive intent of commercials, although they may recognize them as different from the programs with which they appear, and by this standard many children are deceived. In any case, whether or not they comprehend persuasive intent, children become persuaded to want products, ask parents for them, and parents often comply (Comstock, 1991b). Ironically, the viewing of *Sesame Street* does not serve as an introduction to the increased viewing of educational and informational programming but to the increased viewing of animated cartoons, and to a lesser degree, adult comedies (Huston, Wright, Rice, Kerkman, & St. Peters, 1990). Cartoons and comedies might be formidable competition under any circumstances, but the question is moot because the medium does not offer much educational and informational programming for children. Young viewers become socialized to the pleasures of popular entertainment designed as a vehicle for advertising, and the role of television in the rearing of U.S. young in effect becomes circumscribed by its defining paradigm.

References

Bandura, A. (1986). *Social foundations of thought and action: A social cognitive theory.* Englewood Cliffs, NJ: Prentice-Hall.

Barnouw, E. (1982). *Tube of plenty.* New York: Oxford University Press.

Boddy, W. (1991). *Fifties television.* Urbana: University of Illinois Press.

Bogart, L. (1972). *The age of television* (3rd ed.). New York: Frederick Ungar.

Cohen, A. A., Levy, M. R., & Golden, K. (1988). Children's uses and gratifications of home VCRs: Evolution or revolution? *Communication Research, 15*(6), 772-780.
Comstock, G. (1980). *Television in America.* Newbury Park, CA: Sage.
Comstock, G. (1989). *The evolution of American television.* Newbury Park, CA: Sage.
Comstock, G. (1991a). *Television in America* (2nd ed.). Newbury Park, CA: Sage.
Comstock, G. (with Paik, H). (1991b). *Television and the American child.* San Diego, CA: Academic Press.
Comstock, G., Chaffee, S., Katzman, N., McCombs, M., & Roberts, D. (1978). *Television and human behavior.* New York: Columbia University Press.
Condry, J. (1989). *The psychology of television.* Hillsdale, NJ: Lawrence Erlbaum.
Cook, T. D., Kendzierski, D. A., & Thomas, S. A. (1983). The implicit assumptions of television research: An analysis of the 1982 NIMH report on *Television and Behavior. Public Opinion Quarterly, 47*(2), 161-201.
Dorr, A., & Kunkel, D. (1990). Children and the media environment: Change and constancy amid change. *Communication Research, 17*(1), 5-25.
Gerbner, G., Gross, L., Morgan, M., & Signorielli, N. (1980). The "mainstreaming" of America: Violence profile no. 11. *Journal of Communication, 30*(3), 10-29.
Gerbner, G., Gross, L., Morgan, M., & Signorielli, N. (1984). Political correlates of television viewing. *Public Opinion Quarterly, 48,* 283-300.
Greenberg, B. S., & Heeter, C. (1987). VCRs and young people. *American Behavioral Scientist, 30*(5), 509-521.
Hawkins, R. P., & Pingree, S. (1980). Some processes in the cultivation effect. *Communication Research, 7,* 193-226.
Hawkins, R. P., & Pingree, S. (1982). Television's influence on construction of reality. In D. Pearl, L. Bouthilet, & J. Lazar (Eds.), *Television and behavior: Ten years of scientific progress and implications for the eighties: Vol. 2. Technical reviews* (pp. 224-247). Washington, DC: U.S. Government Printing Office.
Hawkins, R. P., Pingree, S., & Adler, I. (1987). Searching for cognitive processes in the cultivation effect: Adult and adolescent samples in the United States and Australia. *Human Communication Research, 13*(4), 553-577.
Hearold, S. (1986). A synthesis of 1,043 effects of television on social behavior. In G. Comstock (Ed.), *Public communication and behavior* (Vol. 1, pp. 65-133). New York: Academic Press.
Hughes, M. (1980). The fruits of cultivation analysis: A reexamination of the effects of television watching on fear of victimization, alienation, and the approval of violence. *Public Opinion Quarterly, 44*(3), 287-302.
Huston, A. C., Wright, J. C., Rice, M. L., Kerkman, D., & St. Peters, M. (1990). Development of television viewing patterns in early childhood: A longitudinal investigation. *Developmental Psychology, 26*(3), 409-420.
Johnston, J., & Ettema, J. S. (1982). *Positive images: Breaking stereotypes with children's television.* Newbury Park, CA: Sage.
Kang, N. (1990). *A critique and secondary analysis of the NBC study on television and aggression.* Unpublished doctoral dissertation, Syracuse University, Syracuse, NY.
Levy, M. R. (1989). Why VCRs aren't pop-up toasters: Issues in home video research. In M. R. Levy (Ed.), *The VCR age* (pp. 9-18). Newbury Park, CA: Sage.
Lichty, L. W. (1989). Television in America: Success story. In P. S. Cook, D. Gomery, & L. W. Lichty (Eds.), *American media* (pp. 207-216). Washington, DC: Wilson Center Press.

Morgan, M. (1988). Cultivation analysis. In E. Barnouw (Ed.), *International encyclopedia of communication* (Vol. 1, pp. 430-433). New York: Oxford University Press.

Paik, H. (1991). *The effects of television violence on aggressive behavior: A meta-analysis.* Unpublished doctoral dissertation, Syracuse University, Syracuse, NY.

Robinson, J. P. (1977). *How Americans use time.* New York: Praeger.

Robinson, J. P. (1990). Television's effects on families' use of time. In J. Bryant (Ed.), *Television and the American family* (pp. 195-210). Hillsdale, NJ: Lawrence Erlbaum.

Robinson, J. P., & Levy, M. R. (1986). *The main source: Learning from television news.* Newbury Park, CA: Sage.

Roper Organization, Inc. (1987). *America's watching: Public attitudes toward television.* New York: Television Information Office.

Tyler, T. R., & Cook, F. L. (1984). The mass media and judgments of risk: Distinguishing impact on personal and societal level judgments. *Journal of Personality and Social Psychology, 47*(4), 693-708.

Wartella, E., Heintz, K. E., Aidman, A. J., & Mazzarella, S. R. (1990). Television and beyond: Children's video media in one community. *Communication Research, 17*(1), 45-64.

9. Cultural Diversity on Saturday Morning Television

BRADLEY S. GREENBERG

JEFFREY E. BRAND

In this evaluation, we take up a major segment of television that is targeted to the youngest of viewers—the Saturday morning offerings on the three commercial broadcast networks, supplemented with the offerings during the same time period (as well as weekdays) by public television. In both cases, the programming content is examined; in the case of commercial programming, a major effort is expended in examining the advertising content, for reasons that will become self-evident.

What did we do? We taped one Saturday morning from 8 a.m. to noon on ABC, CBS, and NBC affiliates in April 1992, and did the same for a PBS station on a weekday morning. From this we obtained 4 hours of CBS network programming, 3 hours from the NBC affiliate —which bumped the 11 a.m to noon network offering with an hour of syndicated wrestling—and 3.5 hours from ABC, with the network bumping its normal 11:30 a.m. to noon offering with the first half of a children's special. So, our less than full-blown empirical analysis was based on 10.5 hours of cartoons from the three commercial broadcast networks supplemented by more than 100 network commercials aired during and between those same programs. In addition, we had a typical 4 hours of PBS offerings for youthful viewers. We watched these tapes and jotted down notes; a month later, we watched the tapes a second time and jotted down additional observations.

Observations about what? Cultural diversity for the purposes of this chapter is limited to ethnic diversity and more particularly to *racial diversity*. We wanted to determine to what extent young Saturday morning viewers were able to see and listen to characters who were African American, Hispanic American, Asian American, or Native American. Then, we wished to examine what those racial minorities did on those shows and in the commercials. To extend cultural diversity into other venues, e.g., occupation, gender nationality, would have required a more comprehensive analytic effort. So, today's lesson focuses on what the major commercial television networks (and public television) have to say, largely implicitly, about race in the United States, in programs and commercials on a Saturday morning. What television has to say about racial minorities for the rest of the week is documented elsewhere (Greenberg & Brand, in press).

Programming on the Commercial Networks

Not a single program on the CBS Saturday morning lineup featured or displayed a minority character in any regular role or even a major role on a single episode—a far cry from its *Fat Albert* days. From *The Muppet Babies* at 8 a.m. through *Waldo* at noon, we did not identify any such regular minority characters. Furthermore, the presence of minorities in one-off roles in these 4 hours was constrained to the following: (a) two minor appearances of a Black policeman in a *Mother Goose* episode, (b) a Japanese-American television repairman with a stereotyped accent whom Garfield intimidated by threatening him with a martial arts attack, and (c) some brown musclemen with foreign accents on *Ninja Turtles* who may have been considered Hispanic, or a dozen other possibilities.

For ABC on this particular Saturday, two shows—*Beetlejuice* and *Ghostbusters*—displayed minorities in major roles and five shows had none at all. The *Beetlejuice* episode presented Ramon, the kid next door, as an obnoxious, dirty Hispanic kid who chose to emulate our hero's burping, among other aversive behaviors. But before the show's end, Ramon learned it is better to bathe, wash your ears, and brush your teeth than be so obnoxious. One of three regular Ghostbusters is a Black American and has the role of mechanic and driver on this weekly show. He participates equally with his comrades in ridding us of ghosts. On this same episode, we saw a retirement center with residents of various races.

On this April weekend, NBC was the runaway winner in the depth and extensiveness of its minority portrayals. First, after its 8 a.m. show, and then at several other program breaks in the morning, NBC posted its own public service campaign on "The More We Know" theme. This featured older and younger Black entertainers with their message to stay in school, study, learn, and do well.

There were some minor minority characters, Black female teenagers in the *Yogi Bear* episode at 8:30 a.m., but this was a tepid prelude to *Pro-Stars* at 9:30, which featured three professional athletes in film and animated forms—Michael Jordan, Bo Jackson, and Wayne Gretzky. This team of two African Americans and one Canadian were superheroes and the White guy was the dummy on the team, a sharp change from earlier mixed-race teams. Jordan was articulate and smart, with Jackson a close second. This story focused on a family whose son, Keith, went astray ("Gangs are bad news"), but eventually learned through the efforts of our heroes to "help those you love," and "it takes a special person to admit when you're wrong." Keith credited his heroes: "It was your faith in me." So these messages came from high-profile minority sources, whose identities in real life were accentuated in their superhero roles as cartoon characters.

NBC's following show, *Wish Kid*, also featured a regular African-American character, Daryl, a young sidekick and counselor to our White hero. But Daryl does not play foil or slave in his second-banana role; he makes regular, significant contributions to the story lines, for example advising our *Home Alone* graduate that, "If you want someone to love you, it should be because they want to, not because you wish it."

So much for racial diversity in television programming on a typical Saturday morning. From 20 separate shows: (a) three programs featured regularly appearing racial minority characters; (b) all racial minority characters who appeared regularly were African American; (c) we found one featured Hispanic American in these 10.5 hours, no Asian Americans and no Native Americans; and (d) all featured racial minority characters were male—the adult minority woman was invisible, and younger minority females, when present, were filler. Racial diversity on Saturday morning commercial broadcast network television programs was rare and restricted.

Advertising on the Commercial Network

NBC typically had four blocks of commercials inside each half hour show; the other two broadcast networks had three commercial breaks. Each break had two to four commercials. In addition, there were network commercials on the hour and half hour between programs. All these we watched, listened to, and thought about. Conclusion: *If you want to see racial diversity on Saturday morning television, watch the commercials and skip the programs.* This judgment may be overly severe, given some programs we have discussed, but it better characterizes the overall locus of this aspect of cultural diversity.

Let us demonstrate advertiser sensitivity to racial diversity by providing detail about 1 hour of commercials across all three networks for the 8 to 9 a.m. Saturday time slot. First, in nearly every commercial break there was at least one advertisement that included a minority character, and many that featured those characters.

1. On the CBS 8 to 9 a.m. shows, the following character representations were observed: (a) Hi-C commercial with a Black boy playing guitar and another Black boy sucking Hi-C through a straw; (b) Black girls blowing bubbles in Blow Pops ad; (c) Wendy's Kids Meals ad featured a Black boy sucking pop and a Black policeman; (d) a Brown boy and Black girl in a group of six kids for McDonald's "Would you believe in magic?" ad; and (e) Honeycomb cereal ad set to rap music with Black boy emerging from cereal box with two nonminority youth.
2. On the NBC 8 to 9 a.m. shows, the following character representations were observed: (a) the same Hi-C, Wendy's, McDonald's, and Honeycomb's commercials seen on the CBS shows in this time period; (b) a Kellogg's ad urging that a good breakfast is essential, featuring a Black boy on a baseball diamond and his family's encouragement; (c) a Kellogg's Corn Pops ad featuring a Black family moving into a new home, and the daughter's quest for the moving box containing that cereal—this ad also had one Black and one non-Black mover; and (d) an ad for Kellogg's Double Dip Krunch with Black and Asian male youths in "blinking" appearances, and close-ups only of Whites.
3. On the ABC 8 to 9 a.m. shows, the following character representations were observed: (a) for Kellogg's Rice Krispies, two Black male youths were featured, with one demonstrating magic tricks; (b) a Burger King ad featuring only animated characters, but with one distinctly Black male youth animation; (c) a Kool Aid ad with a Black girl featured

equivalently to others in commercial; (d) the same Hi-C, Honeycomb, Burger King, and Rice Krispies ads already described; and (e) two commercial breaks on this network had no minority characters during this time period.

This display of advertising in this 1 hour was typical of the other time blocks (9 a.m. until noon). The same ads appeared on all three networks, and several times on each network. It was noted, however, that the appearances of minorities in shows surrounding these 8 to 9 a.m. commercials were far less prevalent and considerably less important than the minority characters in the commercials.

From the 9 a.m. to noon time period, let us identify certain commercials we thought were especially strong purveyors of cultural pluralism: (a) McDonald's advertising campaign urging young people to stay in school and to pay close attention to math, science, and English—the narrator and presenter was a Black electrician; (b) a Bubble Yum ad with Black male youth as announcer and demonstrator; (c) McDonald's urging high school youth to study, with a mixed race cast; (d) a Reebok ad with Sinbad and a Black youth cast including one overweight male, one wheelchair male, one with long, braided hair, and one about 4 to 5 years old; (e) a Lego ad with a Black male as the only demonstrator; (f) Streex (hot wheels) with Black and White males playing alongside each other; and (g) another McDonald's ad featuring a high school mixed race group (with a teenage Black female) choosing a videotape to watch and then watching it together.

Qualitative differences accompanied quantitative ones. The commercials provided by McDonald's and by Kellogg's seriously outshone their direct competitors (other fast food purveyors and other cereal manufacturers). Those companies clearly have taken a stance that their commercials will contain diverse characterizations, but also that their commercials will convey messages to both majority and minority viewers about critical issues—education and health in particular. Furthermore, there were more total commercials from those companies across this time segment, reflecting the quality indicated.

But what about Hispanic Americans? Sorry, but the few we saw were "blinkers," often not seen the first time the tapes were reviewed. So, what about Asian faces? We found two nonblinkers in the 10.5 hours: One Asian girl carried an umbrella in a cookie ad, and one Sumo wrestler in loin cloth stared down a Bubble Yum blower. Native Americans? Not this Saturday, or likely any Saturday.

Thus, Saturday morning television advertisers acknowledge and orient to the youthful Black market, as have their daytime and prime-time evening counterparts. All continue to ignore the other components of racial diversity in the United States in what they put into their advertising.

But all is not sanguine in the Black advertising market on Saturday morning. We chose to begin this section with the positive finding that it is advertisers who reflect more sensitivity (or more market sense) than programmers. But let us identify a series of anomalies we found within this large chunk of Saturday morning advertising that presented Black Americans in reasonable numbers and with reasonable characteristics:

1. There was not a single Black female adult—wife, mother, professional —in any commercial during the entire morning.
2. The few Black adult males presented (in oft-repeated commercials) were all in service occupations—mailman, fireman, policeman, electrician. There were no professionals, no managers, no laborers.
3. Black girls on TV commercials did not play together with White girls when White girls played with advertised toys. Not a single ad for girls' nonfood products—Barbie Pets, Bitsy Bears, Barbie Dolls, Barbie Cosmetics, Ariel—included any minority females. A once-seen ad for Skip-It featured half a dozen White girls playing with this item, but no minorities. The Ariel ad was set entirely to calypso music, but with no connection between that music and any of the characters seen.
4. The award for minimal sensitivity goes to the M&M Olympic commercials. On this Saturday morning, we saw three different commercials in this campaign, which ballyhooed the company as a worldwide sponsor of the Olympics and carried a theme song that talked about "changing the world." Each ad centered on a White competitor who received adoring looks from the multicultural audience in the stands; particularly adoring looks came from Black and Asian kids. Yes, the sports featured in the ads were White-dominated sports—bicycling and gymnastics—but why focus on those sports?
5. The award for poorest timing goes to our local ABC affiliate who chose to run a PSA at 9:30 a.m. urging viewers to protect themselves when involved in a sexual activity. I wonder what questions parents were asked.

Commercial broadcast network programming offerings on Saturday morning containing any component of racial diversity are slim. We suspect it would be equally slim if another component of cultural diversity were selected, for example, occupational diversity. What lessons are available to be learned by our Saturday morning fans? First, we must concede that the commercials may be as attractive to youthful viewers as the programs, at least for the first several times they are seen. All viewers can learn that racial diversity in restaurants, or in chewing gum, or in eating virtually anything is an OK, even attractive, occurrence. But Caucasian viewers also may learn that playing with peers of other races is not something that is done on television. And Black girls may wonder why that is so, why they never see kids who look like them playing with Barbies, for example. Black males can find one or two shows across all three networks that feature them positively, but young Black females will come up short if they try to find any adult female role models. And, Asian-American, Hispanic-American, and Native American youth must look elsewhere for any cultural diversity in role models.

Programming on the Public Television Network

In many television markets across the United States, public television is an option to commercial network programming on Saturday mornings. Where it is not, weekday PBS broadcasting to children long has been the benchmark of quality informational and educational programming for them. This analysis is based on a daily (and weekend) lineup of PBS children's programs, including *Barney & Friends, Zoobilee Zoo, Sesame Street, Mister Rogers' Neighborhood, Reading Rainbow,* and *3-2-1 Contact.*

Those public television programs regularly and frequently featured people of color, people of varying social class, the physically challenged, and people from different parts of the world on the day we taped and analyzed. Moreover, these programs dealt more directly with physical and social differences and portrayed more cross-cultural interactions than did commercial network fare. Here, we review the programs in the time order they appeared, beginning at 8 a.m.

Barney & Friends is a half-hour program that features lessons, games, music, and singing. This episode brought us a 10-year-old African-

American male and Hispanic female, a White male about 7, and an Hispanic female in her early teens. Barney is a purple, stuffed dinosaur who ostensibly comes to life through the imagination of the children. He imparts lessons, initiates games, and guides sing-alongs. The theme of this particular episode was neighborhoods. Barney and the children explored the properties of a neighborhood and pretended to be various members of the neighborhood community. Children interacted freely with Barney and with each other. In one skit designed to remind children about the rules of crossing streets in their neighborhood, the four children were playing with toy figures on a play mat imprinted with neighborhood graphics; the toy figures were all people of color and all the children were playing with these. This episode neither emphasized differences nor advocated diversity, but it did promote integrated play.

Next came *Zoobilee Zoo.* This musical program dresses its characters in costumes reminiscent of the Broadway musical "Cats." The primary theme is working and playing together as conveyed through different animals, played by people of different skin tones (either actual or from makeup). The lead character is Ben Vereen and the animal characters are called "Zoobies." This episode promoted cooperation and interaction through a theme about friends making mistakes and the pitfalls of robots replacing friends.

Sesame Street also shows children how to interact with others and embrace diversity. In this episode, we saw direct and indirect cultural learning opportunities. The corporate sponsor in our area is a large grocery and supermarket chain and the underwriter's announcement uses children—an African-American boy, a White boy, an Asian girl, two White girls, and a physically challenged boy in a wheelchair—to spell out the store name, with each child holding one letter of the store's name.

Indirect cultural learning may occur from segments on *Sesame Street* through skits that include many races or many different character types in a cooperative activity. Examples are pervasive in the program. For example, the program's introduction shows children of several racial, ethnic, and cultural backgrounds playing in a park, playing in the city, running together, and so on. Later, we see two dancers, one a White ballerina, the other an African-American male modern dancer. This episode addressed issues about going to the doctor. In one scene, Louis, a Hispanic adult male, sits on door steps with three young school boys: one African American, one Hispanic, and one White. The four discuss a time when they went to the doctor. Another example is a vignette about recycling in which we see an African-American girl and her mother recycling books. People from many different backgrounds appear at the recycling center. In a musical segment, "My New Computer," 10 children play on a giant computer system. One African-American boy, three White girls, five White boys, and an Asian girl walk on the keyboard, roll over a trackball, and play with giant diskettes. Although some scenes may not include character interactions, segments throughout the program feature individuals of differing ages, dialects, skin tones, dress, geographic origins, and socioeconomic backgrounds.

Some program segments introduce culture more directly. One vignette transported viewers to a Southeastern coastal community where trees are lined with moss, a bluegrass fiddle quintet performs, and folks participate in a community picnic and community fishing. A second segment took viewers to Alaska to learn how isolated Eskimo communities receive health services. We see Eskimo children during routine medical examinations and we visit their families and their community, indoors and out. Later, viewers witness a young boy in a tropical locale climbing a coconut tree. He harvests three coconuts from the tree, climbs down, and proceeds to open and consume their milk and fruit.

Mister Rogers' Neighborhood has fewer participants than other programs on public television. This episode had two White males (plus Fred Rogers), one White female, and an African-American male; the remaining characters were puppets.

Diversity was the theme of this broadcast. At the start of the show, Mister Rogers adds a small angel fish to the aquarium. He notes the different appearance of this fish compared with other fish in the tank and says, "All the fish are different—just like people—each one of us is different, it's wonderful." At the show's close, we go back to the aquarium where Mister Rogers explains this new fish will look different and will act differently because it is in a new "neighborhood." He explains, "It's important that we're all different. We all eat, sleep, we all wake up in the morning, we all get angry sometimes, but each one of us is different."

The Reading Rainbow opened with two Asian girls reading a book on the steps of a housing unit, and blond and Hispanic boys each reading in separate locations. The host of *Reading Rainbow* is Levar Burton, an African-American male about 35. In this segment, we see young and old, people of all skin tones, and a wide range of occupations. As is customary in the show, three books are introduced. The first, *The Dream Eater,* is critiqued by a young Hispanic girl, who explains that the story is based on a myth in Asian culture about a creature who eats bad dreams. The second book is introduced by an African-American girl, and the third by a White boy with a noticeable urban New York dialect.

3-2-1 Contact opened with an African-American male baking bread. Hispanic and White females (his friends) enter and interact casually. As this scene ends, we are transported to a park location where Robert Johnson, an African-American male specializing in diet and nutrition, speaks with a racially mixed group of children about their favorite foods. As he talks, we see a little league baseball team with African-American, Hispanic, and Anglo boys and girls. When we rejoin the kitchen crew, they are discussing the importance of variety in foods—that "Variety is the spice of life."

The most significant cultural information in all the programming we viewed came in a film with various people preparing and eating food. It starts with people rolling tortillas, an Asian girl eating sushi, and an Asian man doing the same. Then, we see an African tribesman preparing meats in smoldering leaves. We go to an African plain with hunters and gatherers while the narrator explains that in some parts of the world "What people eat depends on what they can find." The Africans extract juice from fruits, stalks, and roots. We move to Alaska where Eskimos are eating raw meats or fishing the snow. We see a fowl being cooked in a Southeast Asian hut. Later, Arabs are eating a rice dish from a community bowl. A different African tribe is boiling potatoes and then we are in an Eastern European market where an old woman is buying vegetables. We go back to Africa where children are foraging for grub worms. The short film ends with a white American family and an African American visitor sitting at the table eating a meal. The narrator reiterates, "Variety is the spice of life."

In sum, PBS programs for children yield a rich and broad array of cultural variability. Whereas public television has innovated modes of cultural education, commercial television has yet to adopt, much less improve upon, this content. With singular consistency, people of different races are integral characters in skits, plots, and lessons on public TV. Moreover, the characterization of different races and cultures in these shows is less stereotyped than in commercial network content aimed at children. Commercial entertainment content on Saturday morning primarily ignores the different races, and places its few African Americans in background or service rather than leadership roles, save for athletic superheroes. PBS content emphasizes to its young audience that all kinds of people exist, belong, and are enfranchised in our pluralistic society.

Saturday's commercial television programming is fairly empty as a carrier of multicultural information. Should we be surprised? It's been nearly a decade since the last weekday commercial program for children left the airwaves. There never was more than a handful of them. That weekday time was absorbed by the networks' morning news/talk/interview shows. Thereafter, the networks confined their children's fare to Saturday mornings, with some overlap on Sunday, and some late afternoon specials for teenagers. Given the number of commercials we saw, Saturday morning appears to be a well-sold time period. Yet in 1992, there is no attention to Hispanics, Asians or Native Americans, save in the most offhand manner. We speculate that the networks have accommodated complaints of Black Americans and increased their presence, but have not responded to similar pressure from other cultural segments.

As this chapter is being written, rumors persist that for the next television season (1992-1993), there will be less children's programming on Saturday morning from these broadcast networks. It is anticipated that they will reorient themselves to more adult programming and further abdicate the children's television market to PBS and to available cable television channels, such as Nickelodeon and Disney. For those who expect children's programming to include prosocial, multicultural messages, this may be no considerable loss. Yet, it is difficult to believe that any other source will provide as much programming as now comes from these three networks. Perhaps it is not how much, however, but what kind that should get our attention. Another flow of programming comparable to PBS's offering should do the job.

Reference

Greenberg, B. S., & Brand, J. (in press). Minorities and the mass media. In J. Bryant & D. Zillman (Eds.), *Perspectives on media effects*. Hillsdale, NJ: Lawrence Erlbaum.

10. Rubik's Tube

Developing a Child's Television Worldview

EDWARD L. PALMER

K. TAYLOR SMITH

KIM S. STRAWSER

> Television is . . . a major source of information about what happens in the local community, throughout the country, and around the globe. The medium helps shape our understanding of ourselves, our society, and our place in the world. (Fontana, 1988, p. 348)

And as the world's children catch a glimpse of one another through their television window, perceptions form, stereotypes develop, and expectations abound. No longer will these young be simply children. They will be television portrayals of different children, and this difference can make all the difference in their world of perception, valuing, and interaction.

Cross-Cultural Experience With Television

Various cultures and subcultures spend notably different amounts of time with television and watch for distinctly different reasons. After television was introduced in El Salvador, for example, children who previously had high educational aspirations, lowered them. Israeli children, on the other hand, view television primarily as an information source. For them, subtitles enhance general reading ability, and consequently, television itself increases mental effort in processing (Salomon, 1985).

Television Use Patterns in the United States

Blosser (1988) finds that children's patterns of television use are based on four factors—quantity, frequency, access, and use habits. In the United States, Black children watch more hours of television than any other group. Not only are they the highest quantity users, but the more frequent users as well. Television sets are readily accessible to all groups. One hundred percent of White households report owning a set; 99% of Black and 97.6% of Hispanic families report owning one. Viewing habits vary dramatically across groups. Blacks watch more mealtime television whereas Whites are most likely to have television sets on when no one is watching. This overall framework of differences in viewing frequency and viewing times may suggest far-reaching ethnic and cultural differences. Music and visual image proficiency in Black culture suggest a natural orientation toward electronic media and sound recordings. Whites characteristically have been more oriented toward linear thought—characterized by print media. These differences in orientation create cross-cultural differences in child access to television. To the extent that a given medium provides information and develops skills of significant educational or social value, ethnic differences in access carry lasting social consequences.

For ethnic minority families coming to this country, television becomes a child's social tool and socializing agent. Television provides an easily available and entertaining source of information about the host country, its "American way of life," its norms and its social values. These child viewers can meet new friends, travel to new places, and participate in exotic customs. This "new cultural environment" also helps relieve the loneliness of few social contacts. The U.S.-born child, having experienced a variety of socializing agents, delegates far fewer responsibilities to television than does the ethnic newcomer. Although television's content is equally realistic to both groups, the U.S.-born child is more likely to view it as a means of escape and entertainment (Zohoori, 1988).

Ethnic Portrayals

Beyond the more typical socializing role, television teaches ethnic minority children subtle lessons about themselves and how they are perceived. The portrayals are sparse and almost uniformly negative.

Ethnic minorities join women and the elderly as frequently portrayed television victims (Gerbner & Signorielli, 1990). Prolonged exposure to these stereotypical images inhibits minority children's interest in wanting to be a part of the larger, host society. The end result is a twofold tragedy. On the one hand, these children and their families experience a lowered self-concept. On the other, these same children grow up separate and apart. The television tool through which they sought socialization and integration in the final analysis segregates them.

Child viewers "selectively perceive" ethnic differences in television portrayals. Although heavy television viewing makes ethnic minority children more aware of imbalance, similar viewing among White children creates the belief that minorities are fairly represented. Education level positively correlates with imbalance perceptions across all groups, and program portrayals are seen as slightly more problematic than advertising portrayals (Faber, O'Guinn, & Meyer, 1987).

Where available, ethnic media provide a "safe haven alternative" for identification with one's own culture and background. As the most rapidly growing minority group in the United States, the Hispanic population has the most direct access to alternative media programming. Such media alternatives are most frequently watched by lower-income and elderly Hispanics. With a view toward anticipatory socialization and upward mobility, higher income and younger Hispanics prefer English-language, host-country television (Faber, O'Guinn, & Meyer, 1986). Like their counterparts from other countries (e.g., Africa, the Middle East, South and East Asia), Hispanic children prefer educational programming—their least stereotypical programming option within their host country (Zohoori, 1988). Even here the "television window" is a very narrow one because the United States lavishly exports programming to the rest of the world but imports very little of the programming other countries have to offer child viewers. A greater import-export balance will create child opportunities for a more open and informed worldview.

U.S. Commercial Programming

Commercial television is unique in that program funding comes not from the public sector but from advertisers. As a result, programming executives do not aim to please the customer as much as the supplier. Because of this dilemma, program content sometimes contains inappropriate material for younger viewers, and the content of certain programs serves to create and even maintain sexual and racial stereotypes.

Children's U.S. "television window" has never been without controversy and concern. The birth of television in the late 1940s was welcomed by many, but as popularity grew, so did controversy. Although different issues were addressed in different decades, some remained the same. Loewi and DuMont's original intent in 1948 was to design a programming schedule that would "coincide with the average housewife's routine" (Palmer, 1987, p. 198). However, remnants of this same primitive schedule are still employed today. The result of such a practice is the subtle and even blatant reinforcement of sexual stereotypes. Moreover, during these same early years of television, other ethnic groups were portrayed in a negative light. For example, Blacks appeared as either servants or buffoons. These stereotypical roles have had a far-reaching influence on society's image of certain cultural groups, and more important, children's acquisition of a worldview.

George Gerbner and Nancy Signorielli (1990) have noted that the more time one spends "living" in the world of television, the more that world becomes the viewer's social reality. By evaluating the content of commercials as well as several popular prime-time and children's shows, it may be possible to acquire an idea of the "world" that children live in. For our purposes, a popular season hit from each weekday night and Saturday morning will be assessed and its negative or positive impact ascertained. In addition, the profile of the average child appearing on Saturday morning commercials will be constructed and results reviewed. The programs selected, in order of appearance, include *Evening Shade; Roseanne; Doogie Howser, M.D.; Beverly Hills 90210; The Cosby Show;* and *Wide World of Kids.* Although *Beverly Hills 90210* and *The Cosby Show* both appear on Thursday nights, it is important to look at them and the different messages they convey.

Sex Stereotyping

Throughout the history of television, the representation of females has consistently been lower than males. In a study done in 1980, Butler and Paisley reported that 72% of characters in general programming were male and only 28% were female (Durkin, 1985). However, the male/female ratio of the selected current-season programs was characteristic of the demographics of the overall population with females comprising 51% of characters and males, 49%. It seems then that programming executives today are more concerned with creating programs that reflect the numbers of the general population. But although the sheer numbers of males and females are correct, their roles are not. *The Cosby Show* and *Evening Shade* are both atypical in that the lead female characters are lawyers. However, the other shows place the female characters in stereotypical roles such as housewife (*Doogie Howser, M.D.*) and waitress (*Roseanne*). The female characters on *Beverly Hills 90210* have no real occupation other than students, but they are placed in the typical female sex role through their emphasis on beauty and material goods.

The male characters, on the other hand, are placed in traditional roles such as doctor (*The Cosby Show* and *Doogie Howser, M.D.*), football coach (*Evening Shade*) and workman (*Roseanne*). The males of *Beverly Hills 90210* are shown basking in their masculinity and pursuit of women. This data is also consistent with previous research. Seggar and McGhee (cited in Greenberg & Heeter, 1982) found that in prime time, men were typically lawyers, ministers, store owners, and doctors; women were secretaries, nurses, entertainers, teachers, and journalists. In sum, it appears that television has not undergone a significant change in the portrayal of sex roles since its beginning.

Advertising

Saturday morning cartoons are a major source of entertainment for children. Commercials, interspersed with cartoons, also seek to supplement the child's enjoyment while carrying extremely persuasive messages. But beyond the advertisers' intended message is the "hidden" information that children assimilate.

Children's Saturday morning commercials were monitored from 7 a.m. to 12 p.m. over a 4-week period. The three major networks, NBC, ABC, CBS, as well as a cable channel, Nickelodeon, were viewed. A total of 20 hours of Saturday morning television was watched with 154 commercials being recorded. Results show that Whites are more prevalent than Blacks, Hispanics, Asians, and other non-Whites. Furthermore, Whites are in 100% of commercials but non-Whites are never found exclusively with other non-Whites. Eighty-two percent of the children in the commercials are White, 15% are Black, and 3% are other non-Whites.

Somewhat surprising is the fact that the total number of females is greater than the total number of males, 57% to 43%. Thirty-six percent of commercials contain males only and 36% consist of females only, 27% have both male and female characters. More boys appear in commercials for vehicles and manipulative toys and a greater number of girls appear in doll and household object commercials. Thus, it appears that advertisements directed toward children still embrace decades-old stereotypes of men as breadwinners and women as homemakers.

Racial Stereotyping

Racial stereotyping is especially dangerous because it teaches children that they are different or better than others based on the color of their skin. As Lesley Crosson (1989) states:

> Ideally, our perceptions about people who are different from us are shaped through personal experiences with those people. But the youngster who may not have had an opportunity for social, cultural, or economic interaction with minorities understandably forms his perceptions with the help of TV. If the message transmitted by the medium is distorted, that youngster grows up with dangerous misperceptions of reality. (p. 168)

Thus, when Blacks or other non-Whites are portrayed in negative roles such as criminal suspects or gang leaders, the resulting ideologies children acquire are distorted. Furthermore, a lack of representation on shows produces the mentality of "out of sight, out of mind." During the 1970-1976 TV seasons, for example, 10% of characters were Black, 3% Hispanic, 2.5% Asian, and less than .5% Native American (Gerbner, Gross, Signorielli, Morgan, & Jackson-Beeck, 1979). These representations continue (Gerbner & Signorielli, 1990). Moreover, it seems that when Blacks or other non-Whites are shown, it is in a minority context like *The Cosby Show.* Of the programs selected for review, not one had a regular Black or non-White character other than, of course, Cosby. Conversely, *The Cosby Show* contains no White characters. Television creates two worlds—one White, one non-White with little or no interaction between the two. Weigel, Loomis, and Soja (cited in Greenberg & Heeter, 1982) found that 77% of Black appearance time was found in 18% of shows. Interactions between different racial groups made up less than 2% of all appearances. Furthermore, 89% of Black/White interactions were seen only in a job-related context. The consequences of this practice serve to further widen the boundaries between different ethnic groups. The result is twofold—the majority, guided by television's unflattering images of the minority, avoid contact with minority group members. The minority, aware of television's stereotypes, may not feel motivated to interact with the majority. Thus, television creates a separatist society and discourages interaction between different minority groups.

Developing a Worldview

With a portion of television's message having been sampled, it is now possible to develop a picture of a child's worldview. As previously stated, television creates two worlds—one White, the other non-White. It follows, then, that television also creates different worldviews for different children.

White children learn from television that it is a White world. White characters comprise a large majority of TV roles. Furthermore, Whites, especially men, are depicted in highly professional, powerful settings whereas Blacks and other non-Whites are pigeonholed into less desirable, stereotypical roles. Black men especially bear the brunt of the burden. When a Black couple is shown, they usually appear in the pattern of the weak man and strong woman. And the couples are more likely to be shown exchanging insults rather than engaging in a loving relationship (Staples & Jones, 1985). It is hard for children of any ethnic group to gain respect for Black men when they are portrayed as the exact opposite of how a "real" man should behave. The resulting worldview that White children acquire is an ethnocentric one where they sit atop the hierarchy of ethnic groups.

Non-Whites, conversely, learn that Whites are "superior" to other groups. The impact is especially potent for non-Whites given their heavy reliance on television for information. Bower (cited in Comstock & Cobbey, 1979) has found that persons of low socioeconomic status, frequently minorities, cite learning as a motive for watching television. It is a shame that those who show the most trust in the medium are those who are most deceived by it.

U.S. Educational Programming

Nicholas Johnson (personal communication, 1977) once said that "All television is educational television, the question is what is it teaching?" Just as a child at home learns far-reaching and formative messages parents never intended to teach, a child gradually forms a worldview of peoples and cultures through television's unintentional programming and commercial messages. We have seen how these unintentional messages teach resounding lessons about ethnicity, gender, and age. Who is important? Who is culturally elevated and valued? The messages are subtly and pervasively there in role casting, voice-overs, and scripting. Ironically, the true teaching dimension of television—instructional, educational, and prosocial—faces the formidable challenge of counterbalancing many of the messages learned within television's commercial programming window. Where commercial programming showcases violence as the way to resolve conflicts, educational and prosocial programming spotlights cooperation and mutual understanding. Where commercials themselves showcase products as the avenue to personal happiness, educational and prosocial programming spotlights the value and uniqueness of the individual child. This spotlight has taken a variety of forms and formats throughout the past two decades, and a careful look at format evolution across time suggests that the general landscape has changed.

Instructional television's early, teacher-in-the-tube orientation said little to children about a view of the world, its peoples, and its cultures. Children were taught math, English, or science, but there was no conscious concern for the gender and ethnicity of the accomplished individuals cited in each field. The content area was a product of its own dominant culture and subtly reflected this dominance, but it was largely a basic set of concepts and principles to be learned and to be built upon. As a content area, social studies came closest in developing a child's worldview, but here the teacher also had distinct potentials to present issues and convey values that encompassed nations, peoples, and cultures. Once again, these values reflected the dominant culture as conveyed and learned by the teacher's own experience within it. This was the instructional television counterpart to questions of textbook selection and cultural bias in the school classroom.

Beyond the classroom-on-the-screen, educational and instructional television moved toward more creative program production. Children's Television Workshop and its firstborn—*Sesame Street*—marked a significant new approach to children. Premiering on PBS on November 9, 1970, it was "an anywhere street of learning in an anywhere city or town" (Terrace, 1976, p. 282). All the fine-tuned effectiveness of advertising was now directed toward children in bright, upbeat vignettes. Researchers and producers consciously portrayed multiethnic settings and experiences with ethnic-neutral characters like Big Bird, Bert, and Ernie. The success of this approach has been seen in its capacity to be adapted and programmed in cultures throughout the world.

Just as *Sesame Street* had ushered in the era of educational television, *Mr. Rogers' Neighborhood* ushered in "self-concept" television. Premiering on NET in October 1967, and on PBS in October 1970, it targeted the emotional development of 3- to-6-year-olds (Terrace, 1976). As child viewers we relaxed with our soft-spoken friend as he shared a variety of guests and a "neighborhood of make-believe" designed to help us get in touch with our feelings and cope with our problems. Mister Rogers was safe. Mister Rogers was secure. He was our friend, no matter who we were. And research indicated that the prosocial messages of friendship, persistence, delay of gratification, etc., were behaviorally internalized among low-income child viewers (Friedrich & Stein, 1973; Irving, 1988).

The success of *Sesame Street* and *Mister Rogers' Neighborhood*—coupled with our societal emphasis on education and world competitiveness—spawned a variety of educational programs designed specifically for multiethnic viewing and greater cross-cultural awareness. *The Big, Blue Marble* won Emmy and Peabody awards as a magazine series highlighting the life-styles of children around the world. Each half-hour program featured 7- to 10-minute portraits of children, a "Dear Pen Pal," and serialized dramas promoting international understanding. Sponsored by ITT as a public service, the program premiered in September 1974 and was carried on 180 commercial and public television stations in the United States and in 60 countries abroad (Brown, 1982). No other multicultural program has come even close to a comparable level of international popularity and impact.

Other multicultural programs included *Vegetable Soup* and bilingual programs such as *Villa Alegre, Carrascolendas,* and *Rebop. Carrascolendas,* for example, targeted Mexican-American children in the Southwest United States, helping them to enculturate while simultaneously helping other child viewers to gain appreciation and understanding (Laosa, 1976; Williams & Natalicio, 1972).

Other shows addressed special populations and specific social concerns. *Inside-Out* focused on elementary school children with learning disabilities, helping them cope with expressing their feelings, making new friends, practical jokes, embarrassment, peer acceptance, emotional abuse at home, bullies, and so on. Any child viewer could readily identify with these feelings, but the program and its design carried a special poignancy for this special population (Elias, 1979). *Freestyle* targeted elementary school girls in Grades 4 through 6 and aimed toward changing existing sex role and career stereotypes. These children were encouraged to "think career" in widescale, nonsexist terms, and corresponding male viewers were encouraged to change their stereotypes as well (Johnston, 1983).

Conclusions

Children's educational-programming "window on the world" still holds some gleaming remnants of its illustrious past. Carefully channeled young hands can still find *Sesame Street, Mr. Rogers' Neighborhood, Inside-Out,* and *Self-Incorporated,* and the windowscape reveals newer entries such as *Square One TV* (math) and *Where in the World Is Carmen Sandiego?* (geography). But children around the world need a budding new *Big, Blue Marble,* and it is nowhere in sight.

Equally absent from view are the early pillars in children's commercial television. *Captain Kangaroo* and its CBS host, Bob Keeshan, ran an unprecedented 24 years with a variety of formats and a prosocial commitment, and *Fat Albert and the Cosby Kids* received widespread acclaim for its unique capacity to identify with human feelings, ethics, and values experienced by urban Black teens. A special beauty of the show was its popularity with children of all races (Brown, 1982). U.S. television and its child viewers need a rededication to this caliber of prosocial commitment and cross-cultural appeal.

The acquisition of a worldview comes about through a variety of processes—personal experiences, newspapers, magazines, and television. And of these processes, certainly, television is the most readily available. However, with an increasing emphasis on content, there has been declining attention to multicultural issues and understanding. Programs that are within this area take middle-class United States as their starting point and reflect the ethnocentric view characteristic of our country in general—a view that exports "us" to the rest of the world but imports very little in programming, and consequently, very little in appreciation and understanding. In this deprived environment, stereotypes prevail. *Wide World of Kids* exemplifies this trend as it presents only White hosts and largely limits its "wide world" to the continental United States.

The failure of U.S. programming to provide multicultural shows lies in part with the public. Americans seem content to watch programs exalting the importance of Americans. And who wouldn't? A concerted effort to increase international awareness must be taken. Our *Wide World of Kids* needs to encircle and embrace the globe. In sum, it appears that in order to make American programming better, an un-American approach is needed.

The current impact of U.S. commercial television can be traced to an evolving marketing strategy that has played upon the public susceptibility to closed-minded stereotypes. In the early 1980s, the phenomenon of Rubik's Cube swept the nation into a puzzle-solving frenzy. The goal in solving a Rubik's Cube is to separate the various colors to their respective sides. Similarly, commercial television has pushed peoples of different color further away from one another into isolated and homogeneous social cliques. Although this may not be the explicit objective of commercial television, it is the end result—separating different ethnic groups into distinct elements of society. As a consequence, children acquire worldviews that are as varied as the seemingly endless number of patterns appearing on the faces of the Rubik's Cube.

References

Blosser, B. J. (1988). Ethnic differences in children's media use. *Journal of Broadcasting and Electronic Media, 32*(4), 453-470.

Brown, L. (1982). *Les Brown's encyclopedia of television.* New York: New York Zoetrope.

Comstock, G., & Cobbey, R. E. (1979). Television and the children of ethnic minorities. *Journal of Communication, 29*(1), 104-114.

Crosson, L. (1989). You are what you watch. *Social Education, 53,* 168-169.

Durkin, K. (1985). Television and sex-role acquisition. *British Journal of Social Psychology, 24*(1), 101-113.

Elias, M. J. (1979, November). Helping emotionally disturbed children through prosocial television. *Exceptional Children, 46*(3), 217-218.

Faber, R. J., O'Guinn, T. C., & Meyer, T. P. (1986). Diversity in the ethnic media audience: A study of Spanish language broadcast preference in the U.S. *International Journal of Intercultural Relations, 10,* 347-359.

Faber, R. J., O'Guinn, R. C., & Meyer, T. P. (1987). Televised portrayal of Hispanics. *International Journal of Intercultural Relations, 11,* 155-169.

Fontana, L. A. (1988). Television and the social studies. *Social Education, 52,* 348-351.

Friedrich, L. K., & Stein, A. H. (1973). Aggressive and prosocial television programs and the naturalistic behavior of preschool children. *Monographs of the Society for Research in Child Development, 38*(4), Serial No. 151.

Gerbner, G., & Signorielli, N. (1990, January). *Violence profile 1967 through 1988-89: Enduring patterns.* Unpublished manuscript.

Gerbner, G., Gross, L., Signorielli, N., Morgan, M., & Jackson-Beeck, M. (1979, Summer). The demonstration of power: Violence profile no. 10. *Journal of Communication, 29*(3), 177-196.

Greenberg, B. S. & Heeter, C.(1982). Television and social stereotypes. *Prevention in Human Services, 2,* 37-51.

Irving, V. (1988). *Promoting prosocial behavior to nurture caring in Head Start teachers and children.* Doctoral thesis, Nova University, Fort Lauderdale, FL.

Johnston, J. (1983). *Sex-role orientations in late childhood.* Washington, DC: National Institute of Education.

Laosa, L. M. (1976). Viewing bilingual multicultural educational television: An empirical analysis of children's behaviors during television viewing. *Journal of Educational Psychology, 68*(2), 133-142.

Palmer, E. L. (1987). *Children in the cradle of television.* Lexington, MA: D. C. Heath.

Salomon, G. (1985). The study of television in a cross-cultural context. *Journal of Cross-Cultural Psychology, 16*(3), 381-397.

Staples, R., & Jones, T. (1985). Culture ideology and black television images. *Black Scholar, 16*(3), 10-21.

Terrace, V. (1976). *The complete encyclopedia of television programs 1947-1976* (Vol. 2). South Brunswick & New York: A. S. Barnes.

Williams, F., & Natalicio, D. S. (1972). Evaluating *Carrascolendas:* A television series for Mexican-American children. *Journal of Broadcasting, 16*(3), 299-309.

Zohoori, A. R. (1988). A cross-cultural analysis of children's television use. *Journal of Broadcasting and Electronic Media, 32*(1), 105-113.

11. Conceptual Models of an African-American Belief System

A Program of Research

RICHARD L. ALLEN

The Image of the African to Self and Society

The image presented to the African child, both in the United States and in Africa, provides a basis for what they will be as adults. In what Van Sertima called the "500 year-room" of history, where African people experienced slavery, colonialism, anticolonialism, the African independence explosion, and the rise and fall of civil rights movements in the United States, these images have both negative and positive content (Clarke, 1991). The majority of the imagery in the arts and the news media, however, is negative. African people are rarely portrayed as playing a heroic role, and often are not portrayed at all (Ungar & Gergen, 1991). The tendency to deny, distort, and denigrate the African heritage of African Americans continues also in the public education system designed to train the next generation of Americans. This system has miseducated African-American children to believe they have no African heritage of which they should be proud. It miseducates European-American children, too, by giving them a bogus sense of superiority based on the faulty moral premise that might makes right (Walker, 1991). These images

AUTHOR'S NOTE: The author is grateful for the assistance and the generous support provided by the College of Communication and the Department of Radio-TV-Film at The University of Texas during the conduct of this inquiry. Also, I would like to thank Yvonne Diala, Federico Subervi, and Leah Waks for their careful reading of this draft of the manuscript.

have been put forth by the various institutions in society and the mass media, such as television, radio, newspapers, and literature of all sorts, including that of a religious persuasion. Africans have no control over these images in the mass media, yet the images have influenced African people the world over (Clarke, 1991; Walker, 1991).

The print and the electronic media, and especially cinema and television, have shown African peoples and other people of color in comedic stances and in degrading ways. The depictions have suggested that African peoples are not interested in and do not care about serious matters, are frivolous and irresponsible, and are unable to participate in the mainstream of U.S. society. Television has been notably powerful in implying, suggesting, and maintaining this myth (Comer, 1982; Stroman, Merritt, & Matabane, 1989-1990).

As socioeconomic inequality, specifically in reference to people of color, benefits a small minority at the expense of the overwhelming majority, some cultural apparatus is needed to persuade the exploited group that this inequitable condition is natural (Gray, 1989; Herman & Chomsky, 1989; Winston, 1982). Although historically this cultural apparatus has resided in the religious, political, legal, and educational institutions, in the 20th century, the mass media have become increasingly a prominent force in purveying bourgeois and racist ideological concepts to mass publics worldwide. Moreover, these media, generally termed entertainment, have usually operated negatively for groups residing at the bottom of the social ladder. As the most oppressed of the exploited ethnic groups, African Americans have been portrayed in the media in a manner that reinforces the image of white superiority and supremacy and black inferiority and subordination (Staples & Jones, 1985).

Bourne (1990) noted that the images of African Americans, when not controlled by African Americans, serve a specific purpose for those who control those images, namely to reinforce and rationalize blacks' subordinate place in society. The current black images emanating from Hollywood serve essentially to entertain, to advocate no change, and significantly, to suggest that the current social and political order is legitimate (Ukadike, 1990).

Television has been credited with providing the most influential interpretations of social reality of all the mass media (Allen, Dawson, & Brown, 1989; Allen & Waks, 1990; Gray, 1989; Pierce, 1980; Signorielli, 1990). Further, television has had a particularly important relationship with African Americans. Aside from watching more television than the general population, African Americans are also heavily dependent on television for information about blacks and the black community and tend to use television as a source of information about the world (Dates & Barlow, 1990; McDonald, 1983; Poindexter & Stroman, 1981; Stroman et al., 1989-1990).

Black media may be seen as a filter of African-American information sources pertaining to the general status of African Americans both as a distinct group and in relation to the dominant society. Thus, the black media play a significant role in determining the content of blacks' view of themselves, or stated differently, they influence the content of the African-American racial belief system. The black media, especially the black print media, have served two basic functions: (a) as an agent of social change, and (b) to crystallize black racial consciousness (Allen, Thornton, & Watkins, in press). Although in referring to black media the emphasis is on black print fare, given the importance of television as a medium and purveyor of ideas, it is likely that content pertinent to Africans will be specifically attended to and will be quite influential. Black-oriented television fare in its complexity depicts both accurate and distorted images of African Americans. Thus, its impact on the African-American belief system is both positive and negative (Allen et al., 1989).

Social Structural and Background Antecedents

Race and socioeconomic status remain the two major social factors with the greatest impact on individual African Americans' position in society and their views of themselves individually and of their ethnic group. The two factors remain intertwined, objectively and psychologically (Allen et al., 1989; National Research Council, 1989). The economic position of African Americans remains tied to race, as the differences between blacks and whites in unemployment and poverty rates and occupational structures attest (Farley, 1984; National Research Council, 1989; Reich, 1981). The race and class connections to psychological antecedents have been observed by researchers (M. R. Jackman & R. W. Jackman, 1983; Kilson, 1983; Willie, 1979) and as a consequence, one might expect individual socioeconomic status to be directly linked to the racial belief system. According to some theorists (e.g., Wilson, 1980), as African Americans become more socially prominent, they become more distant from the masses of poorer black people. M. R. Jackman and R. W. Jackman

(1983) noted that lower status blacks have affective barriers against both whites and middle-class blacks, but Kilson (1983) describes the tension-filled position of the black middle-class persons, who are not entirely at home with either the black masses or mainstream white society.

Although some literature suggests that socioeconomic status is related to greater distance from other African Americans, it has also been argued that increased status is associated with a sanguine view of the group as a whole. One notion holds that middle-class blacks would oppose negative stereotypes of blacks because they would be as pernicious to middle-class blacks as to their less affluent brethren, and because higher levels of education are associated with more experience and skill in combating racist and other stereotypical perspectives (Shingles, 1979). Following this line of reasoning, one would expect socioeconomic status to be associated negatively with negative views of African Americans and positively associated with positive views of African Americans. It should be kept in mind that socioeconomic status may be viewed as being composed of such factors as income, education, and occupational status. These three elements, however, may be treated separately, and when they are their independent influence may be different from what is observed when they are aggregated (Allen et al., in press).

Apart from the above social structural variables, much evidence indicates that the black church is particularly influential in fostering an African-American belief system (Dawson, Brown & Allen, 1990). The black church has probably played the most significant role in maintaining the cohesion of black society (Frazier, 1963). It has often been stated that those blacks who have strong religious commitments are the most integrated into the social networks of the black community. Therefore, those who express a strong sense of religiosity have a strong sense of racial identification and consciousness (Morris, 1984).

Religious socialization among African Americans, however, results in believing that God does not foster an uncritical evaluation of African Americans. It may also be argued that religiosity is associated with negative conceptions of the group, as humanity is seen as sinful and the black church is involved in extensive activity to correct the social problems of the African-American community (Dawson et al., 1990).

An African-American Racial Belief System

Two main conclusions may be drawn from a number of studies that have examined blacks' conception of themselves relative to their group. First, most African Americans consider their group identity important. Second, group cohesion, striving and endurance, and the desirability of continuing to inculcate these qualities in future generations seem to be crucial aspects of this identity. These patterns of identity signify a great degree of race consciousness among African Americans to the extent these orientations look at race as an important social characteristic, involving a sense of obligation to all other African Americans and suggesting a commitment to helping the group transcend its current disadvantages (Baldwin, 1980; Bobo, 1983; National Research Council, 1989).

Summarizing, we have provided the background of those influences that have been identified as instrumental in understanding the racial belief system of African Americans. We have examined in broad terms the literature surrounding the antecedents of African American racial belief system, namely, social structural and background variables and communication constructs, especially the mass media, both majority and black. Within each of these broad conceptual categories, there are yet variables to be specified that relate specific social structural and background variables and media constructs to an African American racial belief system.

What follows is the presentation of a program of research and its theoretical development. The steps taken in presenting this research are, first, an investigation of the various dimensions of an African-American racial belief system in terms of its measurement properties and structural invariances across a number of select demographic measures. Second, we examine the explanatory constructs of the derived dimensions of this belief system. That is, the fully developed model with all the constructs we have identified as relevant.

A Program of Research

In our conceptualization of belief systems (Allen et al., 1989), we maintain that belief systems are cognitive structures that tend to facilitate and constrain the work of schemata (specifically, the processing, storing, and organizing of information acquired from the social environment). Further, we maintain that belief systems assist the individual in his or her framing of social reality. The belief system focuses attention on the complementary or conflicting nature of relevant actors' goals and has an impact on the individual's planning, counterplanning, and social behavior (Carbonell, 1981). Cognitive schemata, we contend, actively store and process information and produce expectations about future events and actions (Conover & Feldman, 1980). Heuristic decisions and the access and process of information are made possible by belief systems. The belief system serves the purpose of targeting the perceptions of the understander toward certain characteristics of the actors and the environment and deflecting these perceptions away from other characteristics (Carbonell, 1981).

Much of the theorizing underlying our proffered models may be employed to study other oppressed groups. The categories of the identified constructs should be the same but the concept names and their operationalizations may differ slightly. Instead of referring to black-oriented television or black autonomy, for example, the concept names, and to some degree the measures, would reflect the group under consideration.

We explored an African-American belief system, which we posited comes into being over time, and the strength of the components of this belief system—the cognitive schemata—would vary across individuals based on their position in the society as a whole, their exposure to information sources both within and outside the black community, and the level of their ability and training in processing social information (Allen et al., 1989). The reproduction of this belief system over time is reinforced by the socializing effects of such formal and informal black institutions as the black church and kinship networks, social organizations, and various institutions of the African-American community.

In our studies, we investigated an African-American belief system with respect to five cognitive schema: (a) black autonomy, (b) positive stereotypical beliefs about African Americans (positive stereotypes), (c) negative stereotypical beliefs about African Americans (negative stereotypes), (d) closeness to black masses, and (e) closeness to black elites. To foster clarity and minimize misunderstanding about these constructs, each was given a theoretical definition.

Black autonomy was defined as a component of racial consciousness that signifies the distinctive cultural and racial identity of African Americans. It was conceptualized as an ideological position that suggests that African Americans should build political and social institutions based on group cultural values and interests.

Based on the thesis that individuals tend to assign positive attributes to their group and to reject negative ones (Tajfel, 1982), the two related constructs of positive and negative stereotypes were introduced. Positive stereotype was defined as the acceptance of positive group attribute and rejection of debasing imagery of the group, and negative stereotype was defined as the acceptance of the legitimacy of the notion that blacks do not have social meaning or notions concerning their systemic shortcomings.

Closeness to the black masses was defined as the extent to which the individual has emotional bonds to the racial group and perceives African Americans as sharing a common fate. Closeness to elites was defined as the extent to which African Americans identify with African-American civic and political leaders.

Acknowledging that there is always a gap between the theoretical and the operational definition (Blalock, 1982), we operationally defined the five belief constructs as follows. Black autonomy contained three indicators, each expressed in a 5-point agree-disagree format. These items were: (a) blacks should study an African language, (b) black people should shop in black-owned stores whenever possible, and (c) black parents should give their children African names.

The construct of positive stereotype contained four indicators, each measured on a 4-point very true-not very true at all format: (a) blacks are hard working, (b) blacks do for others, (c) blacks are honest, and (d) blacks are strong.

The construct of negative stereotype contained five indicators, each measured on a 5-point very true-not very true at all format: (a) most blacks are lazy, (b) most blacks neglect their families, (c) most blacks are lying and trifling, (d) most blacks give up easily, and (e) most blacks are weak.

The closeness to black masses contained four indicators, each expressed on a 5-point very close-not very close at all format. The questions were: (a) how close do you feel toward poor blacks, (b) how close do you feel toward religious and church-going blacks, (c) how close do you feel toward middle-class blacks, and (d) how close do you feel toward older blacks.

Closeness to black elites contained two indicators, each expressed on a 4-point very close-not very close at all format. These items were: (a) how close do you feel toward black elected officials; (b) how close do you feel toward professionals (e.g., doctors and lawyers).

A graphic representation of our conceptualization is presented in Figure 11.1. We tested this model with the data from the 1980 National Survey of Black Americans conducted by the Program for Research on Black Americans at the Survey Research Center at the University of Michigan during 1979 and 1980.

We began our analysis by testing how well the model fit, and more particularly, how well the items or indicators were linked to their respective constructs. Here we dealt with the properties of our measurement model.

Throughout our program of research, we used structural equation modeling with latent variables, which has many advantages in performing our tests. For example, we were able to see how well each item performed as an indicator of its latent construct, and we were also able to take into account measurement error.

The major results from our baseline analysis suggest that, first, our model provided a good fit to the data. Second, we found that each of the indicators were good reflectors of their respective constructs. All of the factor loadings were of high magnitude and statistically significant. Moreover, a substantial proportion of variance was explained for each construct. We concluded that for the adult black population in the United States our proposed model seemed adequate and worthy of further pursuit and that the items we used to tap these constructs were reliable.

Given these outcomes, we extended our analysis to the examination of other measurement properties. We compared groups of parameters to test the equivalencies across income and education (Allen et al., in press), gender (Brown, Allen, & Dawson, 1990), and age cohorts (Allen, Chadiha, & Jackson, 1992). Comparisons were done by examining the degrees of fit of the model with different equivalence constraints.

In particular, we evaluated five different specifications. One, we evaluated the null model, which assumed total independence among the observed indicators in our model. The second specification involved the proposed model but included no cross-income, no

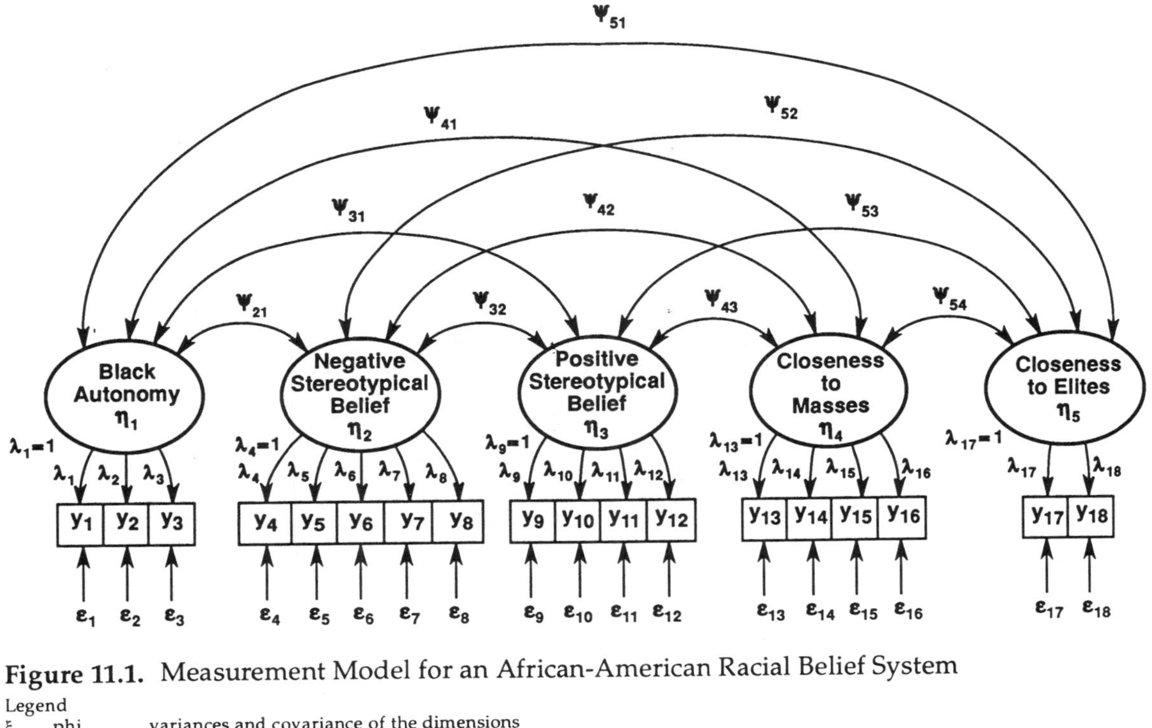

Figure 11.1. Measurement Model for an African-American Racial Belief System

Legend

ξ	phi	variances and covariance of the dimensions
λ	lambda	factor loadings
δ	delta	measurement errors associated with observed indicators of the exogenous constructs
ε	epsilon	measurement errors associated with observed indicators of the endogenous constructs
η	eta	endogenous latent constructs
ψ	psi	variance of covalence of the dimensions

cross-education, no cross-gender, no cross-age cohort equivalences. This is the test of form, or stated differently, of whether the model for the different samples has the same number of latent variables with the same indicators, and the same specification of fixed and free parameters (see Figure 11.1). The third model included equivalence constraints on the factor loadings. The fourth model included equivalence constraints on both the factor loadings and the residual error variances and covariances. The fifth model constrained to be equal, not only the factors and the residual error variance and covariances but also the measure error variances. Models 2 through 5 represent different types of invariance and constitute a hierarchy. For example, the investigation of model 3 assumes that model 2 was not rejected.

It bears mentioning that the acceptance of all five models is a very rigorous test. Usually, if the form of the model provides a good fit across the different samples and the factor loadings are the same across sample, most investigators would find this to be adequate evidence of factorial or structural invariance (Bollen, 1989).

Using the criteria of similarity in model form and similarity in factor loadings as the minimum for accepting structural invariance, our results are instructive. All of the demographic and background variables we tested—income, education, gender, and age cohort—demonstrated structural invariance. Within our hierarchical strategy, income and gender showed the highest degree of structural invariance. They extend to at least invariance of error variances. We may conclude that the model we have proposed to explain an African-American racial belief system has similar meaning or fit equally well across different demographic or background variables.

Our analysis then moved to an examination of mean differences across income, education, gender, and age cohorts. That is, we examined the differences across income, gender, and age cohort groupings on the level to which each endorses our model of an African-American racial belief system. A critical assumption in testing for mean differences is that the measurement and structure of the underlying constructs are equivalent across groups (Bejar, 1980; Bollen, 1989; Drasgow & Kanfer, 1985; Liang & Bollen, 1985). This we demonstrated in the above analyses.

Another point needs to be made with respect to testing mean differences. Whereas most studies of factorial invariance limit the investigation to documenting differences in factor structure (Liang,

Tran, Krause, & Markides, 1989), we went further to explore mean differences across the social structural variables. The typical method of analyzing factor means overlooks the potential differences in measurement structure (e.g., first-order factor loadings). This can lead to ambiguity of results (Liang & Bollen, 1985; Liang et al., 1989). Applications of tests of restrictions on means suggest that there is, at least, invariance of factor loadings (Bollen, 1989).

Taking social structure variables separately, our findings yielded considerable useful information. With respect to income, a test of the factor means suggests that income level does not influence how African Americans relate to the constructs of black autonomy, positive stereotypes, or closeness to the masses.

Conversely, level of income does influence how African Americans relate to the negative evaluation of the African-American community and the degree of closeness to elite groups in that community. The pattern of mean differences suggests that it is the lower income groups who tend to hold more negative stereotypes and to feel closer to elites in the African-American community.

Our examination of factor means across education groups revealed an interesting and rather complex picture. The different educational groups seemed to relate to black autonomy similarly and to have the same notions of positive stereotypes. However, these education groups are quite different with respect to negative stereotypes of the African-American community and their closeness to the masses and the elites. In each case, individuals in the lower educational levels demonstrated the greater mean differences.

Concerning the gender variable, we found that there were no mean differences on any of our five constructs of an African-American racial belief system. That is, African-American men and women do not differ in the level of endorsement of black autonomy, positive and negative stereotypes, and assessment of their closeness to African people and the African-American community.

Finally, when taking into account mean differences in age cohorts, we found no mean differences for the black autonomy or negative and positive stereotypes constructs. On the other hand, the means for closeness to the masses and closeness to elites were significantly different across the three age groups. Specifically, the younger age cohort (17-29) was less likely to express closeness to the masses in the African-American community. The older cohort (55-100), however,

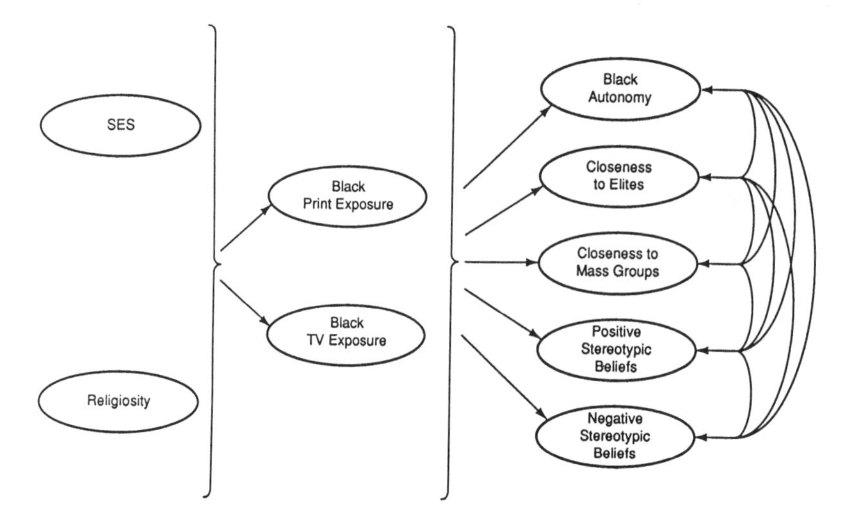

Figure 11.2. Conceptual Model of an African-American Racial Belief System (Adults)

was more likely to express a closeness to the elites in the African-American community.

Antecedents of an African-American Racial Belief System

Having obtained information suggesting that our model was adequate and having indicated factorial invariance to differing degrees across important social structural variables, we moved to the analysis of antecedents or predictors of an African-American racial belief system. A representation of this structural equation model (i.e., the measurement model and the structural model) is presented in Figure 11.2.

At this point, again using a national sample of African Americans, we examined the relationship between several demographic and background variables and their influences on both the media constructs and on the constructs we used to represent an African-American racial belief system. Also, we investigated the impact of black print media and black-oriented television on these belief constructs.

We extended our previous confirmatory factor analysis model by including a number of variables under the category of social structural variables and another set of variables under the category of communication variables.

Social Structural Variables

The social structural variables were theoretically defined and operationalized as follows: Education, income, and occupation status were used to represent an individual's location in the social structure. Education was operationalized as the number of years of formal training the respondent received. Total family income was measured by an item that assessed the income, from all sources, of all persons living in that household. Occupational prestige was coded in terms of degree of prestige.

Religiosity was defined as the extent to which an individual identifies with and participates in an organized religion. The religiosity construct was composed of five items. These items, expressed on a 5-point scale, were: (a) frequency of an individual's reading religious books, (b) frequency of an individual's listening to religious programs, (c) frequency of an individual's praying, (d) frequency of an individual's asking someone to pray for him or her, and (e) degree to which an individual considers him or herself to be religious.

Communication Processes

Black-oriented television exposure was defined as the amount of attention given to content presented on television that depicts the life of African Americans. It was measured by one item. On a 5-point scale, the respondent answered the question on the frequency of watching black-oriented television programs.

Black print media was defined as the amount of attention given to print media owned and produced largely by African Americans for African Americans. It also was measured by one item. On a 5-point scale, the respondent answered the question on the frequency of reading black literature (books, magazines, and newspapers).

Our proposed model indicated a good fit. All of the measurement properties suggested that our model fit the data well. The findings showed that one's place in the social structure and the centrality of religious activity in one's life have powerful and theoretically well understood effects on the African-American racial belief system. Higher placement in the social structure had negative effects on black autonomy, closeness to the black masses, and closeness to black elites.

Taken together these relationships suggest that as African Americans move up the social structure and become more affluent, they are less likely to adopt a view of black identity centered on separation from white society (black autonomy). Simultaneously, they are affectively more removed from the black community, including their own status peers. The negative relationship between socioeconomic status and negative stereotypical beliefs suggests that although those of higher status feel more distant from African people, they also are not as negative toward the African-American community as are lower status respondents. These findings illuminate the importance of continued testing of the effect of social stratification on psychological orientation and social behavior of different elements with the African-American community.

Exposure to the black media was an important predictor of the content of African-American belief schemata. In general terms, the media's position as intermediate interpreters of reality between an individual and his or her environment was substantially confirmed. Television was found to have the most pronounced influence. Although neither black print media nor black-oriented television was found to have significant effects on negative stereotypical beliefs of African Americans, television had statistically significant effects on all the other racial belief constructs. It had a positive effect on the endorsement of positive stereotypical beliefs, black autonomy, and closeness to the masses. It had a negative effect on the closeness to elite elements of the African-American community.

Black print media were related to only one of the five racial belief constructs. That is, exposure to black print media had a negative effect on the endorsement of negative stereotypes about African Americans. The more the exposure to black print media, the less the endorsement of negative stereotypes about African Americans.

Although our model was supported empirically, variations of this conceptualization should be explored across many different subgroups (e.g., occupation, region, or environmental upbringing). This would extend the representativeness of our model and also reveal possible interactions. Also, aside from examining the effects of a more comprehensive measure of black-oriented television and black print media, the effects of the majority media should also be included in our model. Although the study of the black media is very important in illuminating the impact of messages that are more or less in control of African Americans on the African-American racial belief system, at present, more attention is given to the majority media by this population. Finally, and significantly, this model needs to be tested with a sample of children and adolescents. Given the importance of television, and of the media in general, in the lives of children, and especially African-American children, this inquiry would shed light on an important social phenomena. We will discuss this in more detail below.

A Proposed Extension of Our Model for Children and Adolescents: The Media and the Socialization of the African-American Child

We propose that our model, which has generated conceptually rich and methodologically sound findings, should be extended to the study of the most neglected portion of the African-American community—the children (National Research Council, 1989; National Urban League, 1989). Taking into account the array of forces operating to the detriment of the African-American community as we outlined above, the study of the young come to mind. When we peruse such basic facts about the condition that African-American young find themselves, the question arises how do they view themselves and their community. Consider, for example, that half of African children under the age of 6 live in official poverty. A substantial portion of these are parented by poor, isolated teenage girls. Consider further that a high proportion of young African-American men are in prison, in fact more are incarcerated than enrolled in universities (Edelin, 1990). Add to that the fact that many African Americans drop out of high school with little hope or opportunity to obtain a job.

An area of crucial concern for researchers in our field is the socialization (or the process whereby children learn and internalize the ways of their society) of the African-American child living under the onslaught of the forces described above and the extent to which this socialization is influenced by or manifests itself through television. Berry and Mitchell-Kernan (1982) noted that the number of television sets and the hours of usage are increasing and there is evidence that a substantial portion of the audience is relying on television as

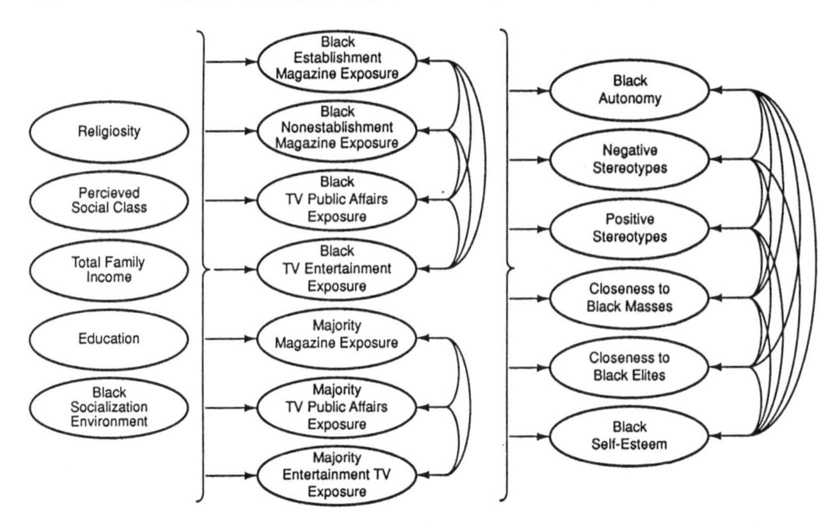

Figure 11.3. Conceptual Model of an African-American Racial Belief System (Adolescents)

a primary source of validating information and perhaps even beliefs and values. They stated further that as a consequence many social observers, and especially those concerned with the development of children, have begun to examine the role of television within the broad context of the socialization process in the United States.

The images that television presents create problems for many African-American children and adolescents. A number of studies have shown how an African-American child may feel ambivalent about his or her racial identity and often will prefer characters on television that do not resemble themselves (Comer, 1982).

With modifications and extensions derived from our exploration of the African-American racial belief system for adults, we propose a revised version of our previous model as an instrument to study the effects of social structural characteristics and communication processes on children and adolescents (see Figure 11.3).

Note that we have included one other exogenous construct, black socialization experience. To provide a broader context for the investigation of television's presumed effects on the internalization of society's images, in our case a racial belief system, we included an endogenous construct, neglected in the adult study, namely, nonblack-oriented television fare, the majority of television content. Moreover, we incorporated a print media construct that pertains to the nonblack print media. Under that heading we included variables for both newspapers and magazines. Finally, we expand the black print media to reflect more fully the variety of types of media.

Because of the desirable measurement properties, these constructs should have several indicators, at least three (Bollen, 1989). What follows is a theoretical definition of these new variables: (a) black socialization experience is defined as the extent of the physical and emotional contact an individual had with the African-American community in the formative years of development; (b) general magazine exposure is defined as the amount and the attention given to information in magazines not owned and not specifically directed to African Americans—this construct is less relevant for preadolescents; (c) general public affairs television exposure is defined as the amount and attention given to news programs or talk shows not specifically directed toward African Americans; and (d) general entertainment television exposure is defined as the amount and the attention given nonnews content not specifically directed to African Americans.

With the same theoretical definitions given for the aforementioned study that examined adults, black print media exposure and black-oriented television exposure may be expanded to include more than one indicator of each construct and each abstract construct may be further separated. For example, black print media may be separated into black established and black nonestablishment press. Moreover, in order to obtain a more comprehensive assessment of these constructs, they may incorporate measures of frequency and amount of attention paid to various kinds of content.

The only new belief construct that is suggested is self-esteem, a concept that historically has been of major concern (Porter & Washington, 1979). It may be defined as a nonracial belief construct. It is the esteem one has for one's individuality regardless of racial group. It pertains to how one feels about the self in a comprehensive sense. Operationally, self-esteem may be tapped, on a 7-point scale, by asking the respondent whether he or she holds a favorable view about himself or herself over a wide range of situations.

The model that we have suggested is most suited for employing survey techniques. Moreover, because external validity is a concern, we think this focus is warranted. Nonetheless, we realize that how we have fashioned our problem and the techniques we have suggested lead to explanations but also some hints on intervention or change. To pursue this area of inquiry, different research questions and designs are needed.

The Formation and Reinforcement of an African-American Racial Belief System

The research problem that is of utmost concern is how or to what extent do African Americans of various ages—particularly the young —and different backgrounds manage to make sense of and transcend the psychological onslaught visited upon them as a group that the majority has viewed with "amused contempt" as described by Dubois (1903).

The question that is of major concern is not merely to describe the state of the community relative to its view of itself, but what can be done to fashion a more favorable, a more empowering, conception by this group. Starting with the young, intervention strategies may be developed to facilitate outcomes that lead to more sanguine and favorable views of self and of the group to which one belongs. This work would involve moving beyond the survey research techniques mentioned above.

What is being suggested here is what is commonly called evaluation research. Rather than a specific method, its purpose is to assess or evaluate the impact of our designated social intervention. Many different research methods may be used in evaluation research (Babbie, 1992), for example, experiments of various kinds and a variety of qualitative research techniques.

A sample of the questions that we plan to explore among young African Americans are: (a) What kind of content (e.g., historical, contemporary, descriptive, explanatory) or combination of content types might influence the view of the self and the group? (b) From which medium does certain content have the most pronounced effect (television, newspapers, magazines)? (c) Is the content most readily accepted when purveyed in a black medium (e.g., black magazines vs. nonblack magazines or black-oriented television vs. nonblack-oriented television)? (d) How effective would the messages be for the various ages group if purveyed thorough video, through story books, through comic books? (e) Within an interactive media format (computer based) that contains a number of aspects of a single topic and allows substantial control to the user, what is its comparative effectiveness?

The measures we will use and that have already been found to be reliable are those identified earlier, namely, black autonomy, closeness to various groups in the African-American community, and stereotypical perspectives of the group. These measures are primarily racially based, but we will also include the more personal, nonracial reference construct of self-esteem. There may indeed be a number of constructs that will be suggested as we acquire qualitative data. In these studies, these constructs will be examined simultaneously. Each will be evaluated relative to the extent to which each is enhanced by the communication interventions. It may turn out that some constructs are enhanced, for instance, self-esteem, and others, for example, negative stereotype, is diminished.

Although the population involved in the evaluation program will be preadolescents and adolescents, greater distinctions between these two broad categories will be made in the analysis. Further, we will measure or control for such variables as gender and socialization environment (primarily black vs. primarily nonblack).

Various experimental designs will be used to examine our research problem. For many of our questions the "true" experiment will be employed. These true experiments will, of course, allow us to control for the factors jeopardizing internal and external validity, as they will allow us to randomly assign individuals to an experimental group. There are a number of such true experiments that may be conducted, depending on which particular research question we examine. Because of certain practical difficulties, we may not be able to employ random assignment, thus we will have to use quasi-experimental designs. A few of the most appropriate designs for answering our research questions are the nonequivalent control groups and the multiple time series designs.

Aside from experimental methods, which will be used as part of the proposed evaluative research, some of the questions we have posed lend themselves to a wide variety of qualitative methods (e.g., intensive interviews, focus groups, case studies). Although there are many differences between quantitative and qualitative research, a fundamental difference is that those operating within a qualitative framework observe and describe information as it occurs within the cultural scene (Hall & Marshall, 1992). These resulting data will likely be much richer and more varied. The inclusion of this qualitative aspect of our program of research is in acknowledgment of the need for both types of research, or what has come to be known as triangulation.

The advantages of the quantitative approach are well known and frequently stated; among neglected unique advantages of qualitative research are its unobtrusiveness and that it occurs in a natural setting. Using qualitative research in our program of research will enable us to obtain a more comprehensive view of the African-American culture and African-American people with respect to their conceptions of self and the group.

Rather than viewing the quantitative and qualitative approaches as being diametrically opposed to one another, we view them as complementary. The qualitative research can be employed to gain a better understanding of the relationships observed empirically. Additionally, our qualitative research may reveal interesting and worthwhile quantitative studies. Finally, it is useful to garner both quantitative and qualitative research, using different oppressed groups to test the same ideas or hypotheses.

In brief, the next stage in our program of research is long and tedious. It has an explicitly interventionist focus. It is orchestrated to have a positive and enduring effect.

References

Allen, R. L., Chadiha, L., & Jackson, J. (1992). *Cohort differences in the structure of an African-American racial belief system.* Unpublished manuscript.

Allen, R. L., Dawson, M. C., & Brown, R. E. (1989). A schema-based approach to modeling an African-American racial belief system. *American Political Science Review, 83,* 421-441.

Allen, R. L., Thornton, M. C., & Watkins, S. C. (in press). An African-American racial belief system and social structural relationships: A test of invariance. *National Sociological Review.*

Allen, R. L., & Waks. L. (1990). Social reality construction: The evaluation of the status and role of women and blacks. *Howard Journal of Communications, 2,* 170-191.

Babbie, E. (1992). *The practice of social research* (6th ed.). Belmont, CA: Wadsworth.

Baldwin, J. (1980). The psychology of oppression. In M. K. Asante & A. S. Vandi (Eds.), *Contemporary black thought* (pp. 95-110). Beverly Hills, CA: Sage.

Bejar, I. (1980). Biased assessment of program impact due to psychometric artifacts. *Psychological Bulletin, 87,* 513-524.

Berry, G. L., & Mitchell-Kernan, C. (1982). *Television and the socialization of the minority child.* New York: Academic Press.

Blalock, H. M. (1982). *Conceptualization and measurement in the social sciences.* Beverly Hills, CA: Sage.
Bobo, L. (1983). Whites opposition to busing: Symbolic racism or realistic group conflict? *Journal of Personality and Social Psychology, 45,* 1196-1210.
Bollen, K. A. (1989). *Structural equations with latent variables.* New York: John Wiley.
Bourne, S. C. (1990). The African-American image in American cinema. *Black Scholar, 21,* 12-19.
Brown, R. E., Allen, R. L., & Dawson, M. C. (1990). *Gender and an African-American racial belief system.* Unpublished manuscript.
Carbonell, J. G. (1981). *Subjective understanding: Computer models of belief systems.* Ann Arbor, MI: UMI Research.
Clarke, J. H. (1991). *Notes for an African world revolution: Africa at the crossroads.* Trenton, NJ: African World Press.
Comer, J. H. (1982). The importance of television images of black families. In A. W. Jackson (Ed.), *Black families and the medium of television* (pp. 19-25). Ann Arbor: University of Michigan, Bush Program in Child Development and Social Policy.
Conover, P. L., & Feldman, S. (1980). Belief system organization in the American electorate: An alternative approach. In J. C. Pierce & J. L. Sullivan (Eds.), *The electorate reconsidered* (pp. 49-67). Beverly Hills, CA: Sage.
Dates, J. L., & Barlow, W. (1990). *Split image: African Americans in the mass media.* Washington, DC: Howard University Press.
Dawson, M. C., Brown, R. E., & Allen, R. L. (1990). Racial belief systems, religious guidance, and African-American political participation. *National Political Science Review, 2,* 23-44.
Drasgow, F., & Kanfer, R. (1985). Equivalence of psychological measurement in heterogeneous populations. *Journal of Applied Psychology, 70,* 662-680.
Dubois, W.E.B. (1903). The souls of black folk: Essays and sketches. Chicago: A. C. McClurg.
Edelin, R. H. (1990). Curriculum and cultural identity. In A. G. Hillard, L. Payton-Stewart & L. O. Williams (Eds.), *Infusion of African and African-American content in the school curriculum* (pp. 37-45). Morristown, NJ: Aaron.
Farley, R. (1984). *Blacks and whites: Narrowing the gap?* Cambridge, MA: Harvard University Press.
Frazier, E. F. (1963). *The Negro church in America.* New York: Schocken.
Gray, H. (1989). Television, Black Americans, and the American dream. *Critical Studies in Mass Communication, 6,* 376-386.
Hall, L. D., & Marshall, K. P. (1992). *Computing for social research.* Belmont, CA: Wadsworth.
Herman, E. S., & Chomsky, N. (1989). *Manufacturing consent: The political economy of the mass media.* New York: Pantheon.
Jackman, M. R., & Jackman, R. W. (1983). *Class awareness in the United States.* Berkeley: University of California Press.
Kilson, M. (1983). The Black bourgeois revisited. *Dissent, 30,* 85-96.
Liang, J., & Bollen, K. (1985). Sex differences in the structure of the Philadelphia Geriatric Center Morale Scale. *Journal of Gerontology, 40,* 468-477.
Liang, J., Tran, T. V., Krause, N., & Markides, K. S. (1989). Generational differences in the structure of the CES-D scale in Mexican Americans. *Journal of Gerontology, 44,* S110-120.

McDonald, J. F. (1983). *Blacks and white TV: Afro-Americans in television since 1948.* Chicago: Nelson-Hall.

Morris, A. D. (1984). *The origins of the civil rights movement: Black communities organizing for change.* New York: Free Press.

National Research Council. (1989). *A common destiny: Blacks and American society.* Washington, DC: National Academy Press.

National Urban League. (1989). *The state of Black America, 1989.* New York: National Urban League.

Pierce, C. (1980). Social trace contaminants: Subtle indicators of racism in TV. In S. B. Withey & R. P. Abeles (Eds.), *Television and social behavior: Beyond violence and children* (pp. 249-257). Hillsdale, NJ: Lawrence Erlbaum.

Poindexter, P. M., & Stroman, C. A. (1981). Blacks and television: A review of the research literature. *Journal of Broadcasting, 25,* 103-122.

Porter, J. R., & Washington, R. E. (1979). Black identity and self-esteem: A review of studies of black self-concept. *Annual Review of Sociology, 5,* 53-74.

Reich, M. (1981). *Racial inequality.* Princeton, NJ: Princeton University Press.

Shingles, R. (1979). College as a source of black alienation. *Journal of Black Studies, 9,* 267-291.

Signorielli, N. (1990). *Cultivation analysis: New directions in media effects research.* Newbury Park, CA: Sage.

Staples, R., & Jones, T. (1985). Culture, ideology and black television images. *Black Scholar, 10,* 10-20.

Stroman, C., Merritt, B. D., & Matabane, P. W. (1989-1990). Twenty years after Kerner: The portrayal of African Americans on prime-time television. *Howard Journal of Communications, 2,* 44-56.

Tajfel, H. (1982). Social psychology of intergroup relations. *Annual Review of Psychology, 33,* 1-39.

Ukadike, N. F. (1990). Western film images of Africa: Genealogy of an ideological formulation. *Black Scholar, 21,* 30-48.

Ungar, S. J., & Gergen, D. (1991). *Africa and the American media* (Occasional paper no. 9). New York: Freedom Forum Media Studies Center, Columbia University.

Walker, S. S. (1991). *Africans and African Americans: Together into the twenty-first century.* Unpublished manuscript.

Willie, C. V. (1979). The inclining significance of race. In C. V. Willie (Ed.), *The caste and class controversy* (pp. 144-154). Bayside, NY: General Hall.

Wilson, W. J. (1980). *The declining significance of race* (2nd ed.). Chicago, University of Chicago Press.

Winston, M. R. (1982). Racial consciousness and the evolution of mass communications in the United States. *Daedalus, 111,* 171-182.

PART III

Television and the Development of a Child's Understanding of Diverse Populations

Television offers portrayals of diverse segments of the population. Through these medium portrayals, some children develop perceptions and attitudes about themselves and others.

Part III includes chapters written by scholars who have studied how the television portrayals of the diverse populations in our society affect the attitude development of our youth toward these groups of people. Although diverse populations are seen more often on television, a consistent theme that emerges in reading the various contributions is that current television programming is still falling short in the way diverse populations are portrayed. For many of the groups represented on the screen, the portrayal is not coming from the phenomenology of the group itself but rather is an interpretation of the group experience by someone who has not shared in the experience. Furthermore, the medium still includes stereotypes in the portrayal of some groups. Still other groups are primarily seen on television when the group membership itself is the focus of the television program, but are usually absent in general programming.

Part III begins with four chapters on the portrayal of the major ethnic or racial minority populations in the United States, and the effect these portrayals have on children's attitudes toward these populations. The contributions include Sherryl Browne Graves on African-American portrayals, Haney Geiogamah and D. Michael Pavel on American Indian and Alaska Native portrayals, Darrell Y. Hamamoto on Asian American portrayals, and Federico A. Subervi-Vélez and Susan Colsant on Latino portrayals.

Finally, the last three chapters in Part III deal with other forms of diversity that cannot be neglected in discussions of television portrayals and the development of children's attitudes. Nancy Signorielli discusses the portrayal of women on television. If nothing else, the portrayal of gender roles on television appears to remain stable in that the status quo is supported.

Two groups that are less studied but clearly emerging as a significant social-cultural influence are the elderly and persons with disabilities. Peter M. Kovaric discusses the diversity that exists among individuals who would be considered elderly although children are presented a very narrow, and often unflattering representation of the elderly population. Elaine Makas reviews the literature that has studied the television portrayal of people with disabilities. Of particular interest are her thoughts as to why persons with disabilities are not more often seen on television.

12. Television, the Portrayal of African Americans, and the Development of Children's Attitudes

SHERRYL BROWNE GRAVES

In the social world of television, characters are overwhelmingly European, male, and middle class, whether one is watching prime-time or children's programming (Downing, 1974; Greenberg, Simmons, Hogan, & Atkins, 1980; Williams & Condry, 1989). Excluding programming in languages other than English, among underrepresented groups, African Americans are the only group appearing in significant numbers (Berry, 1988; S. B. Graves, 1980; Steenland, 1989; Williams & Condry, 1989).

One can conclude, as did a recent American Psychological Association task force (Huston et al., 1992), that minorities, including African Americans, are underrepresented on television, segregated in specific types of content, and rarely engage in cross-ethnic interactions. Although these conclusions are true, a closer examination will reveal exactly how the social role assigned to African Americans is transmitted to child viewers.

African-American characters are more likely to be presented in a highly stereotyped manner than are European American characters in terms of occupational level, social role assignments, and behavioral characteristics (Baptista-Fernandez & Greenberg, 1980; Reid, 1979; Williams & Condry, 1989). After reviewing commercials and children's daytime, nonfiction and prime-time programming, one can conclude that despite almost 40 years of monitoring the portrayal of underrepresented groups on television, African Americans continue to be infrequently seen in many areas of television content.

African-American presentations have a specific age distribution. For example, African Americans tend to be younger than European-American characters in prime-time (Baptista-Fernandez & Greenberg, 1980; S. B. Graves, 1980; Williams & Condry, 1989), and are rarely seen as elderly in commercials (Hiemstra, Goodman, Middlemiss, Vosco, & Ziegler, 1983).

In the area of gender distribution, there is a male-female ratio for African Americans of about two to one in entertainment television (Baptista-Fernandez & Greenberg, 1980). Despite the overall increase in the proportion of females on television from 1970 through the 1980s, the proportion of African-American female characters decreased (Seggar, Hafen, & Hannonen-Gladden, 1981), and they have been confined to situation comedies (Steenland, 1989).

This gender pattern is further complicated when one examines the marital status associated with African-American roles. Among men, fewer African-American than European-American male characters were single, but among women, African-American female characters are more likely to be married than their European-American counterparts (Gerbner, Gross, & Signorielli, 1985).

The African-American family is another area in which particular characterizations regularly occur on television (A. W. Jackson, 1982). African-American families are featured as isolated from other families (Berry, 1982). These family role portrayals are such that the wife is more likely to be presented as being in conflict with her husband, and females in general are more likely to be presented as dominant in the family setting than is true of other family situation comedies (Baptiste, 1986). Among siblings, dominance conflicts are more frequent among African-American sisters and brothers than among siblings in other groups.

The employment and occupational status for African-American characters provides the viewer with another set of expectations. Earlier studies (Barcus, 1983) indicated that African-American characters were less likely to be employed than were European-American characters, but a recent study of 1987 programming (Williams & Condry, 1989) found that minority and majority group members were equally likely to be employed. During the 1970s in prime-time programming, African Americans were less likely to be portrayed in professional or managerial positions than European Americans, despite a general tendency of television to overrepresent these higher socioeconomic levels (Baptista-Fernandez & Greenberg, 1980). On the other hand, a study of children's television (Barcus, 1983) and a study of prime-time programs (Steenland, 1989) found that African- and European-American characters were equally likely to be professionals or managers.

In other occupational areas, among holders of scientific occupations on television, African Americans make up only 2% of the scientist group (Gerbner et al., 1985). Generally, African Americans are more likely to be portrayed as nurses, blue-collar workers, and law enforcement officers (Gerbner et al., 1985; Williams & Condry, 1989). Furthermore, African Americans are more likely to be presented as both victims and suspects or perpetrators of violence (Estep & Macdonald, 1983; L. S. Lichter & S. R. Lichter, 1983; Williams & Condry, 1989). Thus, although the message about the relationship between African Americans and violence is ambiguous, the viewer is nonetheless left with a clear association between aggression and African-American characters.

Television also presents African-American characters as exhibiting specific behaviors or having particular personality characteristics. In a study of dominance patterns on television (Lemon, 1977), African-American characters were more likely to dominate European Americans in situation comedies whereas the reverse was true in crime dramas. African-American characters in integrated shows were more likely to display socially valued characteristics and high social status symbols. Baptista-Fernandez and Greenberg (1980) found that there were differences between African-American and European-American characters in their giving, seeking, and receiving of advice, information, and orders.

Television could be a source of information on how to successfully interact in cross-ethnic situations. However, because African-American characters in prime time are frequently segregated in all-minority, situation comedies or are presented in association with violent acts, there is limited opportunity for meaningful modeling of interracial interactions or for explicit discussions of race relations (Greenberg, 1986; Lovelace, Freund, & S. B. Graves, in press; Pierce, 1980; Williams & Condry, 1989). In a study of children's programs (Barcus, 1983), only 18% of the program segments featured integrated settings where African-American and other minority characters interacted with European characters and racial or ethnic messages were avoided. Cartoon comedies, on the other hand, although employing the most blatant ethnic stereotyping as a content feature, largely avoided the inclusion of African-American portrayals.

In a study (Williams & Condry, 1989) of televised cross-ethnic interaction on children's programs, it was found that 40% of minority characters are presented in segregated environments, precluding the possibility of interracial interaction. When cross-racial interactions occur, the majority of these contacts are presented as positive. In the advertising that accompanies children's programming selections, the contact between the races is more frequent because it takes place in job-related situations.

Among televised roles for youth, ethnic minority youth were three times more likely to engage in positive social interactions with majority group characters than they were to engage in positive interactions with other ethnic minority characters. As with adult roles, only a very small percentage of the identified interethnic encounters showed negative interactions or overt acts of prejudice or racism (D. Jackson, Travis, Williams, & Phillips, 1986; Williams & Condry, 1989).

In an application of a model of interracial interactions, Auletta and Hammerback (1985) found that interactions between African- and European-American major characters are marked by independent communication, whereas interactions among same-group leading characters feature interdependent communication. Independent communication includes judgmental feedback, lack of self-disclosure, unwillingness to collaborate, rejection, and neglect of the other. Interdependent messages, on the other hand, feature feedback stressing understanding, self-disclosure, confirmation of the other, collaboration, and empathic listening. The implication that African Americans are more likely to interact positively with majority group members than with members of their own group reinforces the stereotype that in-group fighting and lack of positive group cohesiveness are characteristic of African Americans.

Television Exposure and Attitude Development

Both the quantitative and qualitative underrepresentation African Americans on television have been shown to influence children's perceptions and attitudes toward African Americans. In general, this research has focused on the impact of these portrayals on only two groups, African- and European-American viewers. Perceptual responses are usually measured in terms of the realism of specific portrayals whereas attitudinal responses are usually measured in terms of the preferences for same-group or different-group stimuli.

There are several theories about how televised portrayals might influence the attitudes of viewers toward other cultural groups:

1. Catharsis theory would suggest that exposure to portrayals associated with powerful human emotions (e.g., aggression or sex), would reduce the amount of these emotions in the viewer.
2. Cultivation theory suggests that content frequently viewed creates a worldview, or a consistent picture of social behavior, norms, and structure based on the stable view of society that television content provides (Gerbner, Gross, Morgan, & Signorielli, 1980).
3. Greenberg (1988) proposes a "drench model." In this view, distinct or unusual television portrayals could overwhelm more mundane roles because of their strength, intensity, or authenticity.
4. Social learning theory predicts that viewing any content will cause children to imitate this content (Bandura, 1977). More recently, this model has evolved to emphasize the role of viewers' needs, interests, abilities, motivations, and self-concepts in the influence process.
5. Constructivism suggests that the child is largely responsible for whatever influence programming has on them. This approach suggests that children actively make sense of the world they live in and that they are particularly responsive to information that helps them develop a better understanding of the world and their experiences (Anderson, 1981, 1983).
6. The uses and gratifications approach (Blumer & Katz, 1974) predicts that there is an interaction between the characteristics of children and the type of content that is likely to influence them. Children actively select television content that gratifies them.

African-American Portrayals and African-American Children

Perceptions and Comprehension of Portrayals

As African-American viewers actively view same-group characters, their perceptions and understanding appear to be related to a number of variables, as constructivism would predict. For example, socioeconomic status is a better predictor of the comprehension of family roles in situation comedies than was ethnicity for African-American elementary school children (Newcomb & Collins, 1979). Further support for the constructivist approach highlights the relevance of age in the effects model. In a study of an episode of *The Cosby Show* (S. B. Graves, 1989), African-American children were more likely than were African-American adult raters to attribute negative characteristics to same-group characters. Moreover, the children were more likely to assign these negative features to younger same-group characters.

Research on the perceived reality of television supports a cultivation model. African-American youth see television as a reflection of real life, except when the portrayals are of the same race group (S. R. Lichter & L. S. Lichter, 1988). However, ethnic group membership predicted perceived realism of *The Cosby Show* for African-American and South African Black children (Brown, Austin, & Roberts, 1988; D. P. Van Vuuren, Bornman, Mels, & M. Van Vuuren, 1990). That is, these subjects found same-group, upper-middle-class characters real or true to life.

Impact on Attitudes

Television programming featuring same-race portrayals have been shown to alter African-American children's attitudes toward their own group (S. B. Graves, 1980). However, the relationship between the nature of the portrayals and the impact on same-group attitudes is mixed. For example, one study (S. H. Graves, 1975) found that cartoons featuring African-American characters, regardless of type of portrayal, produced positive racial attitudes in African-American subjects. This positive effect was strongest when same-group characters were presented in an integrated setting (S. H. Graves, 1975). However, another study (Dorr, S. B. Graves, & Phelps, 1980), featuring prime-time programs, found that exposure to same-group characters produced negative attitudes.

Exposure to same-group portrayals may influence other types of attitudes and perceptions. After exposure to an episode of *Good Times* that featured a gang avoidance theme, African-American children reported that they learned the negative features of gangs and that one should avoid associating with gangs (Anderson & Williams, 1983). In addition, they learned prosocial messages about family cooperation and family support.

Research from the area of the impact of advertising on children offers further insights into the impact of same-group portrayals. African-American children have been found to prefer and to be positively influenced by commercials that have same-group characters (Barry & Hansen, 1973). Certainly, when one looks at the amount of ethnically directed advertising currently on television, there is ample evidence that this finding has been widely accepted by the advertising community.

Programming aimed at counterstereotyping can influence the attitudes of African-American children. In a study of the network program, *Superfriends*, a multiethnic cartoon (LaRose & Eisenstock, 1981), it was found that African-American children reported higher levels of identification with the same-group character than with other-group cast members. A study with African-American preschoolers, using a segment from *Sesame Street* (Lovelace et al., in press), suggests that children attend to positive same-group messages, can recognize positive emotions of a same-group character, and can recall activities of the character and cultural features of the character's environment.

Portrayals and Self-Concept

The relationship between television content and self-concept is such that both the absence of African Americans and exposure to negative same-group portrayals would result in more negative self-concept and self-esteem among African-American youth (S. B. Graves, 1982). Conversely, exposure to positive same-group portrayals would be associated with higher levels of self-concept.

A study of third- to sixth-grade African Americans found that neither high levels of television viewing nor high exposure to programming featuring same-group characters was associated with changes in levels of self-esteem or self-concept (Stroman, 1986). Conversely, a study of *Sesame Street* suggested a positive impact of television on the minority child's self-image, though there was no direct link to same-race portrayals (Filep, Miller, & Gillette, 1971). Thus, the impact of television on self-concept and self-image of African-American children is by no means clear. There is insufficient research to clarify the nature of the relationship between same-group portrayals and self-concept in African-American children.

African-American Portrayals and Other Ethnic American Children

Perceptions and Comprehension of Portrayals

In the area of ethnic perceptions, there is some evidence that European-American adolescents use television as an information source about members of other ethnic groups (S. R. Lichter & L. S. Lichter, 1988). In fact, these groups reported that the roles assigned to other groups were either realistic portrayals or highly positive portrayals. Earlier research suggested that for European-American children, the greater the personal contact with African Americans, the less the perceived reality attributed to African-American television portrayals (Greenberg & Reeves, 1976). For Asian and Latino/American youth, television portrayals of African Americans are thought to be realistic or more positive than their own group portrayals (S. R. Lichter & L. S. Lichter, 1988).

Impact on Attitudes

For European-American children, the nature of the African-American portrayal, positive or negative, generally predicts the direction of attitude change (Dorr et al., 1980; S. H. Graves, 1975). In some instances (Dorr et al., 1980), exposure to any type of portrayal resulted in more positive cross-group attitudes than their initial ethnic attitudes.

There is some suggestion that the presence of intergroup interaction may be a factor in the impact of the portrayals. Some research indicates that African-American characters in integrated settings are more powerful influences than characters in segregated settings (S. H. Graves, 1975; Kraus, 1972). However, research on a Canadian version of *Sesame Street* (Gorn, Goldberg, & Kanungo, 1976) suggests that portrayals of visible racial minorities were equally effective, regardless of the racial composition of the setting.

One investigation related child and parental viewing of television with racial attitudes (Zuckerman, D. G. Singer, & J. L. Singer, 1980). Those European-American third-, fourth-, and fifth-graders who viewed African Americans as less competent and obedient were more likely to watch violent programming. On the other hand, those subjects who rated African Americans as more athletic viewed more programs with African Americans and had mothers who watched fewer violent shows.

Although educational programming has not exclusively focused on the portrayals of African Americans, research on programs designed to create positive racial attitudes and to promote intergroup interaction provides insight into the process by which television may influence attitudes of European-American children. Two years of viewing *Sesame Street* by European-American preschoolers was associated with more positive attitudes toward African and Latino Americans (Bogatz & Ball, 1971).

Another educational program, *Vegetable Soup*, was shown to increase acceptance of other racial groups by European-American subjects (Mays, Henderson, Seidman, & Steiner, 1975). For Latino/a American and Native American children, exposure to the series increased the diversity of children they would consider as potential friends. Asian-American children were unaffected along this dimension. The series was also able to increase identification with the child's own group, particularly for Chicano children, suggesting the role of inclusion in the self-concept and self-identity of children from underrepresented groups.

Conclusion

The need for more research is apparent. As others have indicated (Graham, 1992; McLoyd & Randolph, 1984), there has been a noticeable decrease in research focusing on African-American children. Yet, without additional investigation, it will not be possible to further our understanding of how the portrayals of African Americans influence viewers. Research needs to focus or track both superficial and substantive changes in African-American portrayals. Research must pursue how children make sense of these portrayals and the variables that mediate their perceptions. Research on the process by which these portrayals alter same-group or other-group attitudes and intergroup interaction is crucial as the United States becomes increasingly more diverse. Finally, in the case of African-American children, it becomes important to understand the relationship of same-group portrayals to the development of self- and group identity.

References

Anderson, J. A. (1981). Research on children and television: A critique. *Journal of Broadcasting, 25*(4), 395-400.

Anderson, J. A. (1983). Television literary and critical viewer. In J. Bryant & D. R. Anderson (Eds.), *Children's understanding of television: Research on attention and comprehension* (pp. 297-330). New York: Academic Press.

Anderson, W. H., Jr, & Williams, B. M. (1983). TV and the Black child: What Black children say about the shows they watch. *Journal of Black Psychology, 9*(2), 27-42.

Auletta, G. S., & Hammerback, J. C. (1985). A relational model for interracial interactions on television. *Western Journal of Speech Communication, 49*(4), 301-321.

Bandura, A. (1977). *Social learning.* Englewood Cliffs, NJ: Prentice-Hall.

Baptista-Fernandez, P., & Greenberg, B. S. (1980). The context, characteristics and communication of blacks on television. In B. S. Greenberg (Ed.), *Life on television* (pp. 13-21). Norwood, NJ: Ablex.

Baptiste, D. A. (1986). The image of the Black family portrayed by television: A critical comment. *Marriage and Family Review, 10*(1), 41-65.

Barcus, F. E. (1983). *Images of life on children's television.* New York: Praeger.

Barry, T. E., & Hansen, H. W. (1973). How race affects children's TV commercials. *Journal of Advertising Research, 13,* 63-67.

Berry, G. L. (1982). Research perspectives on the portrayals of Afro-American families on television. In A. W. Jackson (Ed.), *Black families and the medium of television* (pp. 47-59). Ann Arbor, MI: Bush Program in Child Development and Social Policy.

Berry, G. L. (1988). Multicultural role portrayals on television as a social psychological issue. In S. Oskamp (Ed.), *Applied social psychology annual: Television as a social issue* (Vol. 8, p. 118-129). Newbury Park, CA: Sage.

Blumer, J. G., & Katz, E. (1974). *The uses of mass communications.* Beverly Hills, CA: Sage.

Bogatz, G. A., & Ball, S. (1971). *The second year of* Sesame Street: *A continuing evaluation* (Volumes 1 & 2). Princeton, NJ: Educational Testing Service.

Brown, B. M., Austin, E. W., & Roberts, D. F. (1988, May-June). *"Real families" versus "television families": Children's perceptions of realism in* The Cosby Show. Paper presented at the meeting of the International Communication Association, New Orleans.

Dorr, A., Graves, S. B., & Phelps, E. (1980). Television literacy for young children. *Journal of Communication, 30*(3), 71-83.

Downing, M. (1974). Heroine of the daytime serials. *Journal of Communication, 24,* 130-137.

Estep, R., & Macdonald, P. T. (1983). How primetime crime evolved on TV, 1976-1981. *Journalism Quarterly, 60*(2), 293-300.

Filep, R. T., Miller, G. R., & Gillette, P. T. (1971). *The Sesame mother project* (Final Report, ERIC Document Reproduction Service No. ED 055 676). El Segundo, CA: Institute for Educational Development.

Gerbner, G., Gross, L., Morgan, M., & Signorielli, N. (1980). The "mainstreaming" of America: Violence profile no. 11. *Journal of Communication, 30*(3), 10-27.

Gerbner, G., Gross, L., & Signorielli, N. (1985). *The role of television entertainment in public education about science.* Philadelphia: Annenberg School of Communications, University of Pennsylvania.

Gorn, G. I., Goldberg, M. E., & Kanungo, R. N. (1976). The role of educational television in changing intergroup attitudes in children. *Child Development, 47,* 277-280.

Graham, S. (1992). "Most of the subjects were White and middle-class": Trends in published research on African Americans in selected APA Journals, 1970-1989. *American Psychologist, 47*(5), 629-839.

Graves, S. B. (1980). Psychological effects of black portrayals on television. In S. B. Withey & R. P. Abeles (Eds.), *Television and social behavior: Beyond violence and children* (pp. 259-289). Hillsdale, NJ: Lawrence Erlbaum.

Graves, S. B. (1982). The impact of television on the cognitive and affective development of minority children. In G. Berry & C. Mitchell-Kiernan (Eds.), *Television and the socialization of the minority child* (pp. 37-67). New York: Academic Press.

Graves, S. B. (1989). *Impact of African-American television portrayals on minority children: A developmental study.* Paper presented at the biennial meeting of the Society for Research in Child Development, Kansas City, MO.

Graves, S. H. (1975). *Racial diversity in children's television: Its impact on racial attitudes and stated program preferences.* Unpublished doctoral dissertation, Harvard University, Cambridge, MA.

Greenberg, B. S. (1986). Minorities and the mass media. In J. Bryant & D. Zillmann (Eds.), *Perspectives on media effects* (pp. 165-188). Hillsdale, NJ: Lawrence Erlbaum.

Greenberg, B. S. (1988) Some uncommon television images and the drench hypothesis. In S. Oskamp (Ed.), *Applied social psychology annual: Television as a social issue* (Vol. 8, pp. 88-102). Newbury Park, CA: Sage.

Greenberg, B. S., & Reeves, B. (1978). Children and the perceived reality of television. *Journal of Social Issues, 32,* 86-97.

Greenberg, B. S., Simmons, K., Hogan, L., & Atkins, C. (1980). Three seasons of television characters: A demographic analysis. *Journal of Broadcasting, 24,* 49-80.

Hiemstra, R., Goodman, M., Middlemiss, M. A., Vosco, R., & Ziegler, N. (1983). How older persons are portrayed in television advertising: Implications for educators. *Educational Gerontology, 9,* 111-122.

Huston, A. C., Donnerstein, E., Fairchild, H., Feshbach, N. D., Katz, P. A., Murray, J. P., Rubinstein, E. A., Wilcox, B. L., & Zuckerman, D. (1992). *Big world, small screen: The role of television in American society.* Lincoln: University of Nebraska Press.

Jackson, A. W. (1982). *Black families and the medium of television.* Ann Arbor, MI: Bush Program in Child Development and Social Policy.

Jackson, D., Travis, L., Williams, T. M., & Phillips, S. (1986). *Ethnic minorities in Canada: TV's roles in the development of attitudes and stereotypes.* Paper presented at the Canadian Psychological Association, Vancouver.

Kraus, S. (1972). Modifying prejudice: Attitude change as a function of the race of the communicator. *Audiovisual Communication Review, 10*(1), 14-22.

LaRose, R., & Eisenstock, B. (1981). *Techniques for testing the effectiveness of minority portrayals in multicultural children's programming.* Paper presented at the annual meeting of the International Communication Association, Minneapolis, MN.

Lemon, J. (1977). Women and blacks on primetime television. *Journal of Communication, 27*(1), 70-74.

Lichter, L. S., & Lichter, S. R. (1983). *Primetime crime.* Washington, DC: Media Institute.

Lichter, S. R., & Lichter, L. (1988). *Television's impact on ethnic and racial images: A study of Howard Beach adolescents.* New York: American Jewish Committee, Institute of Human Relations.

Lovelace, V., Freund, S., & Graves, S. B. (in press). Race relations in *Sesame Street:* Racial knowledge, attitudes and understanding in preschool children. In M. B. Spencer & G. K. Brookins (Eds.), *Research in minority child development.* Hillsdale, NJ: Lawrence Erlbaum.

Mays, L., Henderson, E. H., Seidman, S. K., & Steiner, V. S. (1975). *An evaluation report on* Vegetable Soup: *The effects of a multiethnic children's television series on intergroup attitudes of children.* Unpublished manuscript, New York State Department of Education.

McLoyd, V., & Randolph, S. (1984). The conduct and publication of research on Afro-American children: A content analysis. *Human Development, 27,* 60-75.

Newcomb, A. F., & Collins, W. A. (1979). Children's comprehension of family role portrayals in televised dramas: Effects of socioeconomic status, ethnicity, and age. *Developmental Psychology, 15*(4), 417-423.

Pierce, C. M. (1980). Social trace contaminants: Subtle indicators of racism in TV. In S. B. Withey & R. P. Abeles (Eds.), *Television and social behavior: Beyond violence toward children* (pp. 249-259). Hillsdale, NJ: Lawrence Erlbaum.

Reid, P. T. (1979). Racial stereotyping on TV: A comparison of behavior of both black and white TV characters. *Journal of Applied Psychology, 64,* 465-471.

Seggar, J. F., Hafen, J. K., & Hannonen-Gladden, H. (1981). Television's portrayals of minorities and women in drama and comedy drama, 1971-1988. *Journal of Broadcasting, 26*(3), 277-288.

Steenland, S. (1989). *Unequal picture: Black, Hispanic, Asian, and Native American characters on television.* Washington, DC: National Commission on Working Women of Wider Opportunities for Women.

Stroman, C. A. (1986). Television viewing and self-concept among Black children. *Journal of Broadcasting and Electronic Media, 30*(1), 87-93.

Van Vuuren, D. P., Bornman, E., Mels, G., & Van Vuuren, M. (1990). Children's perceptions of and identification with the social reality of *The Cosby Show*: A comparison between the USA and South Africa. *South African Journal of Psychology, 20*(2), 70-79.

Williams, M. E., & Condry, J. C. (1989). *Living color: Minority portrayals and cross-racial interactions on television.* Paper presented at the 1989 biennial meeting of the Society for Research in Child Development, Kansas City, MO.

Zuckerman, D. M., Singer, D. G., & Singer, J. L. (1980). Children's television viewing, racial and sex-role attitudes. *Journal of Applied Social Psychology, 10*(4), 281-294.

13. Developing Television for American Indian and Alaska Native Children in the Late 20th Century

HANEY GEIOGAMAH (KIOWA)

D. MICHAEL PAVEL (SKOKOMISH)

An ironic reversal of a truly peculiar, unexpected, and even humorous sort seems to be distinctly possible as the ongoing dilemma of American Indian and Alaska Native people and their tortured relationships with the U.S. communications media—television, motion pictures, video—lumbers and lurches toward the closing credits of the 20th century. After endless decades of arrogant, insensitive and greedy misuse of the Native image, the media have, in the past several years, fallen into a pattern of neglecting, shutting out, and ignoring Native peoples' pleas for fair representation and a role in shaping what goes out on the airwaves. We believe that the opportunities today are better than at anytime before to bring beneficial programming to children by redirecting the media's use of the Native image.

Historical and Contemporary Circumstances

Do American Indians and Alaska Natives have a chance to contribute significantly to the world of television? Can something good and honest, authentic and helpful now get produced? Right now, summer 1992, there are almost no Native characters of substance on television. This absence is welcomed, as we do not have to endure the stereotypes most viewers think Native people are in real life.

The ultimate aim is to rid ourselves of the junk heap of misconceived (and not even well intended) Native-based programming that perpetuates negative stereotypes and trivializes the real-life drama of American Indians and Alaska Natives (Schiere, 1988).

Consider the developments over the arc of Native presence in the product of four major television networks (ABC, CBS, NBC, and PBS). Table 13.1 lists selected series that featured Native characters or Native themes over the last several decades, with remarks as to their effectiveness, lack of positive contributions, or any measurable effect on the U.S. mainstream culture. So fleeting, insubstantial, or infrequent have been the runs of television productions featuring American Indian and Alaska Native characters that it is difficult to adequately assess the impact of the various Native characters on youth as role models, negative influences, or life-style reflections. Probably the most potential for positive role modeling was in the short-lived NBC series, *Spirit of the Wind,* conceived to present a typical Plains tribe struggling to exist and survive in the harsh times of the 1800s. However, the late American Indian actor Will Sampson's (Muskogee Creek) role as Chief Fast Wolf was limited to presiding over a clan of tribespeople who lived in tipis and rode horses. This quaint scenario was further weakened by episodes filled with one predictable crisis after another as the tribe sought to carve out a peaceful life for themselves in the violence-ridden world of the American frontier.

Take, for example, the recent Native characters on television who attract only a passing interest to the new youth sensibilities. These include the borderline wacko sheriff's deputy played by actor Michael Horse (Zuni-Apache) in the short-lived and controversial *Twin Peaks.* Or the "squaw" character with a cool kind of sass played by Elaine Miles (Umatilla) on *Northern Exposure.* Hardly what one would consider proper role models for today's Native children and future generations of Native people. The characters are entertaining but still perpetuate the stereotypical sidekick Native character seen in the media.

Only recently have motion pictures done a slightly better job than their competition on the small box. The film *Dances With Wolves* was an international sensation and euphorically hailed by some Native people as a gateway to Hollywood productions. Finally, here was the big event that could help non-Indian America on the way to understanding a race of people whose cultural and traditional

Table 13.1 Network Television "Indian" Programming

Production	*Year*	*Network*	*Characters*	*Remarks*
Spirit of the Wind	1982	NBC	A tribal family on the plains, circa 1880s. Will Sampson lead role.	Too many predictable crises. Did not make series.
Centennial	1978	CBS	Assorted Cheyenne warriors and half-breeds.	A sprawling, multigenerational saga in which most of the Native characters were lost or obscured by the show's weight.
The Mystic Warrior (formerly *Hanta Yo*)	1984	ABC	Various fake Sioux types.	Very negatively received by Native community.
Mazzola Corn Oil and Margarine Commercial	circa 1970s	Various channels	A modern Indian corn maiden played by a Latina actress	Repeated showing of "positive" Indian image on TV screen. No redeeming image values.
Roanoak	1986	PBS	Members of the extinct Roanoak Tribe of Virginia	Poor production values and leaden, lifeless script
Northern Exposure	1991-1992	CBS	Elaine Miles in "squaw" role.	Updated squaw stereotype. Indians are still a "them" people entity.

integrity had been maligned by countless westerns. After the excitement subsided, "Indians" are still at Square 1: No power, no respected presence, and no production deals. Only the personal tragedy portrayed in other well-received major releases as *Black Robe, Thunderheart,* and *Incident at Oglala* have followed. One can welcome the attention brought by non-Indians to the injustices, but the true accomplishments of American Indians in art, comedy, education, politics, economics, and other endeavors have not received balanced representations in the media. We have to turn elsewhere to find such programming.

Many American Indian and Alaska Native creative artists have been entering the challenging field of filmmaking over the last generation; none of course in the major network arena with sufficient budgets and adequate production opportunities. The early focus for this wide array of creative output was on immediate tribal and family concerns. The intent was to bring attention to the preservation and cultivation of cultural, traditional values, and Native lifestyles while addressing problems stemming from assimilation and alienation. Table 13.2 presents a selected sampling of some of the more outstanding productions that tribal filmmakers produced during the 1980s and early 1990s.

Such filmmakers as Bob Hicks (Creek-Seminole), Phil Lucas (Choctow), George Burdeau (Blackfeet), Sandra Johnson Osawa (Makah), and Chris SpottedEagle (Houma) diligently have gone about the creative tasks of writing, producing, directing, and distributing an impressive collection of short films, documentaries, and video works produced primarily for Native audiences. Many of the more sophisticated and technically advanced of these films are shown annually at the San Francisco American Indian Film Festival, an event that has kept the focus on Native film artists over the last two decades. Positive, culturally sensitive images of American Indian and Alaska Native people and their historic and contemporary life abound in the films. Clearly, this event represents one of many avenues that the major networks could seek out to develop a number of television series, including those directed at children.

Could it be that television, arguably the largest and most influential presence in the life of U.S. youth, is finally ready to enrich the minds of American Indian and Alaska Native children as well as children from other cultures? The combination of recent Native-theme motion pictures enjoying financial success and the absence

Table 13.2 American Indian- and Alaska Native-made Television and Film Programming

Production	*Year*	*Filmmaker*	*Theme*
Images of Indians	1989	Phil Lucas	An in-depth comprehensive examination of the creation of myths, misperceptions, and stereotypes in films and television.
Seasons of Grandmothers	1980	George Burdeau	Depicts the intergenerational relationships in families of the Nez Perce tribe of Idaho from a tribal point of view.
Great Spirit in the Hole	1988	Chris SpottedEagle	Native inmates in federal and state prisons gain spiritual and mental strength from close observance of tribal customs and traditional practices.
Our Sacred Earth	1987	Chris SpottedEagle	Explains clearly, cogently, and succinctly for all viewers the how and why of Native reverence for the land and for all living beings.
Return of the Country	1985	Bob Hicks	A wry comic take on role reversal (and power reversal) for Natives and Whites.
Broken Rainbow	1987	Victoria Mudd	Examines the strengths of traditions and the dangers in losing respect for them.
For the Honor of All	1988	Phil Lucas	Native people find great strength in coming to grips with and understanding one of their most crippling weaknesses.

of any captivating, and inspiring Native characters on today's top hit shows would seem to present many opportunities. Consider that only a fraction of the programming hours each season has anything to do with Native life and issues, and even fewer programs are written, directed, and produced from an entirely American Indian and Alaska Native creative point of view. Add also the increased recognition received by Native artists like actors Graham Green (Canadian Cree), nominated for an Academy Award as best supporting actor in *Dances With Wolves,* or technicians like Buddy Wilson (Pawnee) and Robert Schoenfelt (Sioux). So the answer is yes. It is possible to capitalize on the marketability of Native themes with the Native media talents capable of presenting a powerful and positive message for the benefit of a multicultural youth audience.

Recent Research

Just over a decade ago, research exploring the complexity of human development and its posited relationship with transmitted symbolic features in society indicated that we did not have a good enough understanding "to say how much influence television has on children, or whether its overall effect is good or bad" (Ambron & Brodzinsky, 1979, p. 287). Our understanding of television and its influence on the psychosocial development of children has advanced considerably over the last decade (Dorr, 1986; Huston et al., 1992). Unfortunately, although a growing number of studies examine television's influence on minority children, there is scant literature when the focus turns specifically to American Indian and Alaska Native children. The few studies that do exist recommend a need for a change in media programming philosophy.

Morris (1982) discusses the prominent stereotyping and repetitious distortion of Native culture, historical underrepresentation of American Indian and Alaska Native at all levels of media production, and sporadic or isolated positive visibility. Implications for the mental health of American Indians and Alaska Natives are said to be far-reaching. It is perhaps premature to say that Native children suffer ill effects when confronting erroneous and invalid assumptions of their culture on television. However, "the two major functions of television are to entertain and to inform. Yet in neither of these areas are American Indians accurately or positively depicted, if they are shown at all" (Morris, 1982, p. 200).

Wise and Miller (1983) further elaborate that television media is largely produced by people who reflect the attitudes of non-Indians while catering to a wider audience. Regulated to portrayals of pan-Indianism, the television audience is likely to see an exotic and superstitious culture incapable of stopping the advancement of civilization. Native and non-Native children become sensitive to these negative portrayals: "Even if the message that Indians are second-class citizens is not clearly stated, the subtle influences still come through" (p. 353). For example, in *American Indian Stereotypes in the World of Children,* Hirschfelder (1982) makes reference to a study that found among a sample of non-Indian kindergartners and fifth graders, most students made "negative comments about Indians . . . describe Indians as war-like [or] as lazy and unlawful, breaking into stores or breaking down houses" (p. 12). What a surprise to discover that these are just the kind of images manifested by repeated distorted stereotypes in the fantasy media depicted in many westerns. This suggests that more appropriate media productions coupled with better viewing practices can help make worthwhile contributions to the welfare of Native children.

The need for optimizing television on behalf of Native children becomes even more crucial given recent research indicating that television viewing dominates the out-of-school time of children. The National Center for Education Statistics (1991) national longitudinal survey of eighth graders reported that students spent on average 21 hours of watching television per week compared to 6 hours of homework and 2 hours of outside reading. Aggregated by ethnicity or race, American Indian and Alaska Native children were likely to watch more television (24 hours per week) and do less homework and outside reading than Whites, Hispanics, Asians, and Pacific Islanders. In addition, Severence-King's research (in progress) on the Navajo Reservation found a surprising number of rural homes with satellite dishes, television sets, and VCRs. In light of extensive viewing habits and widespread access to media programming, it seems television can be either constructive or destructive depending on the nature of programming as well as how it is used and the context in which it is understood by the viewer.

The need for appropriate explicit multicultural messages on television is made apparent by the criticism that television serves as an icon to the status quo, especially when considered by ethnicity, race, and gender. For example, Newcomb (1987) sees cultural diversity clouded by the media depiction of the United States as a hegemonic culture, whereas it may be more suitable to say we live in a multifarious society. Morgan (1980) found more acceptance of traditional gender roles in teenage girls than boys, leading to gender stereotypes that adversely affect education and economic opportunities for women. Moreover, Tan's (1979) findings indicate that television's emphasis on physical beauty influences girls' self-image and social relationships in ways that bring undue pressures upon them during critical psychosocial developmental years.

Overall, the media's track record for playing a more satisfactory role in properly socializing American Indian and Alaska Natives is lamentable. However, the media are a grand adventure and such imposing efforts seem to harbor a history of misguided notions. To evolve as a responsible socializing agent, the abeyance of past practices is clearly the next step for the television medium before setting out on a new era of beneficial programming. The following section is introductory in nature and offers advice on how media programming can take a turn for the better in terms of positively influencing the psychosocial development of American Indian and Alaska Native children.

Directing Our Best Intentions

Child Development and Cultural Values

It is helpful to have a basic understanding of the psychosocial development patterns for children 3 to 8 years old when considering the influence of media programming. We complement this discussion with the way values liberally associated with American Indian and Alaska Native cultures might influence their psychosocial development. Neither discussion addresses the complexities of human development nor the ambiguity of values attributed to American Indian and Alaska Native cultures. The purpose of this section is to illustrate how our knowledge of human development and Native cultures can advance appropriate media programming.

Brewer (1992) summarizes and gives examples of physical, social, emotional, and cognitive developmental patterns that children may typically experience. Like physical development, the psychosocial development of children appears to follow a somewhat orderly (but not always) predictable pattern. These patterns can serve as a rough framework for understanding how the larger media environment can positively influence the psychosocial development of Native children.

The social development of children has several important dimensions. For example, the formation of personality, self-esteem, role playing, social skills and relationships, aggression, and sex role identification are prominent elements of how children come to know their community. The emotional development of children can be seen as stages of temperament that children develop while becoming aware of their feelings when having extensive contact and interaction with others. Of special concern is the cognitive development whereby children gain the capacity to use symbolic features of a given cultural setting to think and reason in order to understand society.

The examples of social, emotional, and cognitive developmental patterns among children can be complemented with values liberally associated with American Indian and Alaska Native cultures published in the *American Indian Education Handbook* by the California State Department of Education (1991). Recent research asking teachers of Native children if these values have any influence in their lives "suggest that cultural values influence socialization practices which in turn influence the ways in which children approach learning" (Swisher & Pavel, in press). Our assumption is that values can influence the social, emotional, and cognitive development of children, and that television programming imparts certain values when seen by children day after day, year after year.

For example, two prominent values in Native culture that emphasize social development are cooperation and harmony. The value of cooperation is deeply rooted in the democratic nature of tribal communities, where there is comfort in being part of the community or group. Many Native cultures also acknowledge group harmony in lieu of the personal ego predominant in mainstream society.

Television programming for children could easily impart the values of cooperation through messages that reduce the disparity between working together to achieve a task and competing against one another to see who is the loser. As for group harmony, children can collectively benefit from viewing television that demonstrates how people from different cultures live together rather than looking at programming that emphasizes personal gain. Together, cooperation and group harmony are values that seek to impart in children the genderless ideals necessary to develop a mutually beneficial society. To help children grow up together, it is not as Shakespeare once said, "If it is to be, it is up to me." The Native perspective is more collective and would advocate, "If it is to be, it is up to us."

In another example, Native cultural values that could influence the emotional development of children involve veneration of age and importance of family. Among American Indians and Alaska Natives, veneration of age conveys respect for elders revered for their wisdom and held in high esteem. This contrasts with the mainstream philosophy of overemphasizing youthfulness. When referring to the importance of family, the Native family is characterized by the extended household (versus nuclear), with even distant relatives considered part of the immediate family and humor helping to diffuse tension in members becoming accustomed to living together and telling stories about one another. Media programming aimed at improving the emotional development of children could be realized by showing how elders and other members of the extended community handle anger and frustration appropriately.

Finally, respect for nature is an example of a value imparting Native cultural perspectives about the environment that could have positive benefits to the cognitive development of children. American Indian and Alaska Native cultures respect nature as a way of understanding the complex interrelatedness of life. On the other hand, much of the mainstream culture simply sees the environment as something to exploit for economic gain, even at the risk of leaving nothing for future generations.

One example of a successful effort to blend tribally cultural curriculum with the media enterprise is Primary Reservation Alcohol and Substance Abuse Education (P.R.A.S.E.). Under the direction of Gerald Bruce Miller (Skokomish), P.R.A.S.E. draws upon the traditional values of the Skokomish Tribe to help Native and non-Native children cope with substance abuse. In conjunction with the public television station in Seattle, Washington, P.R.A.S.E. has been developed into a series to help children from all cultural backgrounds to cope with grief, loss, trauma, physical and sexual abuse, and other issues that prevent the healthy development of children. To reach Native children, culturally relevant content is combined with the best practices educators know by casting animals and other characters in tribal lore. The result is that American Indian and Alaska Native children come in contact with programming that helps them cope with adverse experiences affecting their psychosocial development in an entertaining and captivating fashion.

American Indian and Alaska Native Media Talent

We now turn the reader's attention to a growing source of creative talent best able to bring Native-based programming to the television medium. American Indian and Alaska Native film and television producers recently declared their intent to take the initiative in accurately portraying Native people to their own cultures and to the rest of the world, especially in the television medium. In Sante Fe, New Mexico, the year 1992 marked an important effort toward establishing this presence when American Indian and Alaska media talent gathered for the first time as an identifiable group of professional artists to discuss and explore their role in the future of Native-based media programming. They spoke in unity about their purpose: "Our Native American vision, as film and television producers, is to empower ourselves to produce our stories. We will enable our future generations to continue this work from the culture of our people. We say our people deserve their inherent right to dignified and respectful presentation" (*Producer's Statement*, 1990, p. 2).

Over 100 individuals gathered for this historic occasion. Frank Blythe (Cherokee), head of the Native American Public Broadcasting Consortium (NAPBC) in Lincoln, Nebraska, and Jennifer Lawson, programming director for the Public Broadcasting System, were prominent in organizing the gathering. In the *Producer's Statement*, an agenda of goals guided the gathering in its efforts, beginning with the declaration

> We are committed to quality and culturally appropriate productions involving Native Americans. We want any such film and television production to be obligated to:
>
> 1. Insure that proposals are considered without unfavorable political, economic, social, or cultural prejudice.
> 2. Employ Native American film and television producers, directors, writers, technicians, and talent in key roles from initiation of a project and/or production.

3. Support financial and creative opportunities for Native Americans to tell their own stories.
4. Train Native American youth in all media productions.
5. Provide Native American technical assistance on projects and productions that involve our cultures.
6. Benefit Indian communities and individuals through good faith negotiations on ownership of intellectual, published, cultural property. (p. 3)

The hope and conviction was that, "Through such collaboration, all producers and their audiences, Native and non-Native, will be culturally enriched" (*Producer's Statement*, 1990, p. 2).

We share with the reader a brief glimpse of insights shared by selected people in attendance of this historic gathering. A noted American Indian and Alaska Native filmmaker, Phil Lucas (Choctow) sees the future and its many challenges and opportunities as a time when Native people completely control their image in the media via their creative gifts and spirit. Lucas, most of whose creative body of work has been for television, says:

> Films produced by Indian film makers are not always successful with non-Indian audiences. . . . What we are usually guilty of is starting right in with the Indian perspective, which is 180 degrees apart from the American Myth Pool and thus our ideas and thoughts about ourselves are rejected, out of hand, by the mainstream audiences. (Phil Lucas, personal communication, May 24, 1992)

Furthermore, as a final statement, he adds:

> Perhaps, when more of the institutions, both governmental and private, that fund the making of films and videos become more willing to fund Indians to make films that truly express their "voices," then perhaps the Myth Pool will change and be replaced by knowledge, understanding, and appreciation for the differences in our respective cultures. But until then, we as Indian filmmakers will continue to ply our trade in what ever manner and with what ever means we are able to draw unto ourselves. (Lucas, personal communication, May 24, 1992)

George Burdeau (Blackfeet), an award-winning producer-director, has worked in professional television production for the last 10 years in the Los Angeles area. Highly respected among his peers, he echoes Lucas's forecast:

> We know what the issues are and what we need to do to address them. We have the talent and skills and all the creative energy we need to engage in the effort and to be successful. Just thinking about being able to help young Indian people today develop more positive, more honest, and more meaningful concepts of themselves, stronger identities and more positive commitments to helping strengthen tribal life, is perhaps the most powerful motivation for all of us. (George Burdeau, personal communication, May 18, 1992)

A note of caution comes from Bob Hicks (Creek-Seminole), a writer-producer-director whose work includes the award-winning film, *Return of the Country:*

> We need to develop a strong, durable support base to sustain us in our work. We need to get the tribes more involved, and we need to help the tribal leaders develop clearer understandings of the importance of this kind of work and what its contributions can be. That's not going to be easy. But the television networks and the film studios of Hollywood aren't going to do this for us. If we want to create change, we have to empower ourselves to do so. The people, the tribes, will be our most important source of strength and power to do this. (Bob Hicks, personal communication, June 7, 1992)

Final Comments

The decade of the 1990s will unquestionably be a time of historic opportunity for the American Indian and Alaska Native creative community in the area of television and film production. It is clear from a review of past programming, research, and present opinions that there is a need to develop more appropriate media programming for American Indian and Alaska Native children. Past programming generally suffers from a lack of meaningful content and direction or absence of Native characters and themes. There are opportunities to capitalize on the growing source of American Indian and Alaska Native media talent to develop television programming that can enhance the psychosocial development of Native children and children from all cultural backgrounds. If successful, the closing credits of the 20th century will note that U.S. television portrayed the lives of all children in such a way that people looked upon the media as a powerful driving force to social unity.

References

Ambron, S. R., & Brodzinsky, D. (1979). *Lifespan human development.* New York: Holt, Rinehart & Winston.

Brewer, J. A. (1992). *Introduction to early childhood education: Preschool through primary grades.* Boston, MA: Allen & Bacon.

California State Department of Education. (1991). *American Indian education handbook.* Sacramento: California State Department of Education, Indian Education Unit.

Dorr, A. (1986). *Television and children: A special medium for a special audience.* Beverly Hills, CA: Sage.

Hirschfelder, A. B. (1982). *American Indian stereotypes in the world of children: A reader and bibliography.* Metuchen, NJ: Scarecrow Press.

Huston, A. C., Donnerstein, E., Fairchild, H., Feshbach, N. D., Katz, P. A., Murray, J., Rubinstein, E. A., Wilcox, B. L., & Zuckerman, D. (1992). *Big world, small screen.* Lincoln: University of Nebraska Press.

Morgan, M. (1980). *Longitudinal patterns of television use and adolescent role socialization.* Unpublished doctoral dissertation, University of Pennsylvania.

Morris, J. S. (1982). Television portrayal and the socialization of the American Indian child. In G. Berry & C. Mitchell-Kernan (Eds.), *Television and the socialization of the minority child* (pp. 187-202). New York: Academic Press.

National Center for Education Statistics. (1991). *A profile of the American eighth grader: NELS:88 student descriptive summary.* Washington, DC: U.S. Department of Education.

Newcomb, H. (1987). *Television: The critical view.* New York: Oxford University Press.

Producer's statement. (1990). Lincoln, NE: Native American Public Broadcasting Consortium.

Severence-King, S. (In progress). *Navajo community lead: An examination of cultural and biological aspects.* Unpublished doctoral dissertation, University of California at Los Angeles, Los Angeles.

Schiere, T. E. (Ed.). (1988). *Contemporary Native American cultural issues.* Sault Ste. Marie, MI: Lake Superior State University Press.

Swisher, K., & Pavel, D. M. (In press). American Indian learning styles: An assessment of teacher knowledge. *Journal of Educational Issues of Minority Language Students.*

Tan, A. S. (1979). TV beauty ads and role expectations of adolescent female viewers. *Journalism Quarterly, 56,* 283-288.

Wise, F., & Miller, N. B. (1983). The mental health of the American Indian child. In G. J. Powell (Ed.), *The psychosocial development of minority group children* (pp. 334-361). New York: Brunner/Mazel.

14. They're So Cute When They're Young

The Asian-American Child on Television

DARRELL Y. HAMAMOTO

Controlling Images

The purpose of this chapter is to examine the representation of the Asian-American child on independent and network television programs. It will be argued that the Asian-American child as portrayed on television is but one of many "controlling images" that are applied to Asian Americans in general. The "evil genius," "benign mystic," "sidekick," "helping professional," and "newscaster" (female only) are other common examples of controlling images that are part of the Asian-American child's socialization experience. More specifically, the Asian-American child as a television "type" is often used to advance a host of social meanings that are largely congruent with the dominant liberal democratic ideology.

The term *controlling images* is derived from the work of the political scientist Patricia Hill Collins (1990), who has described at great length the domination of African American women via their objectification in popular culture. "Even when the political and economic conditions that originally generated controlling images disappear," Collins writes, "such images prove remarkably tenacious because they not only keep Black women oppressed but are key in maintaining interlocking systems of race, class, and gender oppression" (Collins, 1990, p. 68). Note that Collins brings to her analysis a recognition of the multiple sources of social oppression, including race and class in addition to gender. Until recently, the analysis of media often reflected the white, middle-class bias of the dominant society by giving short shrift to the question of race.

In the observations to follow, *controlling images* is preferred over the more common and weakened term, *stereotype*. A stereotype might possess high truth content or it might not. A stereotype can be "positive" or "negative." A stereotype can be neutral or loaded with ugly meaning. A stereotype is neither inherently demeaning nor necessarily dehumanizing, as the human thought process itself is informed by categories, typologies, and other socially constructed classificatory schemes. But at bottom, the notion of "stereotype" is inadequate because it does not convey the implication that controlling images are a means of exerting symbolic power, and by extension, material control over a given group by the dominant society through discursive practices that compose the television text. Before launching into the discussion of specific television programs that portray the Asian-American child, a brief historical excursus is necessary.

New World Asians

Following the dispossession of Native Americans and the forcible taking of their resource-rich lands, the vast social wealth of U.S. society was created by the labor of African slaves, Mexicans living in territories annexed by the United States, and immigrant peoples from Europe and Asia. The dynamism and growth of U.S. society, in short, is owed to the labor provided by peoples connected by a global system that Immanuel Wallerstein (1979) refers to as the "capitalist world-economy." In the case of Asians, immigration to the United States was regulated according to the shifting needs of capital.

During the periodic crises of capitalist production, the Asian-American population was viewed by Nativists, organized labor, and elected officials as being a yellow blight upon the land. Harsh economic times saw those Asians living in the United States subjected to both extralegal barriers and official measures designed to prevent or restrict their entry into the primary economy. To protect its own short-term interests, white European labor often joined with the capital in excluding nonwhite labor such as Asians (Roediger, 1991; Saxton, 1990).

Any number of means were employed to restrict the participation of Asians in mainstream U.S. economic life. Beatings, lynchings, and other forms of physical intimidation were employed to terrorize

Asian immigrant populations. The forced segregation of immigrant Asians and the development of ethnic enclaves such as "Chinatowns" further precluded the possibility of Asians coming into direct competition with white labor. As if physical and psychological terror were not enough, the state often brought to bear its legislative powers to control almost every aspect of Asian immigrant life including education, marriage, residence, and business activity.

Media Power

Even in societies stratified along racial lines, state and police power can only go so far in enforcing the legal and de facto mechanisms of power that serve to concentrate and maintain power in the hands of the ruling elite. In the United States, enforcing racial inequality becomes even more problematic, because U.S. society is founded upon abstract principles of equality, liberty, and justice. Yet despite the equality revolution of the 1960s, when civil rights legislation extended formal equality to all groups, significant racial divisions and differential access to power resources still remain alongside the abstract principles of liberal democracy.

Beyond the instruments of state power then, a method perhaps even more effective in preserving various forms of antidemocratic privilege and perpetuating social inequality can be found in the explicit messages and underlying ideology borne by the vast media of modern communications. Television in particular has been demonstrably effective in helping to shape attitudes and opinions in addition to creating and maintaining the degree of ideological consensus required to legitimize the capitalist system of power. And as an agent of socialization, television looms ever larger in the struggle for the consciousness of the minority child.

Herbert Schiller (1989) and others have remarked upon the ever-increasing private control of communications and information in large-scale corporate hands. It should come as no surprise that the messages transmitted via television—whether through news and information programs or through entertainment programs—are relatively consistent with the norms, values, and requirements of oligopoly capitalism. But as will be seen below, the socializing influence of the media is not total and not immune to challenge. Even in television, the most extensive of the mass media in scope and influence, it can be observed that TV programs embody social contradictions sufficient to cast doubt (however momentary) upon conventional wisdom. In the episodes of *Bonanza* discussed below, for example, a number of Asian-American controlling images clash with the overall liberal democratic tenor of the program. Such contradictions within television programs implies that the socialization process is never final, never complete.

Children of the West

The television western dominated the airwaves for a period of 10 years beginning in the mid-1950s. Unlike their cinematic counterparts, the television westerns underplayed individual heroism and instead promoted the ideal of community, especially as reflected by the bourgeois family. The television historian J. Fred MacDonald (1987) observes that the program *Bonanza* (1959-1973), for example, conveyed humanistic values that were dramatized in a domestic, family setting. "If in concept the family was the primary social unit of mutual support and shared love," writes MacDonald, "*Bonanza* accentuated the fact that even in times of great challenge, humane interests were critical to lasting effective social values" (MacDonald, 1987, pp. 87-88).

During the broadcast seasons spanning 1961 through 1970, *Bonanza* was among the five top-rated programs according to the Nielsen ratings. For 3 years straight, from 1964 to 1966, *Bonanza* was rated as the Number 1 program. It is no small coincidence that the years of the program's peak popularity reflected the political idealism and sense of expansive possibility associated with the Kennedy-Johnson years. For the social values that MacDonald alludes to were, specifically, those of Great Society liberalism. In this vision of frontier community the stern but fair patriarch of the Ponderosa, Ben Cartwright, presides over an all-male household with Hop Sing fulfilling certain domestic functions such as cooking and cleaning. As in the Great Society, Hop Sing inhabits the same social space as his benefactors by being allowed to live under the same roof as the Cartwrights, but never is he permitted to sit with them at the table.

As stated above, the program *Bonanza* was in step with the social values of Great Society liberalism. Virginia City is the archetypal liberal pluralist society transported back in time, a society that celebrates ethnic and racial diversity and condemns bigotry in all its manifestations. It is an imperfect society, to be sure, but one that can be made better by piecemeal reform rather than through radical transformation. As liberals acting in good faith, the Cartwrights took it as their responsibility to help maintain an orderly world that accepted all those who wished to make a positive contribution to society, whether Asian, Mexican, Native American, or white.

The principle of ethnic pluralism as a model of intergroup relations in U.S. society is well illustrated in an episode of *Bonanza* entitled "A Christmas Story" (Dortort & Oswald, 1966). The episode features Andy Walker, a young singer who has returned home to Virginia City for a visit after having made it big in the world of entertainment. In one particularly telling scene, Andy sings at a Christmas party for a group of orphaned children. The children—Mexican, Native American, Asian, and white—are shown basking in the warm glow of fellow feeling that is associated with the Christmas holidays.

So that the viewer does not miss the point, each child represents his or her respective group by being clothed in ethnically specific attire. There is no hint of how the diverse children became orphans in the first place. And with the exception of Hop Sing, who is seen serving hors d'oeuvres to guests, the adults in attendance do not reflect the diversity of the assembled children. Perhaps even in the Great Society presided over by the benevolent Cartwright clan, an implicit white paternalism is the order of the day.

The Cartwright's abiding commitment to Great Society liberalism was also seen in an episode entitled "The Fear Merchants" (Dortort & Allen, 1970). Unlike most television westerns, where minorities usually play peripheral roles, this particular episode delves somewhat deeply into the life of Hop Sing and his extended family. The Chinese-American characters are shown as trying hard to assimilate into the unique social experiment that is the United States. Lee Chang, Hop Sing's uncle, expresses his sense of gratitude in witnessing the difficult birth of a new nation.

Hop Sing, on the other hand, expresses reservations about U.S. civilization that prove to be well founded when he is jumped by thugs shortly after his conversation with his uncle. As it turns out, the assailants are the henchmen of an attorney by the name of Andrew Fulmer who is running for mayor of Virginia City on a Nativist, anti-Chinese campaign platform similar to that of the Workingmen's party. "Virginia City for Virginia City" reads one of Fulmer's campaign signs.

Ben Cartwright is justifiably upset at Hop Sing's beating, but Hoss asks whether the assault might have been linked to their servant's involvement in "one of those tongs we've been hearing about." But Ben patiently explains to his son Hoss that a "tong" is no more than a "protective association." Hoss is the physical, impulsive, childlike member of the Cartwright household, and he immediately seeks revenge for Hop Sing's beating. But Adam, the eldest Cartwright son and the voice of reason and liberal moderation, warns against retribution. To retaliate would mean only more problems for the Chinese of Virginia City.

Ben travels into town to confront Fulmer about his suspected involvement with Hop Sing's bashing. Cartwright then engages the mayoral candidate in an argument over the "outsiders" who are perceived to be threatening the livelihood of white men. When Ben asks Fulmer who qualifies as an "outsider," Fulmer responds, "It means our town's being overrun by foreigners who are willing to work for nothing. And they're taking the bread and butter out of the mouth of folks like us who built this country." But Ben is not satisfied with Fulmer's definition. Cartwright correctly identifies the underlying anti-Chinese racism of the attorney's seemingly neutral definition when he asks, "By 'foreigner' Andy, who do you mean? The Irish? The Welsh? Or . . . the Chinese?"

Although this episode of *Bonanza* explicitly repudiates racism, it nevertheless dramatizes a central argument of this essay. That is, so long as Asian Americans remain subordinated and infantilized they are tolerated by the dominant society. But once they become direct economic competitors, Asian Americans are liable to be targeted for racist hate and persecution.

Little Orphan Asians

In its first decade, the new medium of television proved an effective tool in creating the proper cold war political mood. It was especially effective in vividly dramatizing the evils of "godless" Asian Communism to the U.S. people. According to the historian J. Fred MacDonald (1985), television "became the most important vehicle through which citizens learned the latest developments in a rivalry that, in simplified terms, matched good Democracy against evil Communism" (p. 101).

In the postwar era, television has been of inestimable help in making U.S. foreign policy understandable and acceptable to the U.S. public by producing programs with high propaganda content. The television portrayal of Asian war orphans is noteworthy in this regard. A virtual television subgenre has developed that exploits the humanitarian impulses of many well-meaning Americans. Such programs, however, do not discuss the extent to which the United States has been responsible for systematically creating the conditions that have given rise to Asian orphanage. The lack of such discussion absolves the United States of responsibility for spreading the misery that attends war and instead places the blame exclusively on the ruling regimes of Communist countries. Further, the authoritarian rule of U.S. client states in East Asia such as South Korea, the Philippines, Thailand, and Indonesia goes unexamined.

Countless families have been displaced, split up, or snuffed out of existence as a result of U.S. military intervention throughout East Asia. Yet there is little concern expressed for such families other than the function they serve in mass-mediated television tales of humanitarian aid offered by caring, compassionate Americans. The orphaned Asian child often has been employed masterfully as a method of graphically dramatizing the evils of Communism to good-hearted Americans. An example of the exploitation of the war orphan is *Korean Legacy*, produced and directed by Baldwin Baker, Jr., a television documentary of the Holt Adoption Agency, which supplied Americans with children orphaned by the Korean War and alone was responsible for placing 6,293 children in the United States between 1955 and 1966 (Kitano & Daniels, 1988).

The baby trade between Asia and the United States has far from ceased. On the contrary, it is thriving. In 1989, Asian countries were still the largest suppliers of children per year (5,000), with Latin America a distant second place (2,600) (McConahay, 1990). Decades after Harry Holt placed his last orphan child, South Korea remains the chief Asian source of babies for American couples unwilling to buy domestically bred spawn (especially if black or brown). A war that was ostensibly fought to stem the tide of Communist influence throughout Asia has had the effect of transforming South Korea into a reliable source of cuddly human capital.

Conclusion

The above discussion concerning the social uses of the Asian and Asian-American child on television spans the 1950s through the 1970s. Just as these representations were shaped by the political currents of their respective historical era, contemporary controlling images of the Asian-American child on television are linked with an ongoing power struggle between those who advocate economic and social justice and the forces of conservative political and cultural reaction. The political right, for example, has valorized "the family" in trying to implement its agenda, an agenda that emphasizes self-help and so-called free market enterprise while minimizing the role of the state in alleviating the effects of economic inequality through various social welfare programs. In sum, the family and all that it symbolizes has become the terrain where fundamental issues of democracy are being contested.

The Asian-American family in specific has been brought into this contest of fundamental issues. The Asian-American family has been pointed to by a number of sources as a model of economic self-help in an age when too many other (nonwhite) groups have grown dependent upon government entitlement programs. Thomas Sowell (1983), for example, points to the "overseas Chinese" as paragons of free market capitalism. Applauding their "sense of purpose and perseverance," Sowell even goes so far as to claim that Chinese-American schoolchildren "were better behaved and more hard working than white students" (Sowell, 1983, p. 49).

Sowell is not the only conservative apologist with a special interest in Asian Americans and their reputed industriousness and politesse. There is also the journalist James Fallows (1989), perhaps better known for his anti-Japanese diatribes. In his impressionistic essay *More Like Us*, Fallows tells the saga of the Nguyen family, a Vietnamese immigrant family in hot pursuit of the American Dream. The Nguyens are refugees who came to this country with nothing, but by the sweat of their brow they became operators of small businesses and home owners as well. By this anecdotal retelling of the Asian-American "success" myth, Fallows hopes to shame less enterprising people into the manic striving and independence it will take to succeed in the new harshly competitive, post-welfare state.

More recently, the conservative wunderkind Dinesh D'Souza (1991) penned a book-length screed complaining that the U.S. university has become the principal site of a "victim's revolution" that has become all-pervasive in society. D'Souza, a research fellow at the American Enterprise Institute, pins much of his argument on the backs of academically high achieving Asian Americans, who he contends are being unfairly denied admission to elite universities to make room for presumably lesser qualified African Americans and Hispanics. Understood correctly, the deceptively flattering portrayals of Asian Americans and their high-achieving children rendered by the minions of the conservative establishment are intended to disarm the proponents of progressive, inclusionary, and democratic social policies that attempt to redress historic patterns of inequality.

As commercial television is inextricably bound to the structures of power in U.S. society, controlling images of Asian-American children are not likely to deviate from the prevailing political orthodoxy. Although some media activists hold out for reform, others out of choice or by necessity have engaged in a vital counter-video/film practice that attempts to capture the full scope and diversity of Asian-American life (Leong, 1991). As corporate oligopolies extend their control of television—perhaps the most important agent of socialization—it becomes all the more necessary to engage in the sustained critical examination of contemporary media. The future of democratic society depends upon it.

References

Collins, P. H. (1990). *Black feminist thought: Knowledge, consciousness, and the politics of empowerment.* Boston: Unwin Hyman.

Dortort, D. (Producer), & Allen, L. (Director). (1970). The fear merchants. *Bonanza* [Television].

Dortort, D. (Producer), & Oswald, G. (Director). (1966). A Christmas story. *Bonanza* [Television].

D'Souza, D. (1991). *Illiberal education: The politics of race and sex on campus.* New York: Free Press.

Fallows, J. (1989). *More like us: Making America great again.* Boston: Houghton Mifflin.

Kitano, H.H.L., & Daniels, R. (1988). *Asian Americans: Emerging minorities.* Englewood Cliffs, NJ: Prentice-Hall.

Leong, R. (Ed.). (1991). *Moving the image: Independent Asian Pacific media arts.* Los Angeles: UCLA Asian American Studies Center and Visual Communications, Southern California Asian American Studies Central.

MacDonald, J. F. (1985). *Television and the red menace: The video road to Vietnam.* New York: Praeger.

MacDonald, J. F. (1987). *Who shot the sheriff? The rise and fall of the television western.* New York: Praeger.

McConahay, M. J. (1990, December 16). The baby trade. *Los Angeles Times Magazine,* p. 14.

Roediger, D. A. (1991). *The wages of whiteness: Race and the making of the American working class.* London: Verso.

Saxton, A. (1990). *The rise and fall of the white republic: Class politics and mass culture in nineteenth-century America.* New York: Verso.

Schiller, H. I. (1989). *Culture, inc.: The corporate takeover of public expression.* New York: Oxford University Press.

Sowell, T. (1983). *The economics and politics of race: An international perspective.* New York: William Morrow.

Wallerstein, I. (1979). *The capitalist world-economy.* Cambridge, UK: Cambridge University Press.

15. The Television Worlds of Latino Children

FEDERICO A. SUBERVI-VÉLEZ

SUSAN COLSANT

Introduction

When Berry and Mitchell-Kernan's (1982) book on television and minority children was published 10 years ago, it contained a chapter about the impact of educational television on the socialization of the Hispanic child. That chapter, by Arias (1982), listed many references to the general subject of television and children but it offered very few sources on research that dealt specifically with *Latino* children. The limited number of citations relevant to this ethnic group was a reflection of the scarcity of research with these youngsters as objects or subjects of inquiry. A decade later, less than a dozen new titles appear in electronic and printed indexes of academic publications. Of the works that emerge in searches using the key words "television" and "Hispanic" or "Latino" children, barely a handful provide valuable new insights or even notions of theories about the uses, exposure, or effects of television on the Hispanic child (e.g., Blosser, 1988; Gandy & Matabane, 1989; Subervi-Vélez & Necochea, 1990).

Apparently, there has been meager funding and/or interest in studying the relationship between television and Latino children. Nevertheless, the need for developing this line of inquiry remains, and in fact, is ever more urgent given the Hispanic population trends documented by the 1990 Census. Not only is this population growing at faster rates than Whites and Blacks, but it is also continuing

AUTHORS' NOTE: Technical support by Sarah Harding, research assistant.

some distinct sociocultural development patterns with respect to media use as well in the availability and growth of Hispanic-oriented television and other entertainment media nationwide.

The purpose of this chapter is to provide an overview of some of the major characteristics of the diverse television worlds that are potentially available to Latino children. Throughout the chapter various concerns are expressed, and unanswered questions are raised about future research on television and the Hispanic child in the United States.

The Sociodemographic Imperatives for Focusing on Latinos

According to reports by the U.S. Bureau of the Census (1991), between 1980 and 1990 there was a 53% growth in the Hispanic population in the United States—from approximately 14.6 million to over 22.4 million. Although still only a fraction of the total national population, the Latino component constitutes over a quarter of the inhabitants of three states: New Mexico (38.2%), Texas (25.8%), and California (25.8%)—this last a state with a 69% growth of its Hispanic population between 1980 and 1990. And in large metropolitan cities such as Miami, San Antonio, and El Paso, the Hispanic minority is in fact the numerical (if not political or economic) majority. Even greater proportions of Latino residents are evident in large and small communities in the Southwest, particularly in border towns and areas very dependent on agriculture.

In the meantime, the number of Latino children in the school systems of the United States has surged from approximately 7.4 million (13%) of the total school-age population in 1980, to over 9.5 million (16% of that total) in 1989 (U.S. Bureau of the Census, 1991). The geometric growth of Hispanic enrollment is most evident in five of the nation's six largest school districts. According to the National Center for Educational Statistics, the top districts and their corresponding Hispanic enrollment for grades K-12 during 1988-1989 were as follows: New York—34%, Los Angeles—59%, Chicago—26% Miami/Dade—44%, Philadelphia—9%, and Houston—41% (National Center for Educational Statistics, personal communication, August 7, 1992). As summarized by Wilson and Gutiérrez (1985), this population explosion is a product of various factors, including increased immigration, higher birth rates, and younger median age among Hispanics. The larger census counts of Hispanics in recent years is also due to the increased validation of and identification with Latino roots and heritage.

Demographic data such as the above should be sufficiently compelling to include Hispanic subjects in almost any study of the use of television and its influence on children or adults. Although such has yet to be the case for academic communications research, the Hispanic market has not gone unnoticed in the business world. Because of the growth of this population and its annual purchasing power estimated at over $177 billion dollars (Acosta, 1991), advertising companies (Lopes, 1991), and even the major political parties, in search of the Hispanic vote, have given more attention to this ethnic group. In fact, survey research businesses such as NuStats (Austin, TX), Hispanic Market Connections (Los Altos, CA), and Strategy Research Corporation (Miami, FL) have profited from numerous studies conducted for clients of Hispanic behaviors, values, and life-styles, including those pertaining to media uses, gratifications, and effects.

One of the principal findings in the commercial and academic-oriented communications research on Latinos is that this group merits distinct attention for reasons that transcend the nominal classification brought by the ethnic label of "Hispanic" or "Latino." The attention is warranted because many Hispanics are indeed distinct in their socioeconomic status and cultural traits. Language and ethnic identification are among the characteristics that have bearing on the present text.

According to Strategy Research Corporation (SRC, 1991), the first language learned by nearly 96% of U.S. Hispanic adults was Spanish. Furthermore, over 70% indicate that they use this language most frequently at home, and approximately 66% say they speak Spanish most frequently on social occasions. In a study by Hispanic Market Connections (1992), in 1991 over 96% of Latino adults surveyed speak Spanish. In fact, 49% of the subjects of that study are "Spanish dependent"; another 34% prefer Spanish.

With numbers such as the above, it is not surprising that in the Strategy Research Corporation (SRC, 1991) survey, at least 79% of U.S. Hispanic children indicate that Spanish is the first language they spoke. The number was relatively lower only in the Southwest (51%). On the other hand, generational differences are very striking when it comes to questions of the language those children speak most frequently in the home. Spanish is predominant in three regions (Northeast 56%, Southeast 56%, Central 68%) whereas both languages, Spanish and English, are used in two regions (Southwest 47%, West 51%). Evidently, exposure to Spanish is a normal part of the everyday environment of the majority of Latino children in most parts of the United States. Furthermore, over 95% of the adults hold the view that it is important that children have the ability to read and write this language (SRC, 1991).

This is not to imply that Hispanic children's media use is predominantly in Spanish. Although much of the available data on this subject is still inconclusive, there are studies showing that when available, Spanish-language media are widely used by Hispanics (Greenberg, Burgoon, Burgoon, & Korzenny, 1983; Hispanic Market Connections, 1991; SRC, 1991). However, for various reasons, some Hispanic children do not have opportunities to learn Spanish either formally or informally. Therefore, those born in the United States or socialized primarily in this country are prone to make greater use of, and even have greater preference for, English-language television. As discussed later on, one of the reasons for this preference may be the greater availability and variety of English-language programs, including those directed to children. Still another reason why Hispanic children may prefer to watch English-language television is that they seek to maintain a common base of entertainment experience with their peers. For children living in mixed neighborhoods, English-language programs are a common denominator they share with their peers. The above notwithstanding, Hispanic children are prone to be exposed to some Spanish-language television, especially if their parents are primarily Spanish speakers and they live in a house where only one television set is available.

In terms of identification, the SRC (1991) study shows that in all regions of the country, the plurality of Hispanic adults and children hold high or moderate degrees of "Hispanic orientation" in their self-identification. For adults, the figures of high Hispanic orientation ranged from 90% in the Northeast to 68% in the Southwest. For children, the high/moderate figures varied from 68%/30% in the Central region to 48%/43% in the Southwest. Altogether, these findings are irrefutable evidence of a very pluralistic (i.e., nonassimilated) population when it comes to at least these two indicators of adaptation.

With sociodemographic conditions such as these, the foundations have long been set for the development and growth of numerous institutions that support the unique opportunities allowed by this segmentable market. It should not be surprising that Spanish-language media, and even some English-language media, are among the largest and most established institutions participating intricately in these dynamics. As documented by Subervi-Vélez (in press), Latino-oriented media in the United States are numerous and growing; they constitute the largest "minority" media in this country. U.S.-based Spanish-language television, with its national availability and distinct children's programming, is thus one of the "television worlds" of the Hispanic child. But before discussing this TV world, the major English-language television world needs to be mentioned.

The English-Language Television World

On almost every account, the foremost television world for children in the United States, be they Hispanic or of any other ethnic background, is the one provided by the English-language commercial and public stations. During the week of April 25-May 1, 1992, ABC, CBS, and NBC broadcast a combined total of 15 hours of children's programming; Fox had an additional 22 hours. The number of different programs of this type in the top three networks was 25, with 17 more at Fox. During that same time period, PBS had nine different children's programs taking up 37 hours. When the full-time children-oriented programs of Nickelodeon and the Disney Channel are added to this scenario, it is evident that English-language television provides the greatest number of hours and variety of children's programs in the United States.

However, ethnic minorities are practically excluded as actors, actresses, or even caricatures in the mainstream commercial programs. If they appear, they are mostly token or stereotypical characters in secondary roles with few lines or with minimal contributions to the story plots. More notable and positive portrayals of Hispanics, African Americans, Asian Americans, and occasionally American Indians, are found primarily in selected PBS and some Nickelodeon programs. But Hispanic characters are particularly absent from commercial entertainment television; a middle-class

Hispanic family has been featured on prime time only once and that was over 10 years ago (Subervi-Vélez, 1990). With few exceptions, this is, in broad terms, the first world of television from which Hispanic children obtain their main entertainment on a daily basis. Even as the short- and long-term effects of this TV world on Latino children continue to go unassessed in academic research, there are two other TV worlds that potentially influence the Hispanic child.

The U.S. Spanish-Language Television World

Spanish-language television programs debuted in the United States as early as 1951 when José Pérez del Río, a Mexican national of Spanish heritage, hosted a weekly entertainment and variety talent search show that was broadcast live on Sunday afternoons from the studios of KERN Channel 5, an English-language station in San Antonio, Texas (Subervi-Vélez, in press). Given the popularity of that show and the interest in Spanish-language programs among the Mexicans and Mexican Americans in the Southwest, entrepreneurs from both sides of the border did not take long to produce other similar programs and eventually establish TV stations dedicated to this purpose.

Today, there are three Hispanic-oriented networks, each with numerous outlets in the major Hispanic markets across the country. Univisión, formerly Spanish International Network, was first established in 1961 with the financial backing of the Azcárraga family, owners of Televisa—Mexico's largest television conglomerate. In 1987, Hallmark Cards, Inc., purchased this network and continued its development. At present, it consists of 14 owned and operated stations, 21 affiliates, plus over 550 cable carriers reaching close to 95% of the Hispanic audience of the United States (Subervi-Vélez, in press). The Telemundo network was established in 1987 by the Reliance Capital Group, an investment company directed by Saul Steinberg. At present, this network consists of 10 owned and operated stations, 22 affiliates, plus contracts with 7 cable carriers that operate in 14 states and the District of Columbia, altogether reaching about 84% of the Latino audience (Subervi-Vélez, in press). The third Spanish-language network in the United States is Galavisión, which was launched in 1979 as a premium cable service under parent company Univisa, Inc., a subsidiary of Mexico's Televisa. In

1988, it started changing into an advertising-based basic cable service company that in addition broadcasts via nine UHF affiliates located in the Southwestern states (Subervi-Vélez, in press). Altogether, the programs of these networks, in particular those directed at the younger viewers, constitute the "second television world" of many Hispanic children. Understanding some of the characteristics of this milieu is one important element for studying Latino children and television in a changing sociocultural world.

First, in Spanish-language television *telenovelas* (soap operas) are the predominant genre in number and hours of programming; there are few Hispanic-American-based productions of adventure shows of almost any type. Nevertheless, these networks offer a limited number of hours with a distinct variety of programs for children. Although the time and shows dedicated to such programming have historically been more restricted than those available on English-language stations, they seem to be increasing. For example, from 1981 to 1988 Univisión broadcast an average of less than 3 hours and about 2.5 different shows a week (weekends included) in children's programming. However, after Hallmark finalized its purchase of Univisión in early 1988, the total number of hours per week of children's programming more than doubled from 4 to 9.5. The doubling was a result of adding a half-hour cartoon in the morning and one in the evening to the usual Saturday morning lineup. This was the first time that Univisión viewers could watch children's programming during the weekdays. For fall 1990, the hours per week nearly doubled again with the inclusion of a 2-hour block, Univisión y los Niños, featuring second-run cartoons dubbed in Spanish by DIC Enterprises. For the fall 1992 season, Univisión was scheduled to broadcast seven different shows during 11 hours specifically targeted to children. This includes a weekday schedule from 6 to 7 a.m., and Saturday and Sunday blocks from 10 a.m. to 1 p.m.

At Telemundo, children's programs averaged 3.5 hours and two different shows per week in mid-1990. This increased to 4 hours and three shows during mid-1991, but promptly decreased in fall 1991 to only 2 hours during one show on Sunday mornings. However, for the fall 1992 schedule, Telemundo is planning to broadcast at least four shows during 14.5 hours for children. This includes a weekday schedule of cartoons from 7 to 9 a.m., a Saturday block from 8 to 11 a.m., and a Sunday slot from 8 to 9:30 a.m. Although past lists of Galavisión's programs were not available for review, from its summer 1992 schedule it was observed that 8.5 hours and three shows were dedicated specifically for the youngest audience. Altogether, for fall 1992, it is expected that Latino children in the United States could potentially have access to 34 hours and 14 different shows of Spanish-language programming geared for their entertainment.

The second and most important point to be made about the U.S. Spanish-language television world for children pertains to the sources and content characteristics of the shows. With few exceptions, the cartoon menu consists of U.S. products dubbed into Spanish. For example, Univisión's schedule includes programs such as *Super Mario Brothers, Super Mario 3, Inspector Gadget,* and *Captain N: The Game Master.* And on June 1, 1992, Telemundo started broadcasting *El Conejo de la Suerte, El Pato Lucas, El Conchito Porky, Silvestre, Piolín,* and *Elmer Gruñón,* better known in the United States as, respectively, Bugs Bunny, Daffy Duck, Porky Pig, Sylvester, Tweety, and Elmer Fudd. Galavisión has no programs of this genre. Sociopsychological implications of Hispanic children's exposure to these shows are probably not that different than the outcomes of exposure to the English-language cartoons. What may well be different pertains to language maintenance. On this topic, Telemundo's vice president for programming commented in 1992 that besides entertaining, cartoons can be a vehicle for promoting and preserving the Spanish language among Hispanic children. The void in academic research on these matters is indeed perplexing.

Aside from the cartoons, most of the programs transmitted over the Spanish-language networks in the United States are products of Mexico, with a few shows coming from Brazil, Peru, Venezuela, Puerto Rico, or Spain. News, talk shows, and variety shows are the core components of the local U.S. productions. Thus, the children's programs follow this same pattern for which Mexico has been the major supplier. At Galavisión, all three of the children's programs are produced and transmitted from that country—*T.V.O.,* one of Mexico's most popular children's shows, featuring games, contests, singing, and dancing; *El Chavo del Ocho,* the perennial and always popular comedian; and *En Familia,* a family-do-it-together educational fun and games show. Telemundo's Mexican imports include the long-running *Kolitas,* a cartoon program in which there is also a studio audience that journeys to a make-believe island for visits with a variety of animal friends; and the now-canceled studio game shows *El País de Caramelo* and its sequel *El Circo Cómplice.* Only

NubeLuz, another cartoon and studio game program that was part of the fall 1992 schedule, originates in Peru.

Most of Univisión's children's programs also originate from Mexico. This includes *El Arbol Azul*, a *telenovela* (soap opera) produced for children; it was on the air from fall 1991 to spring 1992. Current Mexican imports in this genre include *Chespirito*, a slapstick comedy with various wacky characters, and *Carrusel*, another ongoing *telenovela* produced especially for and about children.

The first and only Spanish-language children's program made especially for a U.S. commercial television network was *Pepe Plata*. This half-hour live-action comedy and adventure show, created especially for Univisión by Chris Brough in association with DIC Enterprises of Los Angeles, featured actor Simón Maldonado in the role of the world's richest teenager and hit recording star (à la Richie Rich, the Anglo super rich comic book and cartoon character). Starting in fall 1990, *Pepe Plata* was on the air from Monday through Friday afternoons and Saturday and Sunday mornings in a children's segment called *Platavisión*. This segment contained the cartoons *Aventuras en Plata Hills* (a Spanish-language revoicing of *Beverly Hills Teens*) and *C.O.P.S.* (another animation dubbed from English). The 65 original episodes of *Pepe Plata* included the guest star participation of numerous Hispanic-American actors and actresses, and the recording of a weekly original song that was promoted, along with other *Pepe Plata* merchandise, by DIC Enterprises. These features helped this show win very high ratings, and thus many advertisers, during its first and even second runs. However, after four consecutive showings the same year, the *Pepe Plata* show lost a lot of its appeal, and thus audience, leading it to be replaced by yet another import—*El Show de Xuxa*.

Since it was launched on Univisión on August 9, 1991, *El Show de Xuxa* has been a phenomenal success, continuing the pattern it established in its place of origin—Brazil. The Spanish-language version of this show of dancing, singing, and contests is produced in Argentina before a live studio audience and broadcast via satellite across North and South America. Since the original show's debut in Brazil, the 28-year-old Xuxa has enjoyed unprecedented following. In Brazil alone, her program has achieved an estimated viewership of 33 million, the largest audience ever garnered by TV Globo, the dominant television network in that country. Because of her blond hair, effervescent personality, and flashy costumes of super short shorts and knee-high boots, she can seem like a cross between Madonna and Captain Kangaroo. Nevertheless, Xuxa is such a preeminent superstar for Spanish-speaking and Portuguese-speaking children in Latin America and the United States that prospects for an English-language show are now in the working (Blount, 1992; Cerone, 1992).

One of the commonalties of the children's programs mentioned above (cartoons excluded), be they the local production of *Pepe Plata* or the Mexican, Peruvian, or Brazilian imports, is that they regularly feature Spanish-speaking, Latino-type characters, studio participants, and role models. Telemundo's *Kolitas* has even worked in collaboration with Kolitas International, producers of the show, and Immevisión, the network where the series is broadcast, to have segments in which Hispanic children can call in and participate in contests directly from their homes in the United States. Except for the super blond Xuxa and many of the blond assistants who dance and dress like her, the other children who play games, sing, and jump around in the show are typical Latino kids from a variety of racial backgrounds.

Another commonality of these programs is that when values and moral lessons are promoted in the comic sketches and dramas, particularly in the soap opera *Carrusel,* these tend to reflect similar values and moral lessons traditionally promoted by Hispanic families, especially those of Mexican heritage. Thus, it is not surprising that when Hispanic children have been asked to list their favorite programs or to identify with a television character, some of the responses point to shows and personalities from Spanish-language television (Eastman & Liss, 1980). Unfortunately, other socialization effects of exposure to this television world have yet to be assessed.

Before concluding this segment, it should be mentioned that the future of children's shows on Spanish-language television is contingent on advertisers' validation of them as a vehicle to reach that market. Until now, advertisers have not strongly embraced the Spanish-language children's television format for two primary reasons. First, they are confident that the English-language commercial messages reach Hispanic children, who are expected to be bilingual and watch English-language programs. Little need is seen to take additional risks and incur the costs to market more directly to Hispanic children. Second, advertisers are reluctant to advertise directly to Spanish-speaking children and prefer targeting the income-earning parents. These sentiments run straight through executives in all areas of the industry ("Christmas ads," 1990; "Fisher-Price," 1989; "No fun and games," 1991).

One of the exceptions to this trend has been Mattel, Inc. This children's toy manufacturer was one of the charter advertisers for Univisión's 1990 *Platavisión* series along with McDonald's, General Mills' Cereals, and Proctor & Gamble for its Crest, Hawaiian Punch, Pringle's and Sunny Delight brands. Of special note was that during the 1990 Christmas season, Mattel ran spots on Univisión for its Hispanic Barbie. For about 20 years, Mattel, Inc., has sold Black, Asian, and even Hispanic versions of its legendary Barbie Doll. But the toy company did not make much of an effort to promote those dolls until the Univisión commercial spots. It will be interesting to observe the long-term advertising strategies for the successful *El Show de Xuxa* on Univisión and the new line of dubbed classic cartoons on Telemundo.

The Mexican and Puerto Rican Spanish-Language Television World

The third and final "television world" that has the potential to influence Hispanic children is that which is experienced in their "home" country or the country of their ancestors. Latino children who are born outside the United States or live a number of their early years elsewhere are bound to be exposed to yet another barrage of visual stimuli from the television programs in those countries. U.S.-born Latino children who move to a Spanish-speaking country for a season because of their parents' work, or to visit or stay with relatives and friends, face similar television experiences. A cursory inquiry into the children's television offerings in Mexico and Puerto Rico provides a glimpse of the options found in this world. The brief review is restricted to Mexico and Puerto Rico because the vast majority of U.S. Hispanics immigrate from these two countries.

One of the first characteristics of the children's programs in both Puerto Rico and Mexico is that both make extensive use of dubbed cartoons made in the United States. Spanish-language editions of classic animations such as those acquired recently by Telemundo, plus the perennial *The Flintstones, Tom & Jerry, Popeye,* and the whole Disney gang have long been part of the regular TV features in

Mexico and Puerto Rico. Even *Sesame Street* has been specially produced in Spanish as *Plaza Sésamo* for the Spanish-speaking children in these and other southern countries. In fact, aside from local productions of news, soap operas, and some variety shows, Hollywood productions of all types have been a dominant feature of the airwaves of almost all Latin American countries. Another more recent development of this third television world is the advent of cable and satellite programs transmitted directly from the United States with mostly adult programs, but also some children's shows and channels such as Nickelodeon and Disney. In this respect, as well as the exposure to dubbed Hollywood programs, a child immigrating to the United States from almost anywhere in this hemisphere would find little difficulty in quickly becoming familiar with the television programs of English- or Spanish-language stations in this country. On the other hand, it should also be considered that many children in rural areas of Mexico have few television options whatsoever, and upon their first visit to the United States, face an unprecedented barrage of audiovisual experiences. Studying the effects of these experiences, be they of familiarity or unfamiliarity with children's television, on the adaptation of the immigrant Hispanic child is yet another intriguing but unexplored task.

A second major characteristic of the media systems in both Puerto Rico and Mexico is that many television stations produce some type of children's show in which the local kids are featured taking part in games, contests, singing, dancing, or just having fun with the hosts. Some of the Mexican productions have been mentioned above. Examples from commercial television in Puerto Rico include *El Show de Pacheco,* which has been broadcast for over 20 years, *Burbujitas Gargaritas,* featuring two 17-inch tall moppets, *Chícola y la Ganga,* in which life-size dolls (dressed-up actors) play with the children at the studio, and *El Mundo de Mikey,* hosted by Venezuelan actor Mikey. Even the local public television station produces, in addition to its educational programs, more entertainment-oriented childrens shows such as *Somos Unicos,* with games and songs, and *La Casa de María Chuzema,* featuring the Chuzema house, where children go to play games, sing, and share their concerns.

The portrayals of Latino children that predominate in all of these programs, as well as the other local productions of news, *telenovelas,* talk and variety shows, are relatively much more reflective of the diverse ethnic compositions of those societies. The question that emerges is, what happens to the Hispanic children who upon immigrating to the United States, observe the overwhelming absence (or otherwise preponderant negative images) of "people like themselves" in the mainstream media? For these research questions and many others, it would certainly be imperative to assess the possible differences between the various nationalities of Latino children. For example, the experiences of immigrant Puerto Rican children vis-à-vis the experiences of immigrant Mexican or Central or South American children may have some commonalties, but also significant distinctions with unique implications for their socialization. Furthermore, for a Cuban child living in Miami, the socialization experiences of Spanish-language and English-language television may also be quite different given that in that area there is an environment where Spanish-language television and other media, as well as Hispanic politics and cultural celebrations, are much more supported and validated all across the economic spectrum.

Conclusion

Evidently, the television worlds of many Hispanic children in the United States are potentially more complex than the single television world of Anglo children. This brief presentation of some of the characteristics of the U.S.-based and foreign-based Spanish-language television environments should be only a beginning in the serious analysis of the relationships between any of these worlds and the development and socialization of the Latino child in this country. The questions that need answering are uncountable and the task should not have to wait until the next century when Hispanic children are even less of a minority and much more part of the U.S. majority. A small effort to assess the effect of exposure to Spanish-language versus English-language media on the self-concept of Latino children led to some exciting preliminary findings (Subervi-Vélez & Necochea, 1990). But that was a first exploration that needs follow-up and expansion. It is crucial that we accelerate the understanding and improvement of both Spanish-language and English-language television so that we may also be part of the positive changes of an ever more diverse sociocultural world.

References

Acosta, S. (1991, December). Spending power at $151 billion. *Hispanic Business*, p. 20.

Arias, M. B. (1982). Educational television: Impact on the socialization of the Hispanic child. In G. L. Berry & C. Mitchell-Kernan (Eds.), *Television and the socialization of the minority child* (pp. 203-211). New York: Academic Press.

Berry, G. L., & Mitchell-Kernan, C. (1982). Television as a socializing force within a society of mass communication. In G. L. Berry & C. Mitchell-Kernan (Eds.), *Television and the socialization of the minority child* (pp. 1-11). New York: Academic Press.

Blosser, B. J. (1988). Ethnic differences in children's media use. *Journal of Broadcasting and Electronic Media, 32*(4), 453-470.

Blount, J. (1992, April 19). Xuxa's very big neighborhood. *Los Angeles Times Calendar*, pp. 9-10, 78.

Cerone, D. (1992, April 19). A hit in L.A. Latino homes, Xuxa is working on her English. *Los Angeles Times Calendar*, p. 10.

Christmas ads bypass Hispanic TV networks. (1990, November 26). *Advertising Age*, p. 48.

Eastman, H., & Liss, M. (1980). Ethnicity and children's TV preferences. *Journalism Quarterly, 57*(2), 277-280.

Fisher-Price toys with TV. (1989, February 13). *Advertising Age*, pp. 5-8.

Gandy, O. H., Jr., & Matabane, P. W. (1989). Television and social perceptions among African Americans and Hispanics. In M. K. Asante & W. B. Gudykunst (Eds.), *Handbook of international and intercultural communication* (pp. 318-348). Newbury Park, CA: Sage.

Greenberg, B. S., Burgoon, M, Burgoon, J, & Korzenny, F. (1983). *Mexican Americans and the mass media*. Norwood, NJ: Ablex.

Hispanic Market Connections. (1992). *The national Hispanic database: A Los Angeles preview*. Los Altos, CA: Hispanic Market Connections.

Lopes, H. (1991, December). Who's the leader of the pack? *Hispanic Business*, p. 24.

No fun and games for TV's toy segment. (1991, February 4). *Advertising Age*, p. 32.

Strategy Research Corporation. (1991). *U.S. Hispanic market*. Miami, FL: Author.

Subervi-Vélez, F. A. (1990). Interactions between Latinos and Anglos on prime-time television: A case study of "Condo." In S. Chan (Ed.), *Income and status differences between white and minority Americans: A persistent inequality* (pp. 303-336). Lewiston, NY: Edwin Mellen.

Subervi-Vélez, F. A. (in press). Media. In N. Kanellos & Claudio Esteva-Fabregat (Eds.), *Hispanic American almanac*. Detroit, MI: Gale Research.

Subervi-Vélez, F. A., & Necochea, J. (1990). Television viewing and self-concept among Latino children: A pilot study. *Howard Journal of Communications, 3*(2), 315-329.

U.S. Bureau of the Census. (1991). *Current population reports* (Series P-20, No. 443). Washington, DC: U.S. Government Printing Office.

Wilson, C., Jr., & Gutiérrez, F. (1985). *Minorities and the media: Diversity and the end of mass communication*. Beverly Hills, CA: Sage.

16. Television, the Portrayal of Women, and Children's Attitudes

NANCY SIGNORIELLI

Television is our nation's most common, constant, and vivid learning environment. Americans spend much of their time in the world of television and today newer delivery systems, such as cable and VCRs, provide even more opportunities for viewing. In the average home, the set is turned on for about 7 hours each day and the average person watches more than 3 hours a day. Children and their grandparents watch the most; teenage girls the least (but even this group averages just under 3 hours each day) (Nielsen, 1990). Few people escape exposure to television's vivid and recurrent patterns of images, information, and values.

Television is first and foremost a storyteller—it tells most of the stories to most of the people, most of the time. It is the wholesale distributor of images and the mainstream of our popular culture. Our children are born into homes in which, for the first time in human history, a centralized commercial institution rather than parents, church, or school tells most of the stories. The world of television shows and tells us about life—people, places, striving, power, and fate. It presents the good and bad, the happy and sad, and lets us know who is successful and who a failure. This story-telling function of television is extremely important because it is through these stories that people learn about the world and its peoples.

The role of the mass media, especially television, in the development of people's views of the world, as well as the possible influence of the media on behavior, has been a concern for a long time. During the heyday of motion pictures, the Payne Fund studies (Charters, 1933) examined the role of the movies in children's lives: Who went, what they saw, and what they learned. In the 1950s, around the time television was gaining in popularity, a debate emerged about the potentially harmful effects of comic books (Wertheim, 1954). And since the 1960s, television has been the focus of hundreds if not thousands of studies, many concerned with the relationship between viewing and violence (Baker & Ball, 1968; Huston et al., 1992; Pearl, Bouthilet, & Lazar, 1982; U.S. Surgeon General's Scientific Advisory Committee, 1972).

Socialization, especially sex role socialization, has been a focus of scholars in numerous disciplines, including sociology, psychology, social psychology, anthropology, and communication. Naturally, in each discipline, the term has a slightly different connotation. Psychologists may look at socialization as a form of personal learning, development, or adjustment. Sociologists, on the other hand, use the term to refer to the social processes by which an individual is introduced to the society's or group's culture, and anthropologists see socialization as enculturation.

A common thread in these definitions is the notion that socialization is a social process—the way that people learn about their culture and acquire some of its values, beliefs, perspectives, and social norms. In short, socialization is the way in which an individual comes to adopt the behavior and values of a group. Socialization is an ongoing process; we are socialized and resocialized throughout the life cycle.

Traditionally, the major responsibility for socialization has been the domain of parents, peers, schools, and churches. Over the past 25 years, however, numerous studies have revealed that the mass media play a very important role in the socialization process for both children and adults (Berry & Mitchell-Kerman, 1982; Roberts & Bachen, 1981; Roberts & Maccoby, 1985). The actual processes of media socialization, however, are different from those used by more traditional agents of socialization.

Of all the media, television may be the one most suited for socialization, especially for children. It is found in practically every U.S. home and increasingly in practically every home around the world; it requires only minimal skills for understanding; and its visual nature makes it particularly appealing to youngsters. Television may also play a central role in a child's social life, providing the fuel for conversations and peer group cohesiveness. Finally, television series have a relatively long life. Many programs, once they have completed their first run on a network, go into syndication and are shown, again and again, on independent stations, cable systems, or in other countries. Consequently, media images cannot be thought of as onetime occurrences whose possible effects are limited to one-shot viewing experiences.

A number of factors, including the overabundance and long life of stereotypical and traditional images of males and females in television programming (Signorielli, 1985), have thus contributed to concern about the role of television in gender role socialization. In this chapter, I will review some of the research relating to this area of investigation. I will first examine the basic imagery of male and female roles and then discuss research about television's possible impact on conceptions about gender roles.

Gender Role Images on Television

For the past 20 years, in study after study, men have outnumbered women by two or three to one in prime-time dramatic programming (Davis, 1990; Selnow, 1990; Signorielli, 1985, 1989). Women are likely to be younger than men (Gerbner, Gross, Signorielli, & Morgan, 1980; Vernon, Williams, Phillips, & Wilson, 1991); tend to be cast in traditional and stereotypical roles (Signorielli, 1989); and are more likely to have blond or red/auburn than black or brown hair (Davis, 1990). This is not to say that "liberated" or nontraditional women do not appear on television; it is just that these images are not found consistently. Naturally, most people can easily cite five, six, or more examples of women who are not stereotyped and most of the research examining nonstereotyped roles has focused upon a small number of programs (e.g., Reep & Dambrot, 1987). Consequently, it is easy to forget that the majority of female characters in prime time are found in more traditional roles.

Overall, occupational portrayals on television are varied but stereotyped. Women's employment possibilities are somewhat limited, with clerical work the most common job (Steenland, 1990). Television does not recognize adequately that women can successfully mix marriage, homemaking, and raising children with careers. Rather, programs in which married women work outside the home (e.g., Claire Huxtable on *Cosby*) often focus on the character's home-related role rather than her work persona. Nor does the television world adequately acknowledge the importance of homemaking and raising children: As in the real world, on television the woman who stays home has less status than the one who has a career.

Content analyses on 17 week-long annual samples of prime-time network dramatic programs, conducted as part of the Cultural Indicators project (Signorielli, 1989), sheds some light on the traditional and stereotypical ways in which characters are portrayed. Women are seen less often than men and in many respects may be considered as less important. When women do appear, they usually are younger than the men; they are also more attractive and nurturing; more often seen in the context of romantic interests, home, or family; and are more likely to be victimized. Women are somewhat more likely than men to be married, and if they are married, they usually are not employed outside the home. Only 26% of the women who are employed outside the home are also married or have been married. This schism is not perpetuated for male characters.

Women who are employed outside the home are usually cast in traditional female occupations—nurses, secretaries, waitresses, and teachers. Nevertheless, the world of television does not always accurately reflect women's work roles. There are a number of occupations in the U.S. labor force where women outnumber the men, but in the television world, due to the general overabundance of men, the men outnumber the women. These include teachers and restaurant workers.

Men, on the other hand, are presented as older. They tend to be more powerful and potent than the women and proportionately fewer are presented as married. Significantly more men are employed outside the home, and they usually work in high prestige and traditionally masculine occupations such as doctors, lawyers, police, and other higher status and higher paying jobs. Moreover, among married male characters, about three quarters are employed and one quarter are either not working or their employment status is unknown. Among women, the pattern is reversed—only 3 out of 10 married female characters are also employed, a finding quite different from the "real world," in which more than half of all married women are employed. Thus, the image conveyed by prime-time television is that women, especially if married, should stay home and leave the world of work to men.

Children, including those in the early adolescent years (10 to 15), are underrepresented as well as stereotyped in prime-time programs

(Signorielli, 1987). Boys are more active, aggressive, and unhappy than girls. Girls and boys also differ in regard to their activities; for example, girls are more likely to help with housework whereas boys take part in sports and generally get into mischief (Peirce, 1989).

The Soaps, Children's Programming, Commercials, and Music TV

Women in the soaps (daytime serial dramas) generally have parity with the men and are sometimes presented as equal (Cassata & Skill, 1983; Katzman, 1972) and often quite positively (Downing, 1974). The overall impression, however, is that the traditional woman has life just a little easier and is seen in a more positive light; she often triumphs, whereas the liberated or modern woman is punished or has a harder time (Cantor & Pingree, 1983).

Women are especially short changed and underrepresented on children's programs. In cartoons, studies consistently reveal that men outnumber women by four or five to one (Signorielli, 1991b), and that once again, women are presented in very stereotypical roles (Levinson, 1975; Streicher, 1974). Sex role portrayals also do not differ in programs that are toy based compared to those that are not toy based (Eaton & Dominick, 1991). Public television programs for children, although better on some dimensions, still fall short in relation to basic demography (Dohrmann, 1975; Matelski, 1985). Nor do men fare well in children's programming; they are more likely to rely on aggression and to receive disapproval (Nolan, Galst, & White, 1977).

Like children's programs, commercials are also sex typed and stereotyped (Courtney & Whipple, 1983), with strong links typically made between attractiveness and women (Downs & Harrison, 1985). Research conducted over the last 20 years has revealed that a woman's voice is rarely used as a voice-over and that men are presented as authoritative, even for products used primarily by women (Bretl & Cantor, 1988; Dominick & Rauch, 1972; Lovdal, 1989; W. J. O'Donnell & K. J. O'Donnell, 1978). Although men and women are more equally represented (in numbers) in prime-time commercials, women are very underrepresented in commercials aired during children's programs (Doolittle & Pepper, 1975; Riffe, Goldson, Saxton, & Yu, 1989). Sex typing in children's commercials also exists at the structural level with male-oriented commercials containing more cuts, loud music, and boisterous activity, whereas female-oriented commercials contain more fades and dissolves, soft music, and quiet play (Welch, Huston-Stein, Wright, & Plehal, 1979).

In the past 10 years, music videos have become an important television genre for youngsters, particularly adolescents. Women, however, are very underrepresented in videos (Brown & Campbell, 1986; Caplan, 1985) and stereotyped sex roles abound (Vincent, 1989; Vincent, Davis, & Boruszkowski, 1987). Sherman and Dominick (1986) found that women were presented as submissive, passive, physically attractive, and sensual and were often used as decorative objects, particularly in concept videos. Men, on the other hand, were in control of relationships. Other male images in videos include gang members, thugs, and gangsters whereas female images include nightclub performers, temptresses, servants, and goddesses (Aufderheide, 1986).

It cannot be ignored, however, that there has been improvement in the presentation of women on television over the past 20 years. First, the proportion of women has gone from a quarter to a little more than a third of all characters—a statistically significant increase (Signorielli, 1989). Nevertheless, the number of female characters depends upon program genre. Women make up at least half of the characters in situation comedies and serial dramas, but are practically invisible in action-adventure programs (Steenland, 1990). Second, women's work roles have improved with more women presented in "typically male" occupations. Women are also likely to be portrayed as affluent and rarely have problems with child care, harassment, or sex discrimination (Huston et al., 1992).

Impact of Gender Role Images

The description of television images is an important and necessary first step in understanding the role of television in society. Clearly, one cannot assess effects without knowing what people see. Consequently, as awareness of the images of men and women on television and in other media became known, research turned to examining the impact of these images. One particularly important area of investigation is the cultivation of gender role attitudes in both adults and children. This research is an outgrowth of cultivation theory and analysis, which in its simplest form, tries to ascertain if those who spend more time watching television are more likely to perceive the world in ways that reflect television's dominant, stable, and recurrent imagery (Gerbner, Gross, Morgan, & Signorielli, in press; Signorielli & Morgan, 1990).

Cultivation of Gender Role Images

The influence of the mass media, especially television, upon conceptions relating to gender roles is an important area of investigation. This research differs from research relating to perceptions of gender roles (stereotyping) in programming, "identification" (wanting to be like) with specific characters, and counterstereotyping, because it examines how the media may be shaping people's, and especially children's, views of what it means to be a man or a woman. This, in turn, may aid or abet those goals (occupational, educational, personal) a person may set out to achieve. Clearly, the evidence points to the fact that society's notions of appropriate roles for men and women have changed over the past 20 years (Harris & Lucas, 1976; Signorielli, 1989). What we still must determine is the role the media, notably television, has played (if any) in this process.

The research generally points to the existence of a relationship between television viewing and having more stereotypic conceptions about gender roles. In a study of 3- to 6-year-old children, Beuf (1974) found that those children who watched more television were more likely to stereotype occupational roles. This research also revealed that preschool-aged boys were unable to say "What they would be when they grew up" if they were a girl, whereas the girls always had a response to this question. Gross and Jeffries-Fox (1978), in a panel study of 250 8th-, 9th-, and 10th-grade children, found that television viewing was related to giving sexist responses to questions about the nature of men and women and how they are treated by society. Pingree (1978) found that television commercials influenced children's attitudes about gender role stereotypes. Furthermore, Katz and Coulter (1986) found more gender stereotyping among children who watched a lot of television compared to children who spent a lot of time reading.

Additional support for the notion that television viewing contributes to children's perceptions about appropriate male and female behaviors is found in two studies. Freuh and McGhee (1975), in a study of children in kindergarten through sixth grade, found that those who spent more time watching television exhibited greater sex typing than those who spent less time watching television. McGhee and Freuh (1980) similarly found that heavy viewers had more stereotyped perceptions of gender roles than light viewers. For male stereotypes, there was an interaction effect indicating that among light viewers, the perception of male stereotypes declined with age, whereas among heavy viewers, male stereotypes remained with increasing age. An interaction was not found for the perception of female stereotypes.

Studies by Morgan (1982; 1987) and Morgan and Rothschild (1983) revealed that television cultivates sex role attitudes among adolescents. Morgan and Harr-Mazar (1980) found that television seems to cultivate attitudes about when to form a family and how many children to have. Morgan and Rothschild (1983) also found that children who watch more television were more likely to endorse traditional divisions of labor between the sexes.

Morgan (1982) in a 3-year panel study of sixth- through eighth-grade children found that levels of sexism were higher among all boys and lower-class girls, and that television cultivates notions such as "Women are happiest at home raising children" and "Men are born with more ambition than women." Among girls, amount of television viewing was significantly associated with scores on an index of sex role stereotypes 1 year later, over and above the influence of demographics and earlier scores on this same index; there was no evidence that sex role stereotyping led to more television viewing. For boys, the patterns were reversed: There was no relationship between viewing and sex role attitudes but greater sexism was related to more viewing 1 year later. Overall, this study reveals that television viewing is most likely to make a difference among those who are otherwise least likely to hold traditional views of gender roles, a concept cultivation theory refers to as "mainstreaming."

In a second study of 287 adolescents using measures taken at two points in time, Morgan (1987) found that television viewing made an independent contribution to adolescents' sex role attitudes over time, but that television viewing was not related to some of their specific behaviors in relation to seven specific chores. Signorielli and Lears (1992), in a cross-sectional replication of this analysis with a sample of children in the fourth and fifth grades, also found statistically significant relationships between viewing and having sex-typed attitudes toward chores, but no relationship between viewing and actually doing sex-stereotyped chores. Moreover, attitudes toward sex-stereotyped chores and actually doing girl or boy chores were related but sex specific. Children, particularly those who said they watched more television, who had more stereotyped ideas about who should do which chores, were more likely to do those chores traditionally associated with their gender.

Signorielli (1991a, 1993) found support for the relationship between television viewing and conceptions about male and female roles in two studies analyzing data from the Monitoring the Future Survey fielded in 1985. One of these analyses (Signorielli, 1991a) found that children's conceptions about marriage reflected the ambivalent presentation of marriage in prime-time network programming. Television viewing was positively related to high school students saying they probably would get married, have children, and stay married to the same person. At the same time, there was a positive relationship between viewing and expressing the opinion that one sees so few good or happy marriages that one could question marriage as a way of life. In another analysis (Signorielli, 1993), conceptions about work reflected two contradictory views about work that appear on television. Television viewing was related to adolescents' wanting to have (a) high-status jobs that would also give them a chance to earn a lot of money, and (b) jobs that were relatively easy with long vacations and time to do other things in life.

In another study of the potential effects of television's stereotyped occupational portrayals, Wroblewski and Huston (1987) found that fifth- and sixth-grade children knew about jobs they typically encountered on television as well as experienced in real life. Occupations on television, however, were seen as more sex stereotyped than jobs in real life. The children had more negative attitudes about men holding television's typically feminine jobs than men having jobs that women typically hold in real life. The girls in this sample were particularly positive about television's typically masculine jobs.

Experimental Studies

Further evidence comes from a number of experiments, conducted both in the laboratory and in the field. A laboratory experiment was designed to determine the effects of exposure to beauty commercials "on the perceived importance of beauty commercial themes in social relations on adolescent female viewers" (Tan, 1979, p. 284). The results revealed that high school girls exposed to beauty commercials rated beauty characteristics significantly more important for the role "to be popular with men" than girls who saw neutral commercials. Those girls exposed to beauty commercials also rated beauty as personally more important than those who saw neutral commercials. In addition, Geis, Brown, Walstedt, and Porter (1984) found that women who viewed traditionally sex-typed commercials, compared to men and women who saw reversed-role commercials, emphasized homemaking rather than achievement themes in an essay imagining what their lives would be like in 10 years.

Finally, one of the very few studies having natural control groups of children who had very little, if any, exposure to television (Williams, 1986), revealed changes in conceptions about gender roles after television became available to the control groups. In this study, girls in Notel (town without television) and girls in Unitel (town with very limited television) had weaker gender-typed views than girls in Multitel (town with greater television availability). Two years after the introduction of television into Notel and an increase of television's availability in Unitel, the girls in Notel had become significantly more sex typed and the views of both these girls and the girls in Unitel were similar to the views of the girls in Multitel. Similar results were found for boys in these towns.

Conclusion

This review has explored gender role socialization from a communications research perspective. Overall, research examining the presentation of gender roles on television reveals a stable, traditional image that in most cases is very supportive of the status quo, especially in relation to physical appearance, marriage, and occupational roles.

Research on the impact of such images in regard to conceptions about sex roles points to the existence of a relationship between television viewing and having more stereotypic conceptions about gender roles. In essence, television may be contributing to the maintenance of notions of more limited roles for women in society. The image of women on television has undergone some change during the past two decades; society though has undergone numerous changes, and although things are not yet perfect, they are quite improved. Both men and women know that attitudes relating to the roles of men and women in society are different. How much greater, however, would these changes be if television were truly reflective of the status and role of women in the United States?

References

Aufderheide, P. (1986). Music videos: The look of the sound. *Journal of Communication, 36*(1), 57-78.

Baker, R., & Ball, S. (Eds.). (1966). *Violence and the media.* Washington, DC: U.S. Government Printing Office.

Berry, G., & Mitchell-Kerman, C. (Eds.). (1982). *Television and the socialization of the minority child.* New York: Academic Press.

Beuf, A. (1974). Doctor, lawyer, household drudge. *Journal of Communication, 24*(2), 142-154.

Bretl, D. J., & Cantor, J. (1988). The portrayal of men and women in U.S. television commercials: A recent content analysis and trends over 15 years. *Sex Roles, 18*(9/10), 595-609.

Brown, J. D., & Campbell, K. (1986). Race and gender in music videos: The same beat but a different drummer. *Journal of Communication, 36*(1), 94-106.

Cantor, M. G., & Pingree, S. (1983). *The soap opera.* Newbury Park, CA: Sage.

Caplan, R. E. (1985). Violent program content in music video. *Journalism Quarterly, 62*(1), 144-147.

Cassata, M., & Skill, T. (1983). *Live on daytime television: Tuning-in American serial drama.* Norwood, NJ: Ablex.

Charters, W. W. (1933). *Motion pictures and youth: A summary.* New York: Macmillan.

Courtney, A. E., & Whipple, T. W. (1983). *Sex stereotyping in advertising.* Lexington, MA: Lexington.

Davis, D. M. (1990). Portrayals of women in primetime network television: Some demographic characteristics. *Sex Roles, 23*(5/6), 325-332.

Dohrmann, R. (1975). A gender profile of children's educational TV. *Journal of Communication, 25*(4), 56-65.

Dominick, J. R., & Rauch, G. E. (1972). The image of women in network TV commercials. *Journal of Broadcasting, 16*(3), 259-265.

Doolittle, J., & Pepper, R. (1975). Children's TV ad content: 1974. *Journal of Broadcasting, 19*(2), 131-142.

Downing, M. H. (1974). Heroine of the daytime serial. *Journal of Communication, 24*(2), 130-137.

Downs, A. C., & Harrison, S. K. (1985). Embarrassing age spots or just plain ugly? Physical attractiveness stereotyping as an instrument of sexism on American television commercials. *Sex Roles, 13*(1/2), 9-19.

Eaton, B. C., & Dominick, J. R. (1991). Product-related programming and children's TV: A content analysis. *Journalism Quarterly, 68*(1/2), 67-75.

Freuh, T., & McGhee, P. (1975). Traditional sex-role development and amount of time spent watching television. *Developmental Psychology, 11,* 109.

Geis, F. L., Brown, V., Walstedt, J. J., & Porter, N. (1984). TV commercials as achievement scripts for women. *Sex Roles, 10*(7/8), 513-525.

Gerbner, G., Gross, L., Morgan, M., & Signorielli, N. (in press). Growing up with television: The cultivation perspective. In J. Bryant & D. Zillmann (Eds.), *Media effects: Advances in theory and research.* Hillsdale, NJ: Lawrence Erlbaum.

Gerbner, G., Gross, L., Signorielli, N., & Morgan, M. (1980). Aging with television: Images on television drama and conceptions of social reality. *Journal of Communication, 30*(1), 37-47.

Gross, L., & Jeffries-Fox, S. (1978). What do you want to be when you grow up, little girl? In G. Tuchman, A. K. Daniels, & J. Benet (Eds.), *Hearth and home: Images of women in the mass media* (pp. 240-265). New York: Oxford University Press.

Harris, L. H., & Lucas, M. E. (1976). Sex-role stereotyping. *Social Work, 21,* 390-395.

Huston, A. C., Donnerstein, E., Fairchild, H., Feshbach, N. D., Katz, P. A., Murray, J. P., Rubinstein, E. A., Wilcox, B. L., & Zuckerman, D. (1992). *Big world, small screen: The role of television in American society.* Lincoln: University of Nebraska Press.

Katz, P. A., & Coulter, D. K. (1986). *Progress report: Modification of gender: Stereotyped behavior in children* (Grant No. BNS-8316047). Washington, DC: National Science Foundation.

Katzman, N. (1972). Television soap operas: What's been going on anyway? *Public Opinion Quarterly, 36*(2), 200-212.

Levinson, R. M. (1975). From Olive Oyl to Sweet Polly Purebread: Sex-role stereotypes and televised cartoons. *Journal of Popular Culture, 9*(3), 561-572.

Lovdal, L. T. (1989). Sex role messages in television commercials: An update. *Sex Roles, 21*(11/12), 715-724.

Matelski, M. G. (1985). Image and influence: Women in public television. *Journalism Quarterly, 62*(1), 147-150.

McGhee, P. E., & Frueh, T. (1980). Television viewing and the learning of sex-role stereotypes. *Sex Roles, 6*(2), 179-188.

Morgan, M. (1982). Television and adolescents' sex-role stereotypes: A longitudinal study. *Journal of Personality and Social Psychology, 43,* 947-955.

Morgan, M. (1987). Television, sex-role attitudes, and sex-role behavior. *Journal of Early Adolescence, 7*(3), 269-282.

Morgan, M., & Harr-Mazar, H. (1980). *Television and adolescents' family life expectations.* Unpublished manuscript, Annenberg School of Communications, Philadelphia.

Morgan, M., & Rothschild, N. (1983). Impact of the new television technology: Cable TV, peers, and sex-role cultivation in the electronic environment. *Youth and Society, 15*(1), 33-50.

Nielsen, A. C. (1990). *Nielsen report on television.* New York: Nielsen Media Research.

Nolan, J. D., Galst, J. P., & White, M. A. (1977). Sex bias on children's television programs. *Journal of Psychology, 96,* 197-204.

O'Donnell, W. J., & O'Donnell, K. J. (1978). Update: Sex-role messages in TV commercials. *Journal of Communication, 28*(1), 156-158.

Pearl, D., Bouthilet, L., & Lazar J. (1982). *Television and social behavior: Ten years of scientific progress and implications for the eighties.* Rockville, MD: National Institute of Mental Health.

Peirce, K. (1989). Sex-role stereotyping of children on television: A content analysis of the roles and attributes of child characters. *Sociological Spectrum, 9*(3), 321-328.

Pingree, S. (1978). The effects of non-sexist television commercials and perceptions of reality on children's attitudes about women. *Psychology of Women Quarterly, 2,* 262-276.

Reep, D. C., & Dambrot, F. H. (1987). Television's professional women: Working with men in the 1980s. *Journalism Quarterly, 64*(2/3), 376-381.

Riffe, D., Goldson, H., Saxton, K., & Yu, Y. (1989). Females and minorities in TV ads in 1987 Saturday children's programs. *Journalism Quarterly, 66*(1), 129-136.

Roberts, D. F., & Bachen, C. M. (1981). Mass communication effects. *American Review Psychology, 32,* 307-356.

Roberts, D. F., & Maccoby, N. (1985). Effects of mass communication. In G. Lindzey & E. Aronson (Eds.), *Handbook of social psychology* (3rd ed.). New York: Random House.

Selnow, G. W. (1990). Values in primetime television. *Journal of Communication, 40*(2), 64-74.

Sherman, B. L., & Dominick, J. R. (1986). Violence and sex in music videos: TV and rock 'n' roll. *Journal of Communication, 36*(1), 79-93.

Signorielli, N. (1985). *Role portrayal on television: An annotated bibliography of studies relating to women, minorities, aging, sexual behavior, health, and handicaps.* Westport, CT: Greenwood.

Signorielli, N. (1987). Children and adolescents on television: A consistent pattern of devaluation. *Journal of Early Adolescence, 7*(3), 255-268.

Signorielli, N. (1989). Television and conceptions about sex-roles: Maintaining conventionality and the status quo. *Sex Roles, 21*(5/6), 341-360.

Signorielli, N. (1991a). Adolescents and ambivalence toward marriage: A cultivation analysis. *Youth and Society, 23*(1), 121-149.

Signorielli, N. (1991b). *A sourcebook on children and television.* Westport, CT: Greenwood.

Signorielli, N. (1993). Television and adolescents' perceptions about work. *Youth & Society, 25*(3).

Signorielli, N., & Lears, M. (1992). Children, television and conceptions about chores: Attitudes and behaviors. *Sex Roles, 27*(3/4), 157-170.

Signorielli, N., & Morgan, M. (1990). *Cultivation analysis: New directions in media effects research.* Newbury Park, CA: Sage.

Steenland, S. (1990, November). *What's wrong with this picture? The status of women on screen and behind the camera in entertainment TV.* Washington, DC: National Commission on Working Women of Wider Opportunities for Women.

Streicher, H. W. (1974). The girls in the cartoons. *Journal of Communication, 24*(2), 125-129.

Tan, A. S. (1979). TV beauty ads and role expectations of adolescent female viewers. *Journalism Quarterly, 56*(2), 283-288.

U.S. Surgeon General's Scientific Advisory Committee on Television and Social Behavior. (1972). *Television and growing up: The impact of televised violence.* Washington, DC: U.S. Government Printing Office.

Vernon, J. A., Williams, J. A., Phillips, T., & Wilson, J. (1990). Media stereotyping: A comparison of the way elderly women and men are portrayed on primetime television. *Journal of Women and Aging, 2*(4), 55-68.

Vincent, R. C. (1989). Clio's consciousness raised? Portrayal of women in rock videos, re-examined. *Journalism Quarterly, 66*(1), 155-161.

Vincent, R. C., Davis, D. K., & Boruszkowski, L. A. (1987). Sexism on MTV: The portrayal of women in rock videos. *Journalism Quarterly, 64*(4), 750-755, 941.

Welch, R. L., Huston-Stein, A., Wright, J. C., & Plehal, R. (1979). Subtle sex-role cues in children's commercials. *Journal of Communication, 29*(3), 202-209.

Wertheim, F. (1954). *Seduction of the innocent.* New York: Rinehart.

Williams, T. M. (1986). *The impact of television: A natural experiment in three communities.* New York: Academic Press.

Wright, C. R. (1986). *Mass communication: A sociological perspective* (3rd ed.). New York: Random House.

Wroblewski, R., & Huston, A. C. (1987). Televised occupational stereotypes and their effects on early adolescents: Are they changing? *Journal of Early Adolescence, 7*(3), 283-298.

17. Television, the Portrayal of the Elderly, and Children's Attitudes

PETER M. KOVARIC

Introduction

The one domain in our culture in which one finds consistent diversity is age. With markedly few exceptions, one can find people from a broad range of ages, from the very young to the very old, wherever one looks in real life. Can we expect the same from mediated life? In particular, what can we expect the young to learn about the elderly from television? Like other questions about television's effects on children, this one is really three questions in conceptually separable domains. First, what does television have to say about the elderly; that is, how are the elderly portrayed, and do these portrayals vary by type of programming? What are the demographic and social characteristics of the elderly as they appear on television? Second, how do children process televised information about the elderly? How are television messages about the elderly constructed into beliefs and attitudes about them? And third, what are the beliefs and attitudes that children actually have regarding the elderly as a result of their exposure to television?

The Elderly in the United States

To place television's portrayal of the elderly in context, some background information about the older segment of U.S. society is clearly necessary. Based on 1980 census data (U.S. Bureau of the Census, 1991), it was projected that as of 1995, 13% of the U.S. population would be over 65 years old, and 21% would be over 55 years old. By the year 2000, the latter percentage is expected to rise to 22%. Depending on how one defines "elderly," then, between about one eighth and one fifth of the population falls in that category. By comparison, the number of children 17 years old or younger in 1995 was projected to be 25% of the population, decreasing to 24% by the year 2000. Thus children and adults 55 years and older each comprise nearly one fourth of the population, with slow but steady increases predicted for the older segments and similar decreases for the younger segments.

Ethnicity

Employing revisions of the 1980 census data, estimations for 1989 were that of those over 65, 85% would be non-Hispanic European Americans; 8% African Americans; 4% Latinos; and 2% Asian Americans, Asians, Native Americans, and Aleuts. These figures suggest a somewhat higher proportion of elderly whites than in the population as a whole. Carrying out projections through 1995 to 2000 indicates a slight decrease in non-Hispanic European Americans to 83%, with corresponding increases in all other groups, with African Americans rising to 9%; Latinos to 5%; and Asians, Asian Americans, Native Americans, and Aleuts to 3%.

Gender

The 1989 figures for gender are that 59% of those 65 and older are women and 41% men, figures that are expected to remain approximately the same through 1995 and 2000. These figures vary somewhat within ethnic groups, with the ratio of women to men at 1.5:1 for African Americans; 1.4:1 for non-Hispanic European Americans; 1.4:1 for Latinos; and 1.3:1 for Asians, Asian Americans, Native Americans, and Aleuts. The higher ratio of women to men of course reflect the somewhat longer life expectancy for women.

Health

Although it is commonly perceived that the elderly are more subject to injury and illness than the rest of the population, the census data do not completely bear out this conception. Estimates of injuries in 1988 for people 65 and older suggested that there were

21 injuries per 100 people, which is lower than all other age groups except 45- to 64-year-olds. The figures are slightly higher for males than females in all age groups except the oldest. Rates for acute illness (at least one day) tell a similar story. For upper respiratory illnesses, 18 out of 100 of those over 65 can be expected to become infected, compared to 19 per 100 45- to 65-year-olds, 31 per 100 25- to 44-year-olds, 34 per 100 14- to 24-year-olds, 60 per 100 5- to 17-year-olds, and 91 per 100 children 5 years old or younger. Other respiratory illness and other infections evidence a similar pattern with slightly lower rates overall. For digestive illnesses, those 65 and older show slightly higher rates (6 per 100) than 25- to 64-year-olds, but lower than everyone else. Hospitalization figures, on the other hand, indicate that the severity of illness and injury for the elderly is greater than for younger people. The average hospital stay for those 75 and older was 9 days, 8 days for those 65 to 74. The next highest rates were for adults 45 to 64 and children under 1 year (7 days). Other rates ranged from 4 days to 6 days.

Living Arrangements

For 1989, about 29% of the elderly were projected to live alone, with the rest living in households of two or more people. Of those living alone, 78% were women. Thus a higher proportion of elderly women live by themselves, even taking into account the greater number of women than men over 65. For most of those living alone, it can be assumed that it is not entirely by choice, as 34% of those over 65 are widowed, with an additional 4% divorced and 5% single.

Income and Employment

Poverty is relatively common for those over 65, with 11% living below the poverty level. On a proportional basis, the non-Hispanic white elderly are affected the least, with 10% below the poverty level, whereas 21% and 31% of the Hispanic and African-American elderly, respectively, are impoverished. For each ethnic group, a greater proportion of the elderly live below the poverty level than do 45- to 54-year-olds (by about 50%), but a lower proportion than children under 16 (also by about 50%).

The data on employment of the elderly are more intuitively obvious than some of those reported above, because retirement after the age of 65 is common. For 1989, 58% of the male population between 16 to 19 was employed, increasing to a maximum of 94% of those 35 to 44, then decreasing to 67% of those 55 to 64, with only 17% of those males over 65 working. The figures for women follow a similar pattern: 54% of 16- to 19-year-olds, rising to 76% of 35- to 44-year-olds, then dropping to 45% of 55- to 64-year-olds. Only 8% of those women 65 and older remain employed, though because there are about 50% more elderly women than men, the absolute differences in number of employed elderly women and men is not so great as the proportions lead one to believe.

Victimization

In 1988, crimes against the elderly also occurred at different rates than crimes against the population as a whole. For every 1,000 people 65 and older, there were 22 crimes against persons (rape, robbery, assault, purse snatching, pocket picking) versus 100 crimes for the population as a whole. Crimes against property occurred at a higher overall rate, but were also lower for the elderly: For every 1,000 households headed by a person 65 and older there were 78 crimes (burglary, larceny, auto theft), whereas for the population as a whole there were 170 crimes per 1,000 households.

Television's Representation of the Elderly

Demographic Characteristics of the Elderly on Television

The only way to examine how television represents the elderly is to look at the number of content analyses conducted over the years that have examined how and how often the elderly appear. Of course, content analysis of this type requires coding the age of the characters, which without an explicit reference to a character's age in the story line, may be difficult if one is looking for some "cut point" to distinguish middle-aged characters from elderly characters. Allowing for this difficulty, there has been a general pattern of underrepresentation of the elderly on television, with the caveat that most of the studies were carried out in the 1970s, and may not reflect current practices.

In one of the earliest of these content analyses, Smythe (1954) reports that of all characters in dramatic network programming, only 25% were younger than 20 or older than 50, as opposed to 50% of the actual population. More recently, in a sample of all network programming, Harris and Feinberg (1977) found that 8.3% of the characters coded were over 60 years old, with somewhat more appearing on children's shows, comedies, news and talk programs, and somewhat fewer on game shows, dramas, and soap operas. Northcott (1975) found similar numbers in an analysis of prime-time characters whose appearance lasted more than 2 minutes: 7.5% appeared to be over 60 years old, and only 1.5% seemed over 65.

Other studies have found somewhat smaller representation of the elderly on television. The Cultural Indicators project, which content-analyzed 1 week of network dramatic prime-time fall programming from 1969-1979, along with weekly samples from the spring of 1975, 1976, and 1981, is perhaps the most extensive analysis of programming, and has been reported on by various authors. Signorielli (1983) found that only 6.8% of the 14,037 characters who were coded were between 55 to 64, and only 2.3% were 65 or older. Gerbner, Gross, Signorielli, and Morgan (1980), using a slightly earlier Cultural Indicators sample, also found only 2.3% of the characters were over 65. In the earliest Cultural Indicators report concerning age, Aronoff (1974) found that 4.9% of the prime-time characters coded were functionally elderly. In the only study to report on changes in representations of age over time, Greenberg, Simmons, Hogan, and Atkin (1980) found that the number of characters over 60 appearing in fall network drama of 1975-1977 decreased from 4% to 3% to 2%. In the only exception to these general findings, Petersen (1973), who used a fairly small random sample of prime-time dramatic programming, found that 13% of the characters were played by actors over 65 or seemed to be over 65 in the program in which they appeared.

A few studies have focused on particular genres, and suggest that there is some variability among them. For instance, Greenberg, Korzenny, and Atkin (1979) found that in the 1975-1976 season, 36%, 44%, and 7% of the elderly characters appeared in situation comedies, crime shows, and cartoons respectively. For the same genre of programs, the percentages for the 1976-1977 season were 33%, 29%, and 10%. Levinson (1973) found that 4% of the human characters in Saturday cartoons were elderly, whereas a later study (Bishop & Krause, 1984) found 7%, but in neither case could precise age categories be established for coding because of the general lack of information about cartoon characters. Looking at weekend daytime characters (partly, but not exclusively, cartoons), Gerbner et al. (1980) found only 1.4% were 65 or older. The picture is slightly different on daytime soap operas, of which the elderly comprise a significant audience share and children do not. Cassatta, Anderson, and Skill (1980) found that 15.9% of the characters appeared to be 55 or older, though only 9% were over 60; Elliott (1984) found that 20.6% of the characters appeared to be 50 or older, though only 8% of these appeared to be over 60.

Some of the content analyses proceed further to examine other age-related demographic characteristics. Aronoff (1974) found that elderly men on prime time outnumbered elderly women by a ratio of 2.7:1, which was the same ratio for men to women overall. Gerbner et al. (1980) found a men to women ratio of 2.7:1 in prime time, and 2:1 in children's daytime weekend programming. Signorielli's (1983) prime-time sample produced a ratio of 2.3:1. Higher ratios of men to women were found by Greenberg et al. (1980), ranging from 1.3:1 for 1976-1977 to 4.3:1 for 1975-1976, with 1977-1978 falling between these two ratios. In Petersen's (1973) more restricted sample, the ratio of the number of men over 65 to the number of similarly aged women was 9.7:1. In a more recent study, Dail (1988) found that in popular prime-time family-oriented drama, for those 55 and over, the male to female ratio was 2.5:1.

In only two reports is there an explicit report on ethnicity and age, and then only for whites and nonwhites. Signorielli (1983) found that 87.6% of those characters 65 and older were white. Of the white elderly, women comprised 30.5%; of the nonwhite elderly, women comprised 29.7%. Both of these figures reverse and expand on the numbers in real life. Greenberg et al. (1980) found that 88% (1975-1976), 92% (1976-1977) and 94% (1977-1978) of the characters over 65 were white.

Overall, then, it appears that with the possible exception of daytime soap operas, one of the few genres that children over the age of 5 have neither the opportunity nor the inclination to view, the elderly have been underrepresented by a substantial amount in proportion to their frequency in the population. Conversely, the ratio of elderly men to elderly women on television, rather than being about 2:3 as it is in the population, is not only reversed, but the discrepancy ranges somewhere between about 2:1 and 3:1. This pattern reflects the general preponderance of males on television (e.g., Gerbner et al., 1980; Signorielli, 1983). The only area in which television can be said to come close to reflecting the reality of the elderly is in the relative representation of whites and nonwhites, though of course, in this case, nonwhite representation nearly vanishes because of the underrepresentation of the elderly overall.

Social Characteristics of the Elderly on Television

A number of content analyses have examined various physical, social, and psychological characteristics of the elderly portrayed on television. As with the coding of age, coding of these characteristics requires judgments that are neither completely reliable nor based on universally accepted criteria. Thus they vary somewhat from study to study.

In ratings of health and physical activity, the elderly appear to be in slightly better shape than the rest of the television population. Petersen (1973) found that 82% of the elderly characters were in good health, and that 93% were rated as active. Using somewhat different criteria, Harris and Feinberg (1977) found that portrayals of health problems increased with age, with only 6% of the characters under 50 experiencing health problems, 14% of 50- to 60-year-olds, and 25% of the 60- to 70-year-olds. Interestingly, however, about 13% of the 50- to 70-year-olds were engaged in moderate to high physical activity, compared to only 7-8% of the 30- to 50-year-olds. The relative health of the elderly becomes much more apparent in an examination of daytime soap operas, in which Cassatta et al. (1980) found that 90% of the older characters were in good health while this was not so for characters between 22 to 45.

The social roles in which the elderly are portrayed appear to be moderately varied. Harris and Feinberg (1977) found only one instance of prime-time romantic involvement by a couple over 50, and none by anyone over 60. On the other hand, ratings of authority and esteem increase with increasing age, mainly as a result of increases for males, most of whom appear on news and talk programs (Harris &, Feinberg, 1977). Again, the exception to this general rule is older women on daytime soap operas, who tend to be portrayed as official or unofficial advisors and treated with respect (Downing, 1974; Elliott, 1984), although the number of professionally employed elderly women is considerably lower than that of similarly aged men (Downing, 1974).

Greenberg et al. (1979) examined a number of social characteristics of the elderly in their multiyear analysis. Averaged over the 2 years for which they report data, those characters 60 years and older tended to be upper rather than lower class, but much less frequently than any other age group. In terms of positive social behavior, older adults tended to exhibit and be the recipients of altruism and affection at about the same rates as other age groups. Negative social behavior was more mixed: The elderly were less frequently targets or agents of physical aggression than younger people, but more often agents of verbal aggression.

The Cultural Indicators project provides a number of measures of social characteristics of the elderly. However, rather than using ratings of chronological age to classify characters for these measures, ratings of functional age are employed (children/adolescents, young adults without settled personal and job responsibilities, settled adults, and older adults). Because a smaller proportion of all male characters over 65 (76.7%) versus females characters (90%) are coded as functionally elderly, and because the findings concerning social characteristics only refer to major characters, the following results must be regarded as only suggestive. Results from Signorielli (1983) will be described because they are reported in the most detail; findings concerning the elderly will be compared with those for settled adults and young adults. The Cultural Indicators data suggest that older adults are more likely to be portrayed as handicapped (4.3% vs. 1.8% and 2.1%), and as having physical illness (10.8% vs. 7.3% and 8.7%), but no more or less likely to have mental illness (2.2% vs. 2.2% and 5.0%).

The Elderly in Television Commercials

Only two studies have included data on how the elderly have been treated in commercials, so one must be circumspect about making too much of them. Still, the data are in some ways quite different from those derived from the rest of broadcast programming, and hence bear some comment. Harris and Feinberg (1977) found that although people over 60 represented 10.6% of the characters portrayed in commercials (slightly higher than in the rest of the programming schedule), the ratio of males to females in various age groups varied substantially: In the 20 to 30 age group the ratio of males to females was 1:5.5, whereas for 50- to 60-year-olds it was 1.6:1. Compared to the rest of the programming analyzed, characters in commercials experience increased health problems, and this increase is primarily attributable to the elderly. For instance, 35% of the 60- to 70-year-olds in commercials are portrayed as having some sort of health problem, whereas 25% of the characters appearing in other programming suffer similarly.

In the only other study (Fransher, 1973) directly addressing television commercials and the elderly, the data are not presented in such a way as to allow clear interpretation. Apparently older people were utilized in about 8% of the 100 commercials randomly sampled, and only when the product being advertised was designed particularly for them or when the tone of the commercial was humorous. In an extended analysis of a Pepsi commercial of the time, Fransher argues that advertisers rely on associating their products with youthful, attractive, healthy people, to the near exclusion of the elderly.

Children's Attitudes and Beliefs and Television's Portrayal of the Elderly—Where's the Connection?

From the forgoing discussion, it seems rather obvious that television's representation of the elderly does not begin to approach the reality of their numbers and diversity in this country (Davis & Davis, 1985). Content analyses over the last two decades or so suggest that in television society there are not very many old people in general, that most of them are men, and that although healthy, they are ineffective and relatively powerless, subject to criminal victimization, and so on. Most of these images do not represent reality. Children's attitudes and beliefs about the elderly, although not uniformly wrong or negative, appear to be more like television's characterization of older people than what older people are really like. Further, there is surprisingly little research on children's attitudes and beliefs that directly correspond to many of the television messages about the elderly, an empirical deficit that should be rectified.

Further, although the empirical basis is scant, it is not unreasonable to conclude that children, in the relative absence of other information or experience, are likely to learn at least some of television's rather undesirable lessons concerning the elderly. Some attempts have been made to provide educational experiences for children that will alter their beliefs and attitudes about the elderly. Carstensen, Mason, and Caldwell (1982) found that 15-minute daily reading lessons for 6- to 9-year-olds by elderly tutors improved the children's attitudes toward the elderly. Using a similar approach, preschoolers were found to rank the elderly more positively on all 10 semantic differential scales administered after an 8-week program of daily interactions with teaching assistants 55 years old or older (Dellmann-Jenkins, Lambert, Fruit, & Dinero, 1986). However, Seefeldt (1987) found that preschoolers who visited a nursing home once a week for a year formed more negative attitudes toward the elderly than did a control group. Perhaps not unexpectedly, then, it may be that experiences with the elderly in which they are active, helpful, and effective are more likely to positively affect children's beliefs and attitudes. Assuming that such experiences with the elderly on television would have a similar effect as those in real life, there is certainly a strong argument to be made for efforts to push the television industry toward more visible, more diverse, and at least somewhat more positive representations of the elderly.

Yet these conclusions are based on a commonly asserted connection between the television programming described in content analyses and viewers' social beliefs and attitudes. This connection does not usually take into account the relative frequency with which viewers, in this case children, are actually exposed to the content being analyzed, or the relative importance the viewers ascribe to the content. For example, if there are only a few elderly characters regularly appearing on prime-time television, but those characters appear in extremely popular programs, should they be somehow "weighted" more heavily than characters in less frequently viewed programs? Stated another way, content analysis examines a television menu that might appear to be primarily California Cuisine, but what is actually served to the public might turn out to be more like American Gothic. Put in concrete terms, if all the programming children watched out of what is available was *The Golden Girls; Matlock; Murder, She Wrote; Empty Nest;* and *60 Minutes,* what would one conclude about television's portrayal of the elderly? And what would one expect children to learn about the elderly? From a television diet like this, one would expect child viewers to believe that the elderly are financially secure, mostly employed at high-level jobs, bright, funny, healthy, and assertive. Perhaps, then, it is time to link the images described by content analysis with the images actually consumed by children, which should yield a better idea of what television is actually serving up, and how it is likely to affect them.

Although the example above is obviously extreme, it illustrates several points with respect to the issues of how the elderly are depicted on television and what children are likely to learn from these depictions. First, it is not just what is being broadcast that is important to consider, one must also take into account what is being viewed. Second, what is being viewed influences what is being broadcast. As long as television is primarily a market-driven enterprise, any attempts to diversify its programming will be limited by audience acceptance. If the programming that appeals to children does not feature elderly characters, then the programs that do, no matter how well intentioned, will not be viewed and will most certainly be canceled, at least to the extent that children constitute the primary audience for them. A cursory examination of the November 1991 Nielsen data reveals that of the 20 series most viewed by teenagers, every one features a teenager as a prominent member of the cast, and almost none feature elderly characters on a regular basis. The final point, of course, is that because children actually comprise only a small segment of the viewing audience at any given time (except Saturday mornings), they can only have a small influence on what is available. Yet perhaps this is the one cause for hope in this area: With the "graying" of the United States, the number of programs that appeal to the older members of society is likely to increase, and to the extent that these programs feature a variety of elderly characters *and* can simultaneously appeal to young viewers, primarily by featuring appealing young characters dealing with youth-oriented issues, children's learning more about the elderly can at least become an attainable goal.

References

Aronoff, C. (1974). Old age in prime time. *Journal of Communication, 24*(1), 86-87.

Bishop, J. M., & Krause, D. R. (1984). Depictions of aging and old age on Saturday morning television. *Gerontologist, 24,* 91-94.

Carstensen, L., Mason, S. E., & Caldwell, E. C. (1982). Children's attitudes toward the elderly: An intergenerational technique for change. *Educational Gerontology, 8*, 291-301.

Cassatta, B., Anderson, P., & Skill, T. (1980). The older adult in daytime serial drama. *Journal of Communication, 30*, 48-49.

Dail, P. W. (1988). Prime-time television portrayals of older adults in the context of family life. *Gerontologist, 28*, 700-706.

Davis, R. H., & Davis, J. A. (1985). *TV's image of the elderly.* Lexington, MA: D. C. Heath.

Dellmann-Jenkins, M., Lambert, D., Fruit, D, & Dinero, T. (1986). Old and young together: Effect of an educational program on preschoolers' attitudes toward older people. *Childhood Education, 62*, 206-212.

Downing, M. (1974). Heroine of the daytime serial. *Journal of Communication, 24*(2), 130-137.

Elliott, J. (1984). The daytime television drama portrayal of older adults. *Gerontologist, 24*, 628-633.

Fransher, J. S. (1973). "It's the Pepsi generation...." Accelerated aging and the television commercial. *International Journal of Aging and Human Development, 4*, 245-255.

Gerbner, G., Gross, L., Signorielli, N., & Morgan, M. (1980). Aging with television: Images on television drama and conceptions of social reality. *Journal of Communication, 30*, 37-47.

Greenberg, B. S., Korzenny, F., & Atkin, C. (1979). The portrayal of aging: Trends on commercial television. *Research on Aging, 1*, 319-334.

Greenberg, B. S., Simmons, K. W., Hogan, L., & Atkin, C. (1980). Three seasons of television characters: A demographic analysis. *Journal of Broadcasting, 24*, 49-60.

Harris, A. J., & Feinberg, J. F. (1977). Television and aging: Is what you see what you get? *Gerontologist, 17*, 464-468.

Levinson, R. M. (1973). From Olive Oyle to Sweet Polly Purebred: Sex role stereotypes and televised cartoons. *Journal of Popular Culture, 31*, 561-572.

Northcott, H. (1975). Too young, too old—Age in the world of television. *Gerontologist, 15*, 184-186.

Petersen, M. (1973). The visibility and image of old people on television. *Journalism Quarterly, 50*, 569-573.

Seefeldt, C. (1987). The effects of preschoolers' visits to a nursing home. *Gerontologist, 27*, 228-232.

Signorielli, N. (1983). Health, prevention and television: Images of the elderly and perceptions of social reality. *Prevention in Human Services, 3*, 97-117.

Smythe, D. W. (1954). Reality as presented on television. *Public Opinion Quarterly, 18*, 143-156.

U.S. Bureau of the Census. (1991). *Statistical abstract of the United States: 1991.* Washington, DC: U.S. Government Printing Office.

18. Changing Channels

The Portrayal of People With Disabilities on Television

ELAINE MAKAS

Although we often refer to television as a "medium" (or as part of the collective "media"), we usually do not take into consideration the true meaning of this term—a meaning that may be particularly relevant to a discussion of the portrayal of people with disabilities on television. Webster defines medium as a "go-between" or a "channel of communication." As such, the term can be applied to means of communication ranging from television, radio, and newspapers to psychic individuals who serve at seances as intermediaries between earthly beings and beings in the spirit world. Although the focus of this chapter, obviously, will be on a very technological medium—television—the psychic medium presents a useful analogy by which to introduce the crucial role that television can play in forming and altering attitudes toward persons with disabilities.

A "successful" seance, according to true believers, requires the participants to remain passive and to put their total trust in the psychic. Because the psychic is assumed to be the only one who is in direct contact with the spirit world, his or her interpretation of the information relayed to seance participants is accepted as the truth. Although one might hope that consumers of other types of media would be both less passive and more discerning, the fact remains that we, the listening and viewing audience, often attribute special powers to our modern media and accept on faith the interpretations relayed to us by these media. This is particularly true in cases in which we have relatively little direct contact with those from the "other" world.

Although most nondisabled people have had some contact with individuals who have disabilities, direct contact between these two groups remains quite limited. Certainly, few nondisabled persons know individuals with disabilities well enough for them to share information that is as intimate as that revealed to us by the people who populate our television and movie screens. Even people who have disabilities themselves may be somewhat limited in their associations with others who also have disabilities. As a result, many of us rely heavily on the technological media to serve as our interpreters, giving these media the same power given the psychic medium to accurately portray or to misrepresent information from what many consider to be the "other," somewhat mysterious world of individuals with disabilities.

In some ways, television's role in influencing perceptions of people with disabilities is similar to its role in affecting attitudes toward other groups. We form impressions of a particular group based on our experiences with individual representatives of that group. If we are exposed to relatively few individuals or to individuals in relatively few roles, we have little choice but to form limited stereotypes and to rely on these stereotypes. On the other hand, if we are exposed to numerous individuals who represent a particular group, and these individuals are seen in a wide variety of roles, stereotypes begin to break down, and we have more opportunity to identify areas of commonality between ourselves and them.

Until the 1970s, people of color rarely appeared on television, and those who did were portrayed in roles that matched the stereotypic images held by other people. Virtually all of the African Americans we saw, for example, were athletes, entertainers, criminals, or Steppin Fetchits. Few viewers, including African-American viewers, could identify with these individuals. Nowadays, with greater exposure to persons of color on TV and to a broader spectrum of roles, almost all of us can find some areas in which we are more similar than different.

There are differences, however, in the role that television plays in forming our impressions of people with disabilities compared to its role in influencing attitudes toward members of other minority groups. Some of these differences may simply be the result of a time lag. Although many would argue (and justifiably so) that we have not yet achieved full racial integration, the fact remains that concerted efforts to achieve such integration have been under way for more than 20 years. As a result, most white Americans have come into contact with Americans of color in a variety of real-world settings. Therefore, televised representatives of a racial/ethnic minority group constitute a small percentage of the members of that group whom we "know." Equally relevant to the present discussion is the fact that media producers have experienced both social and legal pressure to monitor and to improve their portrayals of racial/ethnic minority persons, resulting in greater diversity of roles.

Integration into mainstream society of people with disabilities, on the other hand, is a much more recent phenomenon, and real-world contact between individuals differing in physical or mental abilities remains limited. Consequently, our televised "acquaintances" who have disabilities represent a larger proportion of all the people with disabilities whom we "know." Because social and legal pressure to monitor and to improve televised portrayals of persons with disabilities is also relatively recent, the roles given to them still lack diversity.

There is another difference, however, between portrayals of people who have disabilities and portrayals of people from most other minority groups. This difference relates to the nature of the identification the viewer experiences with the individual observed. When seeing a person who differs from her- or himself in terms of race or ethnicity, the viewer knows that the person is from a group that she or he will never join. As a result, the viewer can enjoy discovering commonalities between her- or himself and the televised individual without feeling threatened by these commonalities. Observing a person who has a disability, however, may be more personally threatening, particularly when the media focuses, as it often does, on portrayals of people with traumatically acquired or progressive disabilities. The viewer knows that he or she is susceptible to a similar disability. Therefore, even though (or, maybe, because) the potential for identification with the portrayed individual is greater, the resistance to this identification may also be greater.

In a 1980-1981 analysis of television programming (Makas, 1981), 168 hours of randomly selected viewing of afternoon and prime-time network TV resulted in 40 portrayals of people with disabilities, and 150 hours of specifically targeted viewing of both network and public broadcast television resulted in another 121 portrayals. Research by Turow and Coe (1985) suggests a rather dramatic increase in such portrayals by 1983. Seventy-one of the portrayals reported by Turow and Coe in 90.5 hours of TV viewing appear to meet the criteria used by Makas in her 1980-1981 study. Although systematic, quantitative assessments of televised portrayals of people with disabilities seem to have waned over the past decade, there is a great deal of anecdotal evidence that the frequency of these portrayals has remained high. There are numerous major and minor characters with disabilities on weekly prime-time shows and on daily soap operas, and there are many onetime appearances by persons who have disabilities on regular programs and in movies each week. However, even if we use the most conservative estimate, it is safe to assume that we, as television viewers, "meet" at least one individual who has a disability every 4.2 hours.

On the other hand, actual contact between persons who have disabilities and those who do not remains relatively low. In one study, for example, Makas (1989) asked undergraduate students to specify people with disabilities they had known personally in any capacity (classmates, neighbors, relatives, friends of relatives, etc.). The average student identified only two persons. Although some of the individuals with disabilities the students specified were people they knew "very well," the majority were not. It is also important to note that personally knowing someone who uses a wheelchair does not necessarily enhance one's familiarity with people who are deaf. To gain that particular insight, one may resort to televised "acquaintances."

Research by Langer, Fiske, Taylor, and Chanowitz (1976) suggests that even indirect contact with persons who have disabilities may facilitate actual interaction. Langer et al. found that when given the opportunity to do so unobserved, subjects spent significantly more time looking at photographs of people with visible disabilities than at photographs of nondisabled people. They also found that subjects who had been given an opportunity to clandestinely observe a person with a disability, compared to subjects not given this opportunity, were more comfortable when later interacting with the individual. It is likely that nondisabled people experience competing motives when interacting with an individual whose physical appearance differs from the norm: a curiosity motive to visually examine a unique stimulus, and a social motive to avoid breaking the taboo against staring at a person who has a disability. Langer et al. (1976), therefore, might have identified one way by which this conflict can be resolved. If this explanation is correct, the visual media would seem to be an ideal means by which the public could covertly satisfy its curiosity about disability without breaking social standards, thus leading to more comfortable real-life interactions between persons who have disabilities and those who do not.

Although habituation alone may facilitate actual contact between the two groups to some extent, it is also important to consider the salience of the disability within the situation. If a television viewer only encounters people with disabilities under circumstances in which the disability is the focal point of the portrayal, it is easy for the viewer to conclude that the disability is also the all-encompassing focus of attention for a person who has a disability. The highlighting of one characteristic that differentiates between us, as TV viewers, and those we observe on TV interferes with our ability to acknowledge commonalities. On the other hand, if our televised "acquaintances" are introduced to us as people who only incidentally differ from us physically or mentally, we are more likely to take into consideration other defining factors about them.

Most televised portrayals of people with disabilities, however, do highlight the disability. In the Makas (1981) study, for example, the 161 televised portrayals of people with disabilities seen during the 2-month observation period were classified as either factual or fictional and as either focused on the individual or focused on her or his disability. This classification resulted in four categories: fictional disability, real disability, fictional person with a disability, and real person with a disability. The two categories in which the disability was highlighted encompassed more than 90% of the portrayals. Other researchers have found a similarly high incidence of "disability" portrayals (as opposed to "person with a disability" portrayals) in more recent samples (Cumberbatch & Negrine, 1992; Turow & Coe, 1985).

The largest number of portrayals in the Makas (1981) study fit into the "fictional disability" category. The programs on which they occurred included movies, weekly series, and soap operas. The unifying factor in these portrayals was that the plot necessitated a disability, and as a result, a character with a disability filled the role. (In a few instances, the actor or actress playing the role actually had a disability; the categorization of the portrayal as fictional refers to the story line rather than to the disability itself.) It is important to reiterate that the disability in these cases was more important than any other characteristic associated with the individual portrayed as having the disability.

The second most frequently represented category in the Makas (1981) study was the "real disability" portrayal. Although the individuals seen in these portrayals actually had disabilities and were presented as themselves, their disabilities were still the primary reason for their inclusion on these programs. Several "real disability" portrayals occurred on *That's Incredible,* the "incredible" part being that someone could accomplish a particular task despite his or her disability. Two examples of this type of portrayal were an autistic man who played the piano, and a man with both legs amputated who lifted weights. Although both piano playing and weight lifting require some degree of skill, it was apparent that these two men would not have appeared on national TV had they not had disabilities.

Unfortunately, there were very few "person with a disability" portrayals in the Makas (1981) sample. Among those that did occur, however, was one very positive "real" portrayal on *Neighborhood News Conference,* a program focusing on issues of local interest. Chuck Rich, who is a wheelchair user, served as the moderator for a panel discussion among community leaders. There was no attempt either to overly rely on or to avoid camera angles in which Rich's wheelchair was visible, and there was no mention of his disability. What the television viewer saw was simply a skilled interviewer leading a discussion that had nothing to do with disability.

The rarest of all portrayals in the Makas (1981) study was the "fictional person with a disability" portrayal. Included among the few that did occur were wheelchair users who appeared in nonspeaking roles as extras in the newsroom on *Lou Grant* and in the coffee shop on *Happy Days.* The message relayed by these brief, but very significant appearances was that people with disabilities are a part of everyday life, and they do the same things as everybody else.

The paucity of (both fictional and real) "person with a disability" portrayals in the Makas (1981) study (as well as in the research by Turow & Coe, 1985; Cumberbatch & Negrine, 1992) is disturbing in that it reinforces a very stubborn myth about people with disabilities: that disability is a full-time occupation. Some producers, however, justify the exclusion of "extraneous" individuals who have disabilities from television programming by asserting that they do not wish to exploit people with disabilities. Zola (1985) suggests another reason for this exclusion: "Television and film directors have been reluctant to insert an individual with an obvious physical disability into a minor role where the disability is irrelevant to the story for fear of diverting attention from where the focus of action should be" (p. 12). This limitation of "person with a disability" portrayals may result in self-fulfilling prophesy. If we, as viewers, only see people with disabilities whose disabilities are "relevant," then "irrelevant" disability will indeed be distracting, and persons who have disabilities will certainly feel that they are being exploited.

In addition to an exaggeration of the salience of disability in a person's life, television also presents a distorted image of other characteristics of people who have disabilities. As Zola (1985) points out, the majority of people with disabilities who populate our TV screens are nonethnic, relatively young, unmarried, white males. Cumberbatch and Negrine (1992) note that these demographic biases occur in all televised portrayals, but they are particularly apparent among persons who have disabilities. In their sample of British TV programs, for example, 65% of all individuals who did not have disabilities and 71% of all individuals who did were male. Makas (1981) found 65% of her portrayals of people with disabilities to be male. These results are not consistent with 1984 U.S. Census data, which indicated that only 41% of persons with disabilities were males (J. McNeil, personal communication, July 31, 1992).

The misrepresentation of the ages of people with disabilities is even more blatant. Makas (1981), for example, categorized 57% of her portrayals to be of 31- to 50-year-old persons, and only 9% to be of people over the age of 60. Cumberbatch and Negrine (1992) pointed out that this age bias occurred in their total sample of British TV programs, but it was most apparent in the programs in their sample that were produced in the United States. They reported that 47% of the people observed in this subsample were between the ages of 30 and 49, and only 5% were over 60. In stark contrast, it should be noted that the 1984 U.S. Census placed 24% of people with disabilities in the 35- to 54-year-old category, and 41% in the over 65 category.

Many other similar biases in televised portrayals of persons with disabilities have been found: underrepresentation of racial/ethnic minority group members (Makas, 1981); underrepresentation of married or partnered individuals (Cumberbatch & Negrine, 1992; Makas, 1981); underrepresentation of parents (Makas, 1981);

overrepresentation of professionally employed persons (Makas, 1981; Zola, 1985); overrepresentation of individuals with moderately severe (as opposed to mild or severe) disabilities (Cumberbatch & Negrine, 1992); and overrepresentation of locomotor and disfiguring disabilities and underrepresentation of communication disabilities (Cumberbatch & Negrine, 1992).

It is not enough, however, simply to increase the number and demographic diversity of persons with disabilities who appear on our TV screens. Attention must also be given to the quality of these portrayals. At one time, it was assumed that increased contact between members of different groups would automatically lead to more positive attitudes. However, this simplistic notion was rejected in the 1950s by race relations researchers (e.g., Allport, 1954; Cook & Selltiz, 1955) who pointed out that a large number of contact variables influence the types of attitudes formed. Makas (1989), for example, found that the attitudes of nondisabled people toward persons with disabilities can be influenced positively or negatively by variables such as the pleasantness, frequency, and intimacy of the interaction, and by the relative status of the interactants. These results, in combination with Palmerton and Frumkin's (1969) finding that increased contact is related to both more intense positive attitudes and more intense negative attitudes, suggest that the quality of the contact between groups is at least as important as the quantity of interactions. Although the impact of these variables on attitudes has not yet been tested in terms of vicarious contact through the media, it is very likely that negative televised portrayals of individuals who have disabilities may result in negative attitudes toward people with disabilities in general. This places a special burden on media professionals to assure that whatever vicarious contact does occur is both accurate and positive.

Despite an apparent increase since the Makas (1981) study in the number of persons on television who have disabilities, the majority of these individuals are seen in a very limited range of stereotypic roles intended to set the stage symbolically and to elicit specific emotions from the viewing audience. One common image is that of the person with a disability as evil or sinister.

In other portrayals within this sinister/evil image category, the disability is presented as a symbol of deviance rather than as the cause of deviance. Although the connection between disability and evil is expressed less directly, it is no more subtle. As Biklen (1981) suggests, "It is almost as if script writers had read the early works of the physical anthropologist, Lombroso, who claimed a clear relationship between certain physiological characteristics . . . and criminality" (p. 3). It is useful to note that 16% of the televised portrayals reported by Gardner and Radel (1978) were categorized as "deviant persons," and that Cumberbatch and Negrine (1992) found characters with disabilities in 32% of the crime shows that they monitored (although, in some instances, the person with the disability was the victim rather than the criminal).

Thurer (1980) suggests that this connection between disability and evil is intentionally established during childhood. Disability, she proposes, "simplifies and concretizes abstractions to render them accessible to the young mind. What is left is a definitive shorthand —deformity equals immorality. Pinocchio becomes progressively more disfigured as his integrity slips, as does the portrait of Dorian Gray. . . . Virtue is rewarded with physical grace, so that the ugly duckling turns into a swan; the frog, a king; and the Beast, a prince" (pp. 13-14). Considering the prevalence of these images in books and media targeted specifically toward children, it is not at all surprising to find that children must often be taught (or, more accurately, retrained) not to fear or avoid people with visible disabilities.

According to Longmore (1985), the connection between disability and evil serves a social function as well as a literary one. By linking physical appearance to morality, we can conclude that disability is a punishment for evil, and thus, we can justify our avoidance of people with disabilities and our exclusion of them from mainstream society. Longmore adds that such "justified" exclusion is vividly presented in the media by the fact that the person with a disability, or in some cases, the "monster" is often killed off by the end of the program, often to the great relief of all. Longmore's views are supported by Cumberbatch and Negrine's (1992) finding that people portrayed on television as having disabilities were more than three times as likely as those not having disabilities to be dead by the end of the program.

At the opposite end of the image spectrum, although equally stereotypic and damaging, are televised portrayals of people with disabilities as dependent or pathetic. In one way, as Longmore (1985) suggests, the two images are related in that both reflect a loss of self-control. Disability, according to these portrayals may result in evil (a moral loss of self-control) or in dependence (a physical loss of self-control). A vivid example of the latter is the annual reappearance of Tiny Tim in *A Christmas Carol.* Each December, this pathetic child limps into our consciousness to remind us that we, the "non-disabled majority," must bear the burden of those with disabilities, and that we alone can save "them" by our acts of charity and goodness. Gardner and Radel (1978) categorized 48% of the people with disabilities portrayed in their sample as dependent, and Cumberbatch and Negrine (1992) noted that more than half of the programs observed during their study were "likely to leave the audience feeling sorry for the disabled characters" (p. 54). Kent (1988) suggests that this Tiny Tim image is particularly prevalent in portrayals of women with disabilities: "Generally she is both physically and economically dependent upon others, constantly draining their resources and giving little in return" (p. 93).

The association between disability and dependence leads readily to two other common images on television: that of a person with a disability as the victim of manipulation, and that of the person with a disability as the manipulator. These related images occurred with startling consistency, particularly on soap operas, during the Makas (1981) study, and they continue to recur as primary story lines in the "soaps" in 1992.

The association between disability and dependence, however, can produce an entirely different image. There are many televised portrayals in which assistance is not received, and the person with a disability is allowed to blunder along on her or his own. These portrayals are intended to provide "entertainment" for the viewing audience. Cumberbatch and Negrine (1992) point out, for example, that hearing loss is often used in sitcoms to produce the misunderstanding necessary for a humorous plot. Some of these portrayals are targeted toward adult viewers. Often, however, the audience targeted for these "humorous" portrayals is much younger. Longmore (1985) identifies the most frequently seen of these: "stuttering Porky Pig, speech-impaired Elmer Fudd, near-sighted Mr. McGoo, and mentally retarded Dopey" (p. 31).

Although some of these dependency images are intended to entertain (as in these "humorous" portrayals), and others seem intended to warn (as in the manipulation portrayals), there appears to be an overriding social goal—to make the viewer feel good about himself or herself. By assuring us that people with disabilities are unable to fend for themselves and therefore need the assistance of nondisabled people to survive, we, the "nondisabled majority," can feel superior, and at the same time, benevolent.

Television offers another stereotypic image of people with disabilities that on the surface at least, appears to contradict the dependency portrayals already noted. In this image, the person with a disability is seen as being courageous and inspirational. She or he is presented as someone who has overcome tremendous obstacles. In Wright's (1960) terms, this image presents the "coping" pole of the "coping-succumbing dichotomy," whereas the dependency images reflect the "succumbing" pole. In very British terms, Cumberbatch and Negrine (1992) report that many televised news items in their sample referred to people with disabilities as being "brave and plucky."

In some instances, the person or fictional character is truly successful, although the obstacles overcome have little or nothing to do with the physical limitations of the disability. However, because the focus of the portrayal is the disability, the viewer is left with the impression that the individual's abilities are "gifts" to compensate for the disability (Longmore, 1985). In other instances, the person's achievements involve the surmounting of problems directly linked to her or his disability. According to Cumberbatch and Negrine (1992): "By employing certain stereotypes, for example, the courageous disabled person facing up to adversity, it [TV] does not give an adequate account of the everyday experiences of the majority of people with disabilities and of those close to them who, like the able-bodied more generally, stumble from day to day. . . . People with disabilities, as well as the able-bodied, are then supposed to admire and emulate the courageous few" (p. 88).

Longmore (1985) suggests that one social function of courageous and inspirational portrayals of people with disabilities may be that they validate the power of positive thinking, thus allowing those who do not have disabilities to feel better about themselves. "If someone so tragically 'crippled' can overcome the obstacles confronting them, think what you, without such a 'handicap' can do" (p. 35). Both Longmore (1985) and Zola (1985), however, suggest a second more subtle purpose served by programs that depict overly successful adjustment. Zola notes that these portrayals emphasize "individual traits and actions as the way 'to overcome disability.' This individualizing of the problem of disability is at the same time a way of depoliticizing it. The focus on individual achievement, virtues, and weaknesses thereby denies the critical importance of social, political, and economic barriers to the full participation of people with disabilities in society" (p. 15). Longmore (1985) takes this notion one step further by suggesting that characters without disabilities are frequently the ones with enough insight into the problem to be able to guide the characters with disabilities toward their successful adjustment.

Television has exhibited some change in portrayals of people with disabilities over the past 15 years, due in large part to pressure from disability rights activists, both as individuals and as organizations (e.g., the Media Access Office of the California Foundation on Employment and Disability, Rehabilitation International, EIN SOF Communications). In some instances, this activism has led to a reduction in blatantly negative portrayals. In addition to reducing (to some extent) negative portrayals, TV executives have also increased realistically positive portrayals and neutral portrayals of people who have disabilities.

There are a number of other fictional characters with disabilities who now appear regularly on television programs. Among these portrayals are Benny, a clerk on *L.A. Law* who has mental retardation; Byron, an attorney on *Another World* who uses a wheelchair; David, a therapist on *Another World* who has had a leg amputated; Corky, a young man on *Life Goes On* who has mental retardation; Tess, a deaf attorney on *Reasonable Doubts;* Theo, a college student on *The Cosby Show* who has dyslexia; and Paul, the object of romantic intent of two very attractive women on *Loving* who is a wheelchair user.

There is also an increase in other types of "fictional person with a disability" portrayals. *The Trials of Rosie O'Neill,* for example, includes a wheelchair user who plays a background role as one of the workers in the law office. This image of "ordinariness," which Cumberbatch and Negrine (1992) strongly advocate, however, may be seen most clearly in many of the ads now appearing on TV.

It is also important to acknowledge an apparent increase in "real person with a disability" portrayals. Most show hosts, for example, no longer feel the need to focus on an individual's disability if it is not the specific purpose of the program. *Sesame Street* must be singled out for its continued fine practice of including children and adults with disabilities, both in segments that deal with disability and in those that do not.

Despite the progress made in televised portrayals of people with disabilities, much remains to be accomplished. As seen above, the old stereotypes of people with disabilities still occur frequently on our television screens. Some of these images can be attributed to the rerunning of old programs and movies on network and cable TV. Others, however, though new, still reflect the types of portrayals that are neither acceptable to disability rights activists nor likely to enhance understanding between those who have disabilities and those who do not.

Media executives have demonstrated the ability to change with the times. We as television viewers are no longer offered such a limited number of people of color in an even more limited variety of roles with whom we may seek commonalities. It is time now for the same concerted effort to be made in diversifying our options among persons with disabilities we see on TV. As a result of legislation in the past 20 years, actual contact between people who have disabilities and those who do not is increasing. In the meantime, however, we television viewers will continue to file into our living room, darken the lights, possibly even hold hands, and seek guidance from our medium. Perhaps our medium, the television, can teach us to communicate directly with those who at first glance might appear to be so different than us.

References

Allport, G. W. (1954). *The nature of prejudice.* Reading, MA: Addison-Wesley.

Biklen, D. (1981). Should "The Ugly Duckling" be banned? In D. Biklen & L. Bailey (Eds.), *Rudely stamp'd: Imaginal disability and prejudice* (pp. 1-10). Washington, DC: University Press of America.

Cook, S. W., & Selltiz, C. (1955). Some factors which influence the attitudinal outcomes of personal contact. *International Social Science Bulletin, 7,* 51-58.

Cumberbatch, G., & Negrine, R. (1992). *Images of disability on television.* London and New York: Routledge.

Gardner, J. M., & Radel, M. S. (1978). Portrait of the disabled in the media. *Journal of Community Psychology, 6,* 269-274.

Kent, D. (1988). In search of a heroine: Images of women with disabilities in fiction and drama. In M. Fine & A. Asch (Eds.), *Women with disabilities* (pp. 80-110). Philadelphia: Temple University Press.

Langer, E. J., Fiske, S., Taylor, S. E., & Chanowitz, B. (1976). Stigma, staring, and discomfort: A novel-stimulus hypothesis. *Journal of Experimental Social Psychology, 12,* 451-463.

Longmore, P. (1985). Screening stereotypes: Images of disabled people. *Social Policy, 16*(1), 31-37.

Makas, E. (1981). *Guess who's coming to prime time.* Unpublished manuscript.

Makas, E. (1989). Disabling stereotypes: The relationship between contact with and attitudes toward people with physical disabilities (Doctoral dissertation, George Washington University, 1989). *Dissertation Abstracts International, 50*(5), 2206B.

Palmerton, K. E., & Frumkin, R. M. (1969). Contact with disabled persons and intensity of counselors' attitudes. *Perceptual and Motor Skills, 28,* 434.

Thurer, S. (1980). Disability and monstrosity: A look at literary distortions of handicapping conditions. *Rehabilitation Literature, 41*(1-2), 12-15.

Turow, J., & Coe, L. (1985). Curing television's ills: The portrayal of health care. *Journal of Communication, 35*(4), 36-51.

Wright, B. A. (1960). *Physical disability: A psychological approach.* New York: Harper & Row.

Zola, I. K. (1985). Depictions of disability—Metaphor, message, and medium in the media: A research and political agenda. *Social Science Journal, 22*(4), 5-17.

PART IV

Future Perspectives on Programs for Children

Prior to the establishment of the cable industry, the three major networks, along with syndicators, independent companies, and public television, were the principal broadcasters of programs for children as well as adults. With the introduction of cable companies, the viewing patterns of the U.S. television audience were forever altered. Cable programs especially designed for children became a new competitor for the traditional broadcasting companies. Along with these changes, we were also in a period where new policy issues were being discussed at the federal level, local action groups were raising questions about the role of television in the socialization of children, and selected professional associations were increasing their research on television and children.

In Part IV of this book, we take a critical look at present policies and future directions of television programs in general and those for children in particular. The present and future perspectives of the programming issues are related to public policy and governmental legislation, public television and its special program needs, the challenge to commercial networks and children's programs, and the unique experiences of how a cable channel was born. Then we conclude with an epilogue that highlights the special features of television as a teacher of children.

It is important for the reader to understand that Part IV begins with a major chapter related to policy issues and future programs for children. This extensive discussion is then followed by some equally important commentaries in the area of public, commercial, and cable television.

Dale Kunkel provides the first chapter, considering the future directions of television programming for children with a particular emphasis on the role of federal regulatory policy in influencing program practices. This is an important lead-off chapter because it continues the analysis of the state of programs for children by considering the future implications of the Children's Television Act that was passed by the U.S. Congress in 1990.

Gordon L. Berry provides a commentary on public television, offering some historical information on the creation and early mission of the Corporation for Public Broadcasting (CPB). He follows this historical perspective with a focus on the programming challenges faced by CPB in a changing cultural landscape of people and ideas.

Horst Stipp brings the special perspective of a researcher based with a major network. His chapter provides a broad analysis of the issues related to the personal foci or concerns of the academic researcher and those held by broadcasters, cablecasters, and syndicators. He proposes that the difference between orientations held by broadcasters and academics need to both be considered in studying the viewing behavior of children. Stipp further offers a series of proposals for improving television for children.

Geraldine Laybourne brings the perspective of a broadcast executive and a person committed to a unique view on television programs for children. Her account of how Nickelodeon sought to create a network for children provides a view from an insider on how this organization carved out a place for itself and the children to whom it wanted to give a voice.

Joy Keiko Asamen turns her attention in the Epilogue to a capsule summary on television and its meaning in contemporary society. This final chapter also presents in a clear fashion the complexity of assembling a book like this one on such a complicated subject as television and children, and the medium's impact on what and how they learn from it.

Asamen makes it clear that television is a medium upon which many individuals rely to remain informed on the state of the country and the world. She concludes by stating that the editors of this volume are convinced that television programming, when thoughtfully conceptualized and responsibly viewed, can act as a constructive sociocultural informant.

19. Policy and the Future of Children's Television

DALE KUNKEL

Imagine what a different experience television would be for adults if the only programs offered were situation comedies and action-adventure shows. No evening news, no *60 Minutes*, no music, culture, or drama—only endless episodes built around laugh tracks and good-versus-evil fantasy themes. In such a world, television would no doubt be criticized for a lack of diversity and an overall failure to realize its potential.

Now adjust the focus of this picture to programming for children. There is little need for any imagination, as this characterization encompasses most children's programming aired on commercial television. The range of children's shows provided over the years, especially recent years, has been little more than sitcoms and action-adventure formats, albeit packaged in a genre better known as cartoons.

With the exception of occasional network specials, most commercial broadcasters offer no serious dramatic programs for children, no news or information shows, no series to stimulate children's curiosity about nature, science, or the arts. In short, children's television in the United States suffers from a serious lack of diversity of content, a long-standing affliction that stems from a combination of both economic and regulatory factors. Although this shortcoming was recognized and engaged as a public policy issue more than two decades ago, little movement to redress the situation has been accomplished until recently. Approval by the U.S. Congress of the Children's Television Act of 1990 may herald improvements, but the impact of this landmark legislation remains to be seen.

The purpose of this chapter is to consider the future directions of television programming for children, with particular emphasis on the role of federal regulatory policy in influencing program practices. A new policy framework for children's programming on broadcast television has been established with the implementation of the Children's Television Act. As with most legislation, its provisions appear simple at first glance yet prove to be surprisingly complex. This analysis will detail the key aspects of the new law and assess its implications for the future of children's television.

The Fundamental Limitations Facing Children's Programming

Why does children's television in the United States take the shape it does? The medium is capable of providing a diverse range of programs, including educational content that children are eager to watch and that accomplishes significant learning outcomes. The Children's Television Workshop (CTW), creator of *Sesame Street* and a wide range of other children's shows for the Public Broadcasting Service (PBS), has established an unparalleled record of producing popular and effective educational programs. CTW's success with this work is so great that it now consults with dozens of countries around the world to share its expertise, often collaborating with foreign governments or their broadcast systems to develop children's television projects (Palmer, in press; Palmer, Chen, & Lesser, 1976). It is an irony that CTW's services are not in greater demand in the United States. In fact, the organization has yet to produce a children's series for commercial broadcasting in this country. The reason for this outcome is in one sense quite simple, although at a second level more complex.

The most simple explanation for the lack of educational programming for children is that most television in the United States is driven by fundamental commercial interests. The economics of the industry are such that (with the exception of public broadcasting) two key factors dominate decisions about what content will be aired. First, the material must appeal to the widest possible audience, an axiom popularly referred to as the Law of Large Numbers. Additionally, there is a bias toward presenting programs that will attract viewers with the greatest potential buying power, also known as the Law of Right People. Both of these factors reflect the principle that television broadcasters derive their revenues from advertisers, who are in fact the true "clients" of the industry.

Children between 2 to 12 years of age comprise roughly 16% of the U.S. population (U.S. Department of Commerce, 1991) and thus represent only a small minority of all possible television viewers. Furthermore, their ability to influence consumer purchase decisions is limited and concentrated mostly in a narrow range of products such as toys and foods. Consequently, audiences of children are of relatively limited value to advertisers, and therefore to broadcasters. As a result, children's programs tend to air primarily at times when adults are less likely to view, such as before school hours on weekdays and on Saturday mornings. Even when children's programs are presented during these fringe periods, educational content is generally avoided by commercial stations because such material is more expensive to produce than sheer entertainment-oriented fare. In addition, the most effective educational programming targets a narrow age range of child viewers (in order to best address their learning capabilities), a tactic that limits further still the number of potential viewers. From an economic perspective, the business of programming television stations focuses on attracting the largest possible audience at the lowest possible cost, which is fundamentally at odds with providing educational programs for children.

Despite the importance of these fundamental economic considerations, the broadcast industry does not operate entirely on a free market model. The broadcast airwaves are designated by law as a public resource. Those granted the privilege of a broadcast license must comply with regulatory constraints and obligations established by the Federal Communications Commission (FCC). Under the Communications Act of 1934, the commission is charged with crafting policies that promote the "public interest, convenience, and necessity." Herein lies the more complex dimension that helps to explain why children's television in the United States takes the shape that it does. Although the FCC has grappled extensively with children's television policy since the 1960s, it has consistently failed to craft an approach that generates meaningful levels of educational or informational television programming for children, or otherwise contributes to content diversity (Aufderheide, 1989; Kunkel & Watkins, 1987).

With the exception of the financially limited efforts of public broadcasters, the television industry has largely avoided programming with a strong educational orientation (Huston, Watkins, & Kunkel, 1989; Watkins, 1988). This shortcoming has hardly gone unnoticed. Since 1969, child advocates have petitioned the FCC for the creation of policies that would require each broadcast television licensee to deliver some minimum level of such service. At several points throughout the 1970s, the commission seemed close to adopting this type of regulation. Yet at each key decision point, the agency chose to eschew any formal requirements, instead relying on vague standards that called for stations to make "meaningful efforts" to provide a "reasonable amount" of educational children's programming (FCC, 1974, p. 39398). The commission hoped that this approach would generate the desired improvements without the need for formal regulation, and stated so publicly:

> It is believed this report will help to clarify the responsibilities of broadcasters with respect to programming and advertising designed for the child audience. We believe that in these areas every opportunity should be accorded to the broadcast industry to reform itself because self-regulation preserves flexibility and an opportunity for adjustment which is not possible with per se rules. (FCC, 1974, p. 39402)

Reliance on the Marketplace as Public Policy

If the 1970s held the threat of regulation as leverage to increase broadcasters' efforts at children's programming (a technique termed the "raised eyebrow" approach to regulation; cf. Cole & Oettinger, 1978), the 1980s was a time when there was little pretense about the possibility of governmental intervention, at least from the FCC. When it took office in 1981, the Reagan administration brought with it a new philosophy of government, known as the "marketplace approach," to guide the exercise of its regulatory powers. This perspective emphasized the virtues of a competitive marketplace, holding that the public would benefit from the increased competition facilitated by the removal of governmental rules and regulations that impact the business sector. Applied to broadcasting, this meant the government ought to allow public demand to define the "public interest" that stations were licensed to serve rather than relying on the judgments of regulators (Fowler & Brenner, 1982). The rationale was that if a particular type of content was in the public's interest, then it would be widely viewed and hence be of economic value to the broadcaster; in contrast, content that attracted only small audiences would be presumed to be of little value for the public.

Consistent with this philosophy, the FCC (1984a) issued a new policy on children's programming that essentially relieved most stations from any obligation to serve the child audience. Casting aside long-standing complaints of marketplace failure (i.e., that broadcast television offered little content of value for children), the commission redefined the relevant marketplace. That is, the FCC ruled that the needs of children could be served by a wide range of program services, including cable, satellite, videocassettes, and public television, as well as by the commercial broadcast media. In determining the appropriate level of service for children, a broadcaster could now take into account "the alternative program services offered to children in the relevant [community]" (FCC, 1984a, p. 1704). Thus, in most cases where alternatives were available, a broadcaster would have no responsibility to serve the child audience under this policy. Children's needs could be met through the alternative sources available in the marketplace.

This revision led to some palpable changes in broadcast practices. Even the relatively small amount of educational programs that had been provided previously on commercial television essentially disappeared once the FCC deregulated children's television. One study from Kansas (Kerkman, Kunkel, Huston, Wright, & Pinon, 1990) documented a significant decline in children's educational programs shortly after the commission signaled its intention to deregulate. Another from Illinois (Wartella, Heintz, Aidman, & Mazzarella, 1990) reported that commercial broadcasters failed to provide a single educational program for children during a sample week in 1987. A third study (Waterman & Grant, 1987) produced the same finding in the much larger Los Angeles market. With the government no longer interested in broadcasters' efforts for children, educational programming clearly waned.

That is not to say that children's programming was in short supply during the 1980s. Although children's programming declined on some outlets, such as network television, it increased on others, such as independent stations and cable (Frazer, Gross, & Kadlec, 1986;

Siemicki, Atkin, Greenberg, & Baldwin, 1986). Yet little content that was new or different seemed to be provided. The most prevalent approach proved to be cartoon shows designed to promote products to children, a format known as the program-length commercial (Kunkel, 1988).

Program-length commercials had long been prohibited by the FCC as contrary to the public interest because they blurred the distinction between program and commercial matter (FCC, 1969; 1974). Such blurring poses particular problems for young children who already experience difficulty in distinguishing more traditional commercial messages from adjacent program content. However, this policy too was deregulated consistent with the marketplace philosophy (FCC, 1984b) and once it was, the program-length commercial format grew tremendously, driven largely by the potential profits at stake. For example, revenues from the sale of licensed products based on the *Teenage Mutant Ninja Turtles* program totaled $1.1 billion by the end of 1991 (Lazzareschi, 1991).

A New Policy Framework: The Children's Television Act

These developments triggered a surge of congressional interest in children's television policy, which had in the past been left primarily to the discretion of the FCC. One of the key concerns raised was the issue of equity in access to the new nonbroadcast technologies that the commission had relied upon to lessen broadcasters' burden to program for children. Many in society's lower income groups cannot afford the cost of cable or other alternative sources of children's programming, and others who can, reside in rural areas that are unlikely ever to be wired for cable service. Such families were not well served by the marketplace approach to children's television favored by the commission.

Once it became clear that the FCC had abandoned any effort to regulate in this area, legislators began to pursue their own course of action. A complex and protracted political debate spanning several years ensued (Kunkel, 1991a). The final product of this debate was the Children's Television Act of 1990, a rare piece of legislation amending the Communications Act and establishing a new framework for children's television policy.

The act, which was implemented as of January 1, 1992, includes four primary elements. First, it established that each station must provide educational and informational programming for children (but in no specific amount) in order to qualify for license renewal. Second, it limited advertising during children's programs to no more than 12 minutes per hour on weekdays, 10.5 minutes per hour on weekends. Third, it authorized the creation of a National Endowment for Children's Educational Television to be administered through the Department of Commerce. Finally, the act ordered the FCC to reexamine the issue of children's program-length commercials to determine whether its 1984 decision to deregulate such content was appropriate.

As with all legislation applicable to broadcasting, the regulatory provisions of the act must be interpreted and applied by the FCC. It is through this process that the conceptual issues addressed in the act are translated into detailed operational policies with which broadcasters must comply. In assessing the likely impact of this legislation on broadcast practices, it is important to examine the FCC's approach to implementing the new law.

Implementation of the New Children's Programming Requirement

The language of the new programming requirement in the act stipulates that each broadcaster shall serve "the educational and informational needs of children through the licensee's overall programming, including programming specifically designed to serve such needs." To implement the requirement, the FCC must determine the age range of "children" whose needs must be served; what programming will qualify as "educational and informational" content; and the extent of program efforts required, among other concerns. All of these decisions were rendered in the commission's report and order implementing the act (FCC, 1991a) and its response to requests for reconsideration (FCC, 1991b).

For purposes of the programming requirement, children are defined as those 16 years of age and under. This reflects a change from the past, when the commission's policies on children's programming defined children as 12 years and under (advertisement restrictions remain due to younger children being limited in their ability to recognize and defend against television advertising). The key rationale for this new position is that the Children's Television Endowment established by the act is chartered to support educational programming for children up to age 16. The commission thought it prudent to interpret the act so that educational programs funded through the endowment could count toward a station's fulfillment of the programming obligation when they are aired. However, not all segments of the child audience must be served; it is up to each broadcaster to determine the mix of programming they will present and the age ranges to be targeted. Any content intended for viewers 16 years of age and below qualifies as children's programming, regardless of whether it targets an audience aged 2 to 16 or 15 to 16.

Probably the most difficult and certainly the most important ruling implementing the act is the FCC's definition of educational and informational content. Former FCC Commissioner Nicholas Johnson is widely attributed with the observation that "all television is educational; the only question is—what is it teaching?" Reflecting this perspective, many broadcasters argued that the commission should not establish any formal definition of educational and informational programming, and instead should defer to the good faith judgments of licensees. In contrast, the advocacy group Action for Children's Television argued in a brief to the commission that only nonfiction content should be considered.

Rejecting both of these positions, the FCC chose a middle-ground definition of children's educational programming contained in a brief commissioned by the Donald McGannon Communication Research Center (Kunkel, 1991b): "Programming that furthers the positive development of the child in any respect, including the child's cognitive/intellectual and social/emotional needs, can contribute to satisfying the licensee's obligation to serve the educational and informational needs of children" (FCC, 1991a, p. 2114). This two-pronged formulation is meant to encompass the broad range of content that could be of value to children and still provide some delineation of the boundaries of the requirement as a means to hold stations accountable for compliance.

Cognitive/intellectual needs entail the development of fundamental conceptual skills and thinking abilities, such as the capabilities needed for handling symbolic information in its many different forms, such as language or mathematics. Also falling within this realm is "fact-gathering," or gaining knowledge about the concrete aspects of the real world, along with the cognitive capabilities required to organize, store, retrieve, and analyze such information. Social/emotional needs involve gaining an understanding of the world of people, rather than objects and facts. Examples of topics that have been successfully taught by television include family relations, racial tolerance, understanding one's emotions, and prosocial behavior.

When programming that is geared toward general audiences includes content addressing either of these two realms, then it may be counted as service to children in the licensee's overall programming. In addition, each station is expected to provide at least some programming specifically designed for children. There is no quantitative requirement for either type of service. Furthermore, nothing in the act stipulates that there must be any regularly scheduled programs, or even that the "programming" provided be of a particular length.

This latter ambiguity led several parties in the media industry (e.g., National Association of Broadcasters, Walt Disney Company) to argue that the commission should consider public service announcements and other short-segment content (i.e., 30- and 60-second "drop-ins") that hold educational value for children as fulfilling the obligation. The FCC initially adopted this proposal, embracing this type of content as "particularly appropriate" because "such material is well suited to children's short attention spans" (FCC, 1991a, p. 2115). Faced with a petition for reconsideration from the American Psychological Association (Kunkel, 1991c) refuting the commission's narrow perspective on children's attentional capabilities, the agency clarified that it would expect some traditional-length programming to demonstrate compliance, but that short segments could also be counted toward fulfilling the obligation (FCC, 1991b).

Assessing Compliance With the Children's Programming Requirement

Because the nature of the children's programming requirement mandates a broad level of service rather than any specific quantifiable obligations, enforcement of its provisions will be accomplished only at the time a station's license renewal application is processed.

Presently, television stations are licensed for a period of 5 years. When a station applies for license renewal, it must submit to the FCC a summary list of its programming efforts that fulfill the required service to children. Stations are also required to maintain such lists in their public file available for inspection at the station, although there is no uniform reporting requirement regarding any supporting information explaining how or why a given program is deemed to be educational.

In processing a license renewal application, the FCC serves as a reactive body. Rather than independently evaluating the adequacy of a station's efforts on this or any other service criterion, the agency plays a role similar to that of a judge in a legal proceeding. Its function is to weigh any claims filed by parties who oppose the renewal application and then to determine whether or not awarding the license renewal is in the public interest. In essence, then, the system basically operates on a presumption of compliance, although that presumption is rebuttable. To challenge a station's claim of compliance with the children's programming requirement, a petition to deny the license renewal must be filed with the commission outlining the perceived inadequacies.

To the extent that child advocates wish to encourage more and better educational programming, active participation in the process of holding local broadcasters accountable for their children's programming efforts is essential. The precedents established in cases challenging stations' license renewal applications will ultimately determine "how much is enough" in terms of service to the child audience. Although the Children's Television Act may provide the leverage needed to accomplish meaningful improvements, it is unlikely that such outcomes will emerge without some prompting on the part of advocacy groups at both the local and national level.

The fact that license renewals occur only once every 5 years, along with the fact that successful license challenges are extraordinarily rare, suggests the need for interested parties to engage in a dialogue with broadcasters in their community to communicate their concerns about a station's performance. Regardless of whether a station's license renewal is imminent, broadcasters have much to gain by responding to valid concerns brought to their attention. By resolving any concerns in advance of the license renewal process, a station can avoid the costly delays and complications that occur when the commission is forced to investigate objections raised formally in a petition to deny. It is only at this point that a station may be called upon to defend the veracity of its claim that certain children's programs are indeed educational in nature.

As stations are licensed at the local level, the participation of community groups, educators, and others interested in children's welfare presents the most effective means of ensuring compliance with the children's programming obligation. No national organization can have the same degree of familiarity with a station's level of performance as a local resident. At the same time, national leadership is needed to provide advice and counsel for local participants to assist them in understanding the complex nature of the broadcast licensing system and the details of the FCC's rules for children's programming.

For more than 20 years, the advocacy group Action for Children's Television (ACT), led by long-time President Peggy Charren, has played a prominent role along these lines. Once the Children's Television Act was approved, ACT distributed materials nationwide to help explain the provisions of the bill and also created a videotape "It's the Law" to assist community activists. Shortly thereafter, however, Charren announced she was disbanding the organization at the end of 1992. Charren (cited in Du Brow, 1992) stated, "We think we've done what we set out to do, and now it's up to the people to make it work" (p. F1). Charren has endorsed a new Washington-based public interest advocacy group, the Center for Media Education, to pick up where ACT has left off. The center is developing plans to assist local community groups in monitoring children's programming to assess stations' compliance with the new requirements.

Revisiting the Issue of Program-Length Commercials

The growth of children's program-length commercials (PLCs) that resulted from the FCC's deregulation of its policy prohibiting such content (FCC, 1984b) triggered complaints from groups such as ACT and led to congressional concern. In approving the Children's Television Act, the Congress did not rule directly on this issue, but approach is a common means by which the Congress attempts to rein in independent regulatory agencies when it disagrees with their actions.

In deregulating its PLC policy, the FCC had ruled that marketplace forces would effectively keep in check any excessive commercialization, rendering government regulation unnecessary. The surge in PLCs that resulted from deregulation certainly called that assertion into question. After the reconsideration mandated by Congress, the commission indicated it would reinstate its ban on PLCs. That position is misleading, however, as the agency redefined program-length commercials in a manner that would encompass practices already prohibited by a different FCC policy and that only rarely occur. The new definition of a PLC offered by the commission is "a program associated with a product in which commercials for that product are aired" (FCC, 1991a, p. 2117).

A long-standing policy that was never deregulated was the FCC's restriction on "host selling." Host selling refers to the use of children's program characters in ads placed adjacent to the program in which they appear. Since 1974, this policy has effectively banned the practices that the commission now defines as a PLC. In children's television today, the characters are the products; it is difficult to conceive of program-related products that would not involve a popular program character and hence violate the host selling policy when aired adjacent to the character's show. By redefining a program-length commercial as tantamount to host selling, the commission has purportedly reinstated a restriction on PLCs without actually limiting any existing program practices. In fact, under the new definition of PLCs, it would be possible for a program to include unlimited product promotions within the body of the show so long as the broadcaster did not present any "traditional" 30- or 60-second ads for the related products at the same time. Thus there is little reason to expect the commission's new PLC policy to accomplish any reduction in the use of children's programs to promote toys and other products to children.

National Endowment for Children's Educational Television

A final aspect of the Children's Television Act that lies beyond the purview of the FCC is the creation of the children's television endowment. Although the idea of establishing an endowment had emerged in the past, it lacked any serious consideration until the publication of a book entitled *Television and America's Children: A Crisis of Neglect* by Edward L. Palmer (1987), long-time director of research for CTW. Palmer provided both an impassioned plea documenting the need for such an endeavor, as well as a detailed blueprint for how it could work. The book was well received by policymakers, who were already engaged in debates about the regulatory aspects of the Children's Television Act when it was released.

Daniel Inouye, chair of the U.S. Senate Subcommittee on Communications, was enthusiastic about the proposal and invited Palmer to be the chief witness at a hearing exploring the topic (U.S. Senate, 1989). Shortly thereafter, Inouye introduced a bill to create the endowment, and that measure was ultimately joined with the children's television regulation bill that was working its way through Congress.

The role of the endowment is to provide grants for the production of children's educational programming. Any content supported must be directed to those 16 years of age and under. Programs that receive support can only be shown on noncommercial television for the first 2 years after they have been produced, although they may appear on commercial stations after that time so long as they are aired without commercial interruption. Recommendations about the funding of proposals will be made by an advisory council appointed by the secretary of Commerce, who will administer the endowment.

Inouye's initial proposal, which called for $10 million per year, was more generous than the level of funding finally approved in the Children's Television Act. The act authorized the endowment at a level of $2 million for fiscal 1991 and $4 million for fiscal 1992. However, under federal government funding procedures, authorization merely allows the opportunity for monies to be appropriated; actual appropriations require separate legislative action by Congress. Authorization alone does not guarantee that any funding will occur.

In the first year authorized, fiscal 1991, no monies were appropriated, and from a functional perspective, the endowment did not exist. At least three factors contributed to this situation: the huge federal budget deficit, the administration's explicit refusal to request any monies for the endowment in its budget proposal, and the fact that no pressure was brought to bear on the administration or Congress by advocacy groups who supported the effort. An initial appropriation of $2 million was obtained for fiscal 1992, but the measure came relatively late in the funding cycle and administrators have been slow in getting the operation under way. The Secretary of Commerce announced the initial appointments to the advisory board in summer 1992, with only 2 months remaining in the fiscal year. Thus, the initial monies appropriated were expected to be rolled over to 1993 for expenditure. A new authorization of $5 million for fiscal 1993 has been approved by Congress, and an appropriation of $2-3 million is expected.

Given that the cost of producing a year's worth of episodes of a single children's program typically exceeds the entire budget appropriated to date for the endowment, this endeavor clearly cannot be expected to reshape the overall children's programming environment. Should it establish a successful foothold, however, the concept holds the potential to grow into a more formidable enterprise.

Implications for the Future

With all of this new policy framework, is there reason to expect that the future of children's programming might look any different than the past? To address this question, one should consider the likely impact of each of the three new policies discussed in this chapter.

The centerpiece of the Children's Television Act is its educational programming requirement. Stations that were scheduled for license renewal in 1992 have been ordered to demonstrate compliance with the requirement from October 1991 to their renewal application date (which varies geographically). One can therefore gain a sense of the nature of the program efforts stimulated by the act by reviewing the initial license renewal applications filed with the FCC in 1992.

The information reported here is strictly anecdotal and based on a modest random sampling of the license renewal applications pending at the FCC at midyear. Despite this caveat, an obvious pattern is evident that encompasses every case examined: The principal strategy for claiming compliance is to assert that existing programming (in many cases content that has been available and aired for years) fulfills the children's requirement, as opposed to providing any new material developed explicitly in response to the act. This pattern cuts across both independent and network stations.

Although this assessment is only preliminary, it appears that the prevalent strategy for demonstrating compliance with the Children's Television Act is grounded largely in staking claims that existing program practices fulfill the requirement. It is conceivable that the general lack of any new program efforts uniquely responsive to the act is influenced by the lag time required between approval of a program concept and its actual development and production, and that it is simply too soon for new programming efforts to have emerged. Such an explanation, however, discounts the fact that the law was originally approved in October 1990, a year before the FCC's initial implementation of its programming provisions.

These developments stand in contrast to the concerns that motivated the Congress to approve the Children's Television Act. During the debate surrounding the legislation, it was repeatedly alleged that broadcasters' current level of service to children was inadequate. Yet despite these claims, the industry response to the children's programming requirement seems to reflect the perspective that the status quo is not so bad after all, or more specifically, at least it fulfills the provisions required by the legislation Congress enacted. That position does not bode well for the future impact of the new programming requirement. If precedent establishes that the existing level of service provided by most stations accomplishes compliance with the new requirements, there will be little incentive for future innovations or improvements in educational programming.

The other two aspects of the new policy framework directly affecting programming, the program-length commercial restriction and the children's television endowment, also offer little reason to expect substantial changes in the overall environment of children's television. The endowment has received scant resources to date, and even if it were funded more generously, its projects can never be shown with commercial interruptions, a requirement that would seem to limit their viability for commercial stations. In addition, the PLC policy that the FCC "reinstated" in fact accomplishes little if any limitation on the growing commercialization of children's programming. This conclusion was underscored recently when Fox Broadcasting announced plans to develop a new program in collaboration with Frito-Lay based on the snack food company's animated character Chester Cheetah, which appears in ads for Cheetos products (Bernstein, 1991). The plan was quietly dropped after vehement complaints by child advocates, but the fact that such content is now permitted (so long as no traditional commercials for Cheetos appear during the show) even though the FCC maintains it has outlawed program-length commercials demonstrates the true nature of the policy.

Conclusion

The unavoidable conclusion seems to be that despite the new policy framework, there is little cause for immediate optimism about improvements in children's television. Yet if Krasnow, Longley, and Terry (1982) are right that most all communication policy reform comes in small incremental steps, then perhaps there is cause for optimism. Although the Children's Television Act alone may not reverse the shortcomings in children's television that have existed for decades, it may well represent the first in a series of steps designed to realize that goal. Moreover, it remains to be seen whether the FCC will accept the liberal claims offered by broadcasters about the nature and extent of their educational programming for children. If public interest activists succeed in challenging some of these claims as part of the license renewal process, a more stringent precedent may well be established for characterizing programming as educational or informational in the future. So long as commercial broadcasters continue to offer little children's programming that is truly of educational value, policymakers can be expected to continue to seek new and more aggressive means of altering that pattern.

References

Aufderheide, P. (1989). Reregulating children's TV. *Federal Communications Law Journal, 42*, 87-106.

Bernstein, S. (1991, December 25). Frito-Lay, Fox draw up cartoon plans. *Los Angeles Times*, p. F15.

Cole, B., & Oettinger, M. (1978). *Reluctant regulators: The FCC and the broadcast audience*. Reading, MA: Addison-Wesley.

Du Brow, R. (1992, January 9). Watchdog for kids' TV to resign. *Los Angeles Times*, p. F1, F10.

Federal Communications Commission. (1969). In re: Complaint of Topper Corporation concerning American Broadcasting Company and Mattel, Inc. *Federal Communications Commission Reports, 21*(2d), 148-149.

Federal Communications Commission. (1974). Children's television programs: Report and policy statement. *Federal Register, 39*, 39396-39409.

Federal Communications Commission. (1984a). Children's television programming and advertising practices: Report and order. *Federal Register, 49*, 1704-1727.

Federal Communications Commission. (1984b). Revision of programming and commercialization policies, ascertainment requirements, and program log requirements for commercial television stations. *Federal Register, 49*, 33588-33620.

Federal Communications Commission. (1991a). Policies and rules concerning children's television programming: Memorandum opinion and order. *Federal Communications Commission Record, 6,* 2111-2127.

Federal Communications Commission. (1991b). Policies and rules concerning children's television programming: Memorandum opinion and order. *Federal Communications Commission Record, 6,* 5093-5105.

Fowler, M., & Brenner, D. (1982). A marketplace approach to broadcast regulation. *Texas Law Review, 60,* 207-257.

Frazer, Gross, & Kadlec, Inc. (1986). *Independent thinking: An overview of the independent television industry.* Washington, DC: Author.

Huston, A., Watkins, B., & Kunkel, D. (1989). Public policy and children's television. *American Psychologist, 44,* 424-433.

Kerkman, D., Kunkel, D., Huston, A., Wright, J., & Pinon, M. (1990). Children's television programming and the "free market" solution. *Journalism Quarterly, 67,* 147-156.

Krasnow, E., Longley, L., & Terry, H. (1982). *The politics of broadcast regulation* (3rd ed.). New York: St. Martin's.

Kunkel, D. (1988). From a raised eyebrow to a turned back: The FCC and children's product-related programming. *Journal of Communication, 38*(4), 90-108.

Kunkel, D. (1991a). Crafting media policy: The genesis and implications of the Children's Television Act of 1990. *American Behavioral Scientist, 35*(2), 181-202.

Kunkel, D. (1991b, February 20). *Reply comments in the matter of policies and rules concerning children's television programming* (Testimony before the Federal Communications Commission). New York: Donald McGannon Communication Research Center, Fordham University.

Kunkel, D. (1991c, May 10). *Petition for reconsideration in the matter of policies and rules concerning children's television programming* (Testimony before the Federal Communications Commission). Washington, DC: American Psychological Association.

Kunkel, D., & Watkins, B. (1987). Evolution of children's television regulatory policy. *Journal of Broadcasting & Electronic Media, 31,* 367-389.

Lazzareschi, C. (1991, December 23). Rapid-paced turtle sales starting to slow down. *Los Angeles Times,* p. D1.

Palmer, E. (1987). *Television and America's children: A crisis of neglect.* New York: Oxford University Press.

Palmer, E. (in press). *Toward a literate world: Television and literacy education. Lessons from the Arab world.* Boulder, CO: Westview.

Palmer, E., Chen, M., & Lesser, G. (1976). *Sesame Street:* Patterns of international adaptation. *Journal of Communication, 26*(2), 109-123.

Siemicki, M., Atkin, D., Greenberg, B., & Baldwin, T. (1986). Nationally distributed children's shows: What cable TV contributes. *Journalism Quarterly, 63,* 710-718, 734.

U.S. Department of Commerce. Bureau of the Census. (1991). *Statistical abstracts of the United States.* Washington, DC: U.S. Government Printing Office.

U.S. Senate. (1989, April 12). *Education, competitiveness, and children's television. Hearing before the Subcommittee on Communications* (Serial No. 101-169). Washington, DC: U.S. Government Printing Office.

Wartella, E., Heintz, K., Aidman, A., & Mazzarella, S. (1990). Television and beyond: Children's video media in one community. *Communication Research, 17,* 45-64.

Waterman, D., & Grant, A. (1987). *Narrowcasting on cable television: An economic assessment of programming and audiences.* Paper presented to the annual conference of the International Communication Association, Montreal.

Watkins, B. (1988). Improving educational and informational television for children: When the marketplace fails. *Yale Law and Policy Review, 5,* 344-381.

20. Public Television Programming and the Changing Cultural Landscape

GORDON L. BERRY

Public Television: The Challenge

This commentary is driven by the proposition that public television in the 1990s and into the next century must continue and even reinforce its efforts to provide quality programs for a wider spectrum of U.S. society in general, and children in particular. The ever-changing cultural landscape composed of many diverse people, languages, family patterns, gender issues, religions, life-styles, and changing layers of social classes will have a profound impact on how the leadership of the Corporation for Public Broadcasting (CPB) and its creative partners go about the business of serving the broader society. Although the focus of this paper is on the importance of public television continuing to be proactive in developing programs for children throughout the emerging diversification of the United States, it is clear that to accomplish this task there will be a need for CPB to have an adequate base of: (a) sustained funding; (b) continued development of creative talent that will reflect our nation's diversity; (c) reinforcement of cooperative relationships with business, private groups, and foundations; (d) increased attention to building grass roots and general public support among broad sectors of the viewing audience (children and adults); and (e) political leadership on all levels that believes in the concept that there is an important informational, educational, creative, and entertaining mission for a public broadcasting system in the United States.

It is both natural and appropriate for us to place the challenges of meeting the cultural and social changes in our country on the creative shoulders of public broadcasting (although CPB includes both public radio and television, the focus of this chapter is on the latter), because it is a child of both the U.S. Congress and the White House. In fact, following the signing of the Public Broadcasting Act of 1967, which created the Corporation for Public Broadcasting, the first meeting of its board was held in the White House (Corporation for Public Broadcasting, 1987). The two parents of this broadcasting child, coupled with selected social action groups, have not always been open to its creative and developmental growth, but the mandate given to it by the 1967 act was to (a) develop television and radio systems that would reach and serve *all* Americans with alternative programming; (b) develop connection services that would link the public broadcasting stations nationwide; (c) help support those stations; (d) help ensure production of high-quality programs from diverse sources; and (e) provide training, instruction, recruiting, research, and development. This mandate is still a part of CPB's core commitment (Corporation for Public Broadcasting, 1987).

Public broadcasting in the United States today fundamentally consists of the licensees of local public radio and television stations. The Corporation for Public Broadcasting is, however, the manager for most of the federal money allocated for public broadcasting. Other organizations that are part of the industry include the Public Broadcasting Service (PBS), the National Association of Public Television Stations (NAPTS), National Public Radio (NPR), American Public Radio (APR), and the National Federation of Community Broadcasters (NFCB), which provide networking, distribution, production, or representation services to individual stations (Corporation for Public Broadcasting, 1989).

New forms of legislation have been enacted over the years to assist CPB to maintain its mission in a changing cultural landscape. For example, the Public Telecommunications Act of 1988 (Pub. L. 100-626) requires the Corporation for Public Broadcasting to report annually on the provision of service to minority and diverse audiences by public broadcasting and public telecommunications entities. This includes programming, minority employment and training, and efforts to increase the number of minority public radio and television stations eligible for financial support from the CPB. The act defines minority and diverse audiences as racial and ethnic minorities (interpreted to encompass the racial and ethnic groups with special legal protection, i.e., African Americans, Asian Americans,

Hispanics, Native Americans, and Pacific Islanders); recent immigrant populations (e.g., Latin American, Caribbean, Asian, and other newcomers to the United States within the last decade); persons for whom English is a second language; and adults who lack basic reading skills (Corporation for Public Broadcasting, 1989).

Significantly, any discussion of new or old legislation aimed at reaching broad and diverse audiences ultimately must return us to the special needs of children. After all, it is they who are in their developmental years, and are in the process of forming early opinions about themselves and others in society. Both public and commercial television can, for some of these developing children, present images, portrayals, places, and language patterns from which they draw correct and incorrect impressions. Any faulty cultural information, if not modified by other traditional agents of socialization (e.g., family, school, religious institutions, and sometimes the peer group) can form the basis for becoming a part of a child's belief system.

Children's programs from the public sector have not, of course, received the same intense scrutiny and criticism as those from commercial television. The creative work of the Children's Television Workshop (CTW), and its cooperative relationships with PBS, national foundations, and U.S. industry has come to symbolize the types of quality programs that are aired on public television. In addition, a number of local stations in the public network have also distinguished themselves with first-rate general programs for children that have met a variety of needs. Related to this notion, it is important to point out that *Sesame Street, The Electric Company, 3-2-1 Contact,* and *Square One TV* are general programs that also give special attention to the needs of children from minority backgrounds, the disabled, those experiencing learning difficulties, and those from lower socioeconomic circumstances (Palmer, 1988).

Public Television: Meeting Future Programming Needs

Looking at the future landscape for public television and those who will be called upon to write, direct, and produce programs for children, my premise for meeting a broad spectrum of needs is very basic: Public television is one of the main bridges that can span the educational, informational, and entertainment multicultural gorge that our children will need to cross in the future.

To accomplish this bridging process, CPB must reach *out* to both the creative community and people in other fields to develop the characters, settings, and the themes for the cultural landscape of the future. At the same time, the creative community must reach *into* the multiplicity of cultures for story ideas and program elements that will present to children some of their own folkways, languages, music, art, literature, heroes, and heroines, as well as to expose them to these same cultural experiences of others (Berry, 1992). In a dynamic, information-laden environment, wrote Richard Adler (1975), the problem is not how to get a message to the receiver, but how to get his or her attention. In a changing cultural landscape, I would argue that both getting and receiving the message must be accomplished as a collective process.

There should be nothing in this position that would suggest that future programs for children need be preachy or a sixth day of school. Children, like adults, desire a diversity of form and style in their public television offerings. A point to remember is that public television grew to exist in this country not as a matter of national policy, but because many people and organizations help to nourish it, and in no area is the need clearer than in children's programming to nurture the capacity to add diversity to the available viewing choices (Palmer, 1988). That is to say, children, like adults, need a level of creative diversity in their program content, style, format, and characters. Children also need programming that will stimulate their imaginations, assist them in their social development, inform them of their place in the world, introduce them to the world of others, and offer content that will cause them to reach for ideas. All of these needs must, of course, be placed within a framework of understanding that children are not miniature or little adults, but boys and girls who should have the type of program content that will meet their social, psychological, and physical stages of development.

Public television, as an institution, clearly faces a special set of challenges as it moves into the future. Programming for children will always feel the push and pull of the decisions made concerning the larger issues faced by public broadcasting in the United States (the same is probably true with commercial children's programs). As the future planning and decision making goes forward, however, none of it can ignore the important challenge of providing creative programming that will expose developing children to the beauty and the challenges of a culturally diverse country and world.

References

Adler, R. (1975). Understanding television: An overview of the literature of the medium as a social and cultural force. In D. Carter (Ed.), *Television as a social force: New approaches to T.V. criticism* (pp. 23-47). New York: Prager.

Berry, G. L. (1992, April). *The challenge of public television programming to inform, entertain, and empower.* Paper presented at the meeting of the Aspen Institute for Communications and Society Program, Wye, MD.

Corporation for Public Broadcasting. (1987). *A report to the people, 20 years of your national commission to public broadcasting.* Washington, DC: Author.

Corporation for Public Broadcasting. (1989, July). *To know ourselves: A report to the 101st Congress on public broadcasting and the needs of minorities and other groups pursuant to P.L. 100-626.* Washington, DC: Author.

Palmer, E. L. (1988). *Television and America's children: A crisis of neglect.* New York: Oxford University Press.

21. The Challenge to Improve Television for Children

A New Perspective

HORST STIPP

In this country, academic research as well as public debate on issues relating to children's television usually focus on topics like these: What are the effects of television on children? How can negative effects be reduced? How can positive effects be increased? The provisions of the 1990 Children's Television Act are primarily a result of the research and the debate on these issues. The act seeks to increase the amount of educational and informational programming and to reduce the amount of commercial content in order to enhance positive and to diminish negative consequences of television exposure.

Broadcasters, cablecasters, and syndicators usually focus on a very different topic: Which programs do children want to watch? This is a question that is very rarely considered by academics, and most would probably argue that an emphasis on program popularity is detrimental to the goal of improving children's television.

As a researcher at a broadcast network, I have often been confronted by this seemingly wide gap between academic and commercial orientations. In my opinion, that gap is largely based on a misunderstanding, an outgrowth of a traditional separation between academic and commercial research in this country. I think that understanding children's viewing preferences can help improve children's television. Therefore, I want to propose a new perspective that combines these two orientations and uses both research on television's effects and research on the factors that determine children's

Table 21.1 What Children Watch, 1992

Prime Time	*Rating*	*Saturday AM*	*Rating*	*Monday-Friday Afternoon/Other*	*Rating*
Full House	18	*Ninja Turtles*	10	*Darkwing Duck* (Syndicated)	8
The Simpsons	16	*Garfield*	8	*Tiny Toons Adventures*	7
Home Improvement	16	*Bugs Bunny*	7	Wrestling	7
Dinosaurs	15	*Back to the Future*	7	*Talespin*	7
Step by Step	15	*Darkwing Duck* (Network)	6	*Ninja Turtles*	6
Family Matters	15				
America's Funniest Home Videos	14				
America's Funniest People	13				
Fresh Prince	13				
Baby Talk	13				

SOURCE: Nielsen; NBC Research.
NOTE: Rating points represents percent of 2- to 11-year-olds who watch average telecast.

viewing behavior. The emphasis in this chapter will be on showing how research on children's viewing behavior can be used to meet the challenge of improving children's television.

What Children Watch

Table 21.1 shows children's favorite programs during the 1991-1992 television season. The figures represent the percentage of 2- to 11-year-olds watching the average program minute in each episode. Rather than ranking them independently of when the programs are shown, they are listed separately for prime time, Saturday morning, and weekday afternoon/other time periods. The reason for this presentation of the data is to demonstrate two facts that have important implications for devising strategies to improve children's television.

First, most of the programs that children watch are not what we generally call children's programs and they are not shown on Saturday mornings. The highest rated programs are shown during the first hour of prime time; most are family situation comedies. No Saturday morning show reaches the audience levels among children of the top 10 prime-time shows. Children's programs shown during weekday afternoons (and at other times) reach audience levels that are comparable to Saturday morning shows. As those programs are typically shown 5 days a week, most children watch them more often than once-a-week Saturday morning programs. Thus, weekly exposure to some highly rated weekday afternoon programs does rival exposure to children's favorite prime-time shows. Overall, about 10% of children's viewing is devoted to Saturday morning TV, 20% to weekday afternoons, and 25% to prime time. In addition, there is substantial viewing of a variety of programs at other times, especially on weekends.

The second noteworthy finding from these data is that children choose their programs from a wide variety of sources. The top programs include network prime-time shows and Saturday morning programs, but also syndicated programs that are shown on nonnetwork stations. In addition, there is exposure to cable programs (even though none of the individual shows ranks high enough to be included on this short list) and there is a good amount of viewing of one public TV program, *Sesame Street* (ratings for *Sesame Street* are not included on the list of favorites among 6- to 11-year-olds; the program does achieve high ratings among 2- to 5-year-olds). Finally, over three quarters of children have access to a VCR and there is clear evidence that they frequently use it. For starters, a very large portion of best-selling videos and a substantial portion of top rentals consists of children's movies and programs. Unpublished data available to NBC Research indicate that children also see many adult-oriented movies with other family members on VCRs. Although this material is rarely considered in discussions about children and television, we can assume that young children cannot distinguish between program sources and that the delivery system is irrelevant for possible exposure effects.

Much of the attention of researchers and the public debate has focused on children's programs and on the networks' Saturday morning fare. The conclusions from these findings are clear: If we want to improve children's television, we have to direct our attention beyond narrowly defined children's programs, beyond the traditional television networks, and even beyond local stations and cable.

The Effect of Children's Program Choices

It is quite easy to assess what children choose to watch. The above discussion has identified the most popular programs and pointed to key parameters of children's viewing behavior. Assessing *why* children make these choices is more difficult, especially in the context of this brief chapter. We need to address this question because the reasons behind children's program choices are the main factors that determine whether or not children will watch programs with educational and informational content (as defined by the FCC).

Because of the proliferation of local stations and increased cable penetration, most Americans, including families with children, have access to over 20 channels. Even those without cable usually have more than 10 choices, and during times when children watch, several stations offer programming directed at children. In addition, as pointed out above, children's choices go beyond children's programs and they choose from a broad range of programming from broadcast, cable, and video sources. Is there diversity among the many choices? Most of the programs available have little educational or informational content.

However, there are diverse choices: In New York, for example, during children's peak viewing time of 4 p.m. on weekdays, there is *Sesame Street, Carmen Sandiego,* and *Square One.* Only *Sesame Street* gets a large audience, but only among 2- to 5-year-olds. Similarly on Saturday mornings, when a commercial broadcaster presents the highly acclaimed *Not Just News,* most children choose entertainment competition on other channels. An analysis of Saturday morning network programming during the last 20 years shows that many attempts to expose children to "better" programs were frustrated by children's lack of interest in watching them (Stipp, Hill-Scott, & Dorr, 1987). Thus, the problem is not lack of choices or of diversity, but that over three quarters of the children who watch choose an entertainment program.

In considering explanations for this viewing behavior by children, I suggest that we consider the cultural context in which U.S. children grow up. When it comes to choosing between entertainment programs and educational fare, children's viewing behavior is really very similar to their parents—more than three quarters of adults choose noneducational, noninformational programs during most times of the day. And although most parents agree that children should watch better programs, forcing them to watch certain programs strongly contradicts some of the most fundamental values of this society, including values about the way children should be brought up. Parents may place certain limits on the amount of viewing, recommend some programs and prohibit others, but most parents give children considerable freedom to choose. In addition, we need to face the fact that not all parents agree with the values of educators. For example, the programs of the World Wrestling Federation would not be among boys' most popular programs if parents strongly disapproved. Ratings data indicate that a fair portion of parents/fathers watches that program with their children.

In addition to these cultural factors, there are economic, technological, political, and other influences that affect children's viewing. But to a large extent, children's viewing is determined by the choices of children and their parents. Over several decades, most attempts by public broadcasters and broadcast and cable networks to get children to watch educational and informational programs had limited success. (The exception, among 2- to 5-year-olds, is *Sesame Street*.) If we want to improve children's television, we have to recognize these realities.

Toward a Comprehensive Perspective

Calling attention to the effect of the viewer on her or his television diet, and on the program schedule itself, appears necessary because of a rather unique tradition in U.S. communications research. As pointed out in the introduction to this chapter, many U.S. communications researchers are primarily interested in the medium's effects on the viewer; the viewers' effects on the medium are rarely explored. This is not true outside of the United States.

In my view, a narrow focus on TV effects limits our perspective and can easily lead to biased findings. If we dismiss the impact of culture on the medium or ignore the role of children's developmental characteristics, values, and preferences in shaping their TV preferences, we will understate the viewer's active role in determining the medium's effect and develop exaggerated notions about the medium's impact (for more detail on this point of view see McGuire, 1986; Stipp & Milavsky, 1988).

Of course, the reverse is also true. If one were to focus exclusively on what children want to see, one would overlook possible negative consequences of certain program content. I am certainly not advocating that we abandon TV effects research. Rather, I am calling for a more comprehensive perspective.

A recent paper by Entman and Wildman (1992) appears to mirror the view expressed here, namely, that an extended framework is needed to guide communications policy. The authors point to the viewer as gatekeeper, remind us that increased program diversity may have little impact on what is viewed, and raise the issue of a "higher good" (such as having many cultural and educational programs on the air) versus the individual's desire to choose freely—which may mean avoiding those valuable programs.

The challenge to improve television programs for children, then, lies primarily in these three facts: (a) children have access to a large and increasing number of programs and program sources; (b) overwhelmingly, children choose entertainment programs that do not qualify as educational or informational; (c) most parents do not coerce their children to watch educational or instructional programs, and they do not prohibit them from watching popular entertainment programs designed for children or for family viewing.

Improving Television for Children

We have a good body of knowledge on television's effects on children in a variety of areas, ranging from cognitive development (Anderson & Collins, 1988) to socialization of the minority child (Berry & Mitchell-Kernan, 1982), which can be used to improve the effectiveness of programming. More research in these areas would be desirable. However, I suggest that we place more emphasis on the areas listed below.

First, more research on why children reject so many educational and informational programs is needed. Such new research efforts should make use of the knowledge and research resources of commercial broadcasters.

Second, we need to consider all the material that children watch on their television sets, and not focus on a narrow slice of children's TV diet such as cartoons or network programs. Syndicated fare, cable, and videocassettes are very much a part of children's television.

Third, we can take advantage of the experience of broadcasters who have tried different strategies to improve the quality of children's television. I have had the privilege of being involved in such efforts since the late 1970s. A 1987 paper that describes these efforts (Stipp et al., 1987) shows why the scientists and programmers who worked together in this process abandoned a strategy of placing informational programs on the schedule and instead opted for prosocial content in entertainment programs that large numbers of children watched. The decisive role of children's preference for entertainment programs in an increasingly competitive environment is evident. But it is also clear that children will watch and accept positive messages in an entertaining environment.

Most people, from educators to broadcasters, would agree that improving programs that children watch is desirable. This common goal should be reflected in a common effort to bring all our knowledge together, to look at the facts without prejudice, and to conduct new research to cope with the challenge of making good programs that children (and their parents) will watch.

References

Anderson, D. R., & Collins, P. A. (1988). *The impact on children's education: Television's influence on cognitive development* (Working Paper No. 2). Washington, DC: Office of Educational Research and Improvement, U.S. Department of Education.

Berry, G. L., & Mitchell-Kernan, C. (Eds.). (1982). *Television and the socialization of the minority child.* New York: Academic Press.

Entman, R. M., & Wildman, S. S. (1992). Reconciling economic and non-economic perspectives on media policy: Transcending the "marketplace of ideas." *Journal of Communication, 42*(1), 5-19.

McGuire, W. J. (1986). The myth of massive media impact: Savaging and salvaging. In G. Comstock (Ed.), *Public communication and behavior* (Vol. 1, pp. 173-257). Orlando, FL: Academic Press.

Stipp, H., Hill-Scott, K., & Dorr, A. (1987). Using social science to improve children's television: An NBC case study. *Journal of Broadcasting and Electronic Media, 31*(4), 461-473.

Stipp, H., & Milavsky, J. R. (1988). U.S. television programming's effects on aggressive behavior of children and adolescents. *Current Psychological Research and Reviews: Social Issues on Television Violence, 7,* 76-92.

22. The Nickelodeon Experience

GERALDINE LAYBOURNE

A Channel Is Born

Nickelodeon, "the young people's channel," began cablecasting on April Fool's Day in 1979. In the beginning, Nickelodeon was created by cable operators who needed a service for families and children. To parents, Nickelodeon was a commercial-free, 13-hour-a-day, cable channel that showed programs they wanted their kids to watch. To kids, Nick was the "green vegetables" on the TV menu—something their parents said was good for them, not something they really craved. In those days, Nickelodeon really was not about kids at all.

By 1984, cable TV was booming all over the United States, but the landscape for kids remained pretty bleak. The time was right to transform Nickelodeon into a real network for kids. To find out how, we turned to the experts: kids themselves.

We actually started by showing our experts a slew of commercials aimed at them, selling everything from cereal and toys to movies. We watched their response and listened as our audience analyzed how they were being sold to, what appealed to them, and what turned them off. We learned our first lessons about condescension, cute, hype, and being turned off by perfect Hollywood kids.

We moved next to more profound questions like: What do you like about being kids? We were astounded at the response we got. Overwhelmingly, kids told us they like being kids because they were afraid of growing up. They had heard about teen suicide, teen pregnancy, and drunk driving. One child confessed he was sure when you became a teenager your brain shrank! They could not imagine how they could cope with all of this. It became clear to us that kids needed a haven where they could just be kids.

In our research, we also found out how tough it is to be a kid. It is an adult world out there. Kids get talked down to and everybody older has authority over them. For kids, it is "us versus them" in the grown-up world: you're either for kids or against them. Either you think kids should be quiet and behave or you believe kids should stand up for themselves and be free to play around, explore, and be who they really are. We were on the kids' side and we wanted them to know it.

A New Nick

Then and there, Nickelodeon decided to do what nobody else was doing—raise a banner for kids and give them a place on television that they could call their own. In doing this, we reevaluated everything from the program lineup to the logo. We replaced Nick's original inflexible silver ball logo with a bold, brash and ever-changing orange loop that can take as many shapes as kids can imagine. This became the symbol of Nickelodeon's new identity and mission, and in January 1985, we relaunched as a network dedicated to empowering kids, a place where kids could take a break and get a break.

To guide us in our mission, we created a list of promises to shape all the work we do at Nickelodeon. We know that keeping a promise is one of the most important things you can do for a kid. At Nickelodeon, we promise kids:

Nickelodeon is the first kids' network. Nickelodeon is the first to recognize kids' need for a network to call their own. Nick is the first and only place that puts kids first.

Nickelodeon is the only network for you. Although a lot of other TV channels say they are for kids, Nickelodeon is the only network that serves kids in a consistent and reliable way. Nick talks directly to kids and appeals to their sense of humor. Nick is the place where kids come to take a break and get a break. Nick empowers kids by saying to them, "You're important—important enough to have a network of your own."

Nick is kids. Kids like to see other kids on TV, so Nick is not just for kids, it is about kids—kids sliding through guck, goofing around in school, playing with their pets. Nick is not about perfect kids or the generic "everykid" usually seen on TV. At Nickelodeon, no one expects kids to be brainy or dumb, or popular or weird. At Nick, it is okay to be whoever you are.

Nickelodeon is what you want. Nickelodeon listens to kids to find out what they want from their network. No Nick programs or promotions go on the air unless they are Nick-tested and Nick-approved. Nickelodeon is what kids want, not just what adults think kids want.

Nickelodeon is everyday. Nick is not a part-time kids' network. Nickelodeon is always there, from breakfast to bedtime, everyday, whenever kids want to watch. Nick is their home base, a place kids can count on and trust.

Within 6 months of the launch of the new Nickelodeon, we moved from being the lowest to the highest rated network on basic cable. Kids heard our call. For example, Nickelodeon is present in 56 million homes, and seen by 6 million kids in an average hour.

Keeping an Ear to the Ground

It is not easy remembering what it is like to be a kid or to know what it is like to be a kid today. You are probably having trouble yourself remembering what it was like being a kid. Remember riding bikes with your friends? Playing pretend games? Doing poorly on a test? Thinking people who were 30 were old . . . and that you would never be? When you came home from school, there was probably warm soup and mom waiting to greet you and let you unload the problems of the day.

Today's kids are growing up in single-parent homes and households where both parents work. They often come home to an empty house, or at best, a housekeeper. We realized that kids need to have an understanding friend, a friend that unconditionally likes them.

Do not get me wrong. I do not think television can replace a parent or a friend, but it can be a place where kids can tune in without being bombarded with the same sensationalized stories about the world. A place where they can relax—a haven where they can just be kids.

To stay true to our audience, every year Nickelodeon conducts, on average, 150 research studies with focus groups of 9- to 12-year-olds. In these intimate sessions, containing 10 kids and a moderator, kids have the opportunity to express openly their likes and dislikes, their wants and desires.

On a larger scale, Nickelodeon, in conjunction with our own or another research firm, conducts the largest study of young Americans ages 6 to 17, called Youth Monitor. Since 1987, this tracking survey has measured children's and teenagers' attitudes and consumer behavior annually.

The researchers' job is not to put a personal stamp of approval on our projects. The mission of research is to facilitate the process so creative producers can feel they have done their best work and that the product actually improves.

Research at its best can excite producers and inform writers. At its worst, it is used for political purposes and control. As much as I embrace research, in the wrong hands, with the wrong motivation, it can be an enemy of creativity and risk taking.

Giving Kids a Voice

Surveys and research are the first steps in empowering kids—Nickelodeon's central mission. As part of the Nickelodeon Experience, when kids are given self-esteem and a voice, they are encouraged to make choices.

On Nickelodeon, they are given the opportunity. Every year, Nickelodeon's "Kids' Choice" gives kids the chance to vote their favorites in movies, TV, music, and sports—a mini-Academy Awards where kids are the experts. Every election term, kids also get their chance to vote for the president of the United States with "Kids Pick the Prez." The count is followed on the air so that kids can see that their vote matters.

Making Sense of the World

Kids are aware and concerned about other national issues around them, beyond the world of entertainment and the presidential election. Headlines like racial tension in Los Angeles and the rest of the country, Magic Johnson contracting the HIV virus, and the war in the Persian Gulf have made kids confused, sad, and angry.

Because kids, for the most part, are "Home Alone" and bombarded by sensationalized images in the media, it is important to provide an outlet that explains the issues in a language they understand—hence the creation of *Nick News.*

Whereas network television dispenses its news in sound bites and incomplete stories, *Nick News* aims to tell the story from beginning to end, and provides a forum for kids to express their opinions, beliefs, and feelings. *Nick News* fulfills the promise of cable television and makes the future TV experience brighter for kids everywhere.

All the World's a Playground

What is the Nickelodeon Experience? It is not far from being in a playground where there are no rules, everyone is welcome, and imagination runs wild. It is not necessary to watch Nickelodeon for the Experience. It just takes knowing, or remembering, what it is like to be a kid again.

Epilogue

What Children Learn From Television and How They Learn It

JOY KEIKO ASAMEN

A particularly powerful force in the contemporary socialization of children is television. Unlike a parent, teacher, or other significant persons in the child's life, television provides a "window to the world" beyond the immediate culture of the child's family and neighborhood.

Much discussion has occurred regarding the benefits and drawbacks of television viewing. Yet, the reality is that most households in the United States have televisions, and children spend a significant amount of time viewing that which is offered. Television is here to stay; therefore, a more constructive mind-set would be to perceive television as a social-cultural educational medium. And as is the case with any educational medium, time and effort must be spent in learning more about what television is capable of doing and not doing toward the education and socialization of our youth.

We have endeavored to present to the diverse audiences for which this book has been written the thoughts and recommendations of scholars from communications studies, psychology, and other related fields who have made the television viewing practices of children the focus of their research efforts. Furthermore, we have sought the reflections of broadcasters involved in creating television programs for children.

What Children Learn From Television

Television, when used wisely, can make a significant contribution to the social-cultural education of children. So what do children learn from this "audiovisual tapestry"?

Television offers children a unique opportunity to see the world as perceived by others. By being exposed to the attitudes, values, views, thinking, and behaviors of cultures beyond the confines of the child's own phenomenology, the child has an opportunity to learn more about herself or himself. Of course, the caveat here is whether what children learn about themselves from television is best left unlearned. Here, we must all take on our share of the responsibility for ensuring that children benefit from their experience with this medium.

As educators, we must be prepared to teach children and their parents to become wise consumers of this visual medium. As researchers, we must continue to persevere in our efforts to better understand the television viewing practices and needs of young viewers. And as broadcasters and media executives, we must commit ourselves to meet the challenge of offering children and their parents programming that is sensitive to the social-cultural diversity that exists while being entertaining.

How Children Learn From Television

Offering children programs that reflect the "cultural tapestry" of our world may in part be hindered by the diverse opinions among scholars as to the learning mechanism associated with television viewing. So what do we know about how children learn from this visual medium?

A complex issue is attempting to understand exactly how children learn from television. From reading the chapters written by the various contributors, it is apparent that there is no consistent way in which the learning process is theoretically conceptualized. On the other hand, it appears that television viewing is more often seen as an active process rather than an exclusively passive one by those individuals who study this medium. Of course, the quality of the interaction is tempered by the child's own stage of cognitive development.

Clearly, our understanding of the precise mechanism that explains how children learn from television is still in need of further study. On the other hand, children do learn from their television viewing experiences just as they learn from observing and interacting with their parents, siblings, peers, teachers, and other significant individuals in their life. Television is unique in that through a child's interaction with what appears on the screen, the child embarks on a set of social-cultural experiences unlike any she or he probably has had an opportunity to experience in person. For some children, what they view on television may be their only opportunity to share in this "cultural tapestry."

We are a nation that exists in a world experiencing social unrest, economic crisis, political change, and cultural diversification. Television is a medium upon which many individuals rely to remain informed about the state of our union and the world as a whole. This interdependence that has emerged between viewer and this visual medium places tremendous responsibility on the shoulders of those individuals who make television viewing practices their business and those of us charged with helping children to use it wisely. It is our conviction that television programming, when thoughtfully conceptualized and responsibly viewed, can act as a constructive social-cultural informant.

Author Index

Subject Index

About the Contributors

RICHARD L. ALLEN, Ph.D., Associate Professor, Department of Communication, University of Michigan, Ann Arbor, MI 48109.

JAMES A. ANDERSON, Ph.D., Professor and Chair, Department of Communication, University of Utah, Salt Lake City, UT 84112.

JOY KEIKO ASAMEN, Ph.D., Associate Professor, Graduate School of Education and Psychology, Pepperdine University, Culver City, CA 90230.

GORDON L. BERRY, Ed.D., Professor, Graduate School of Education, University of California at Los Angeles, Los Angeles, CA 90024.

JEFFREY E. BRAND, Ph.D. Candidate, Mass Media Ph.D. Program, Michigan State University, East Lansing, MI 48824.

MABEL CHUNG, Student, Communication Studies Program, University of California at Los Angeles, Los Angeles, CA 90024.

SUSAN COLSANT, Ph.D. Student, The University of Texas at Austin, Austin, TX 78712.

GEORGE COMSTOCK, Ph.D., S.I. Newhouse Professor, S.I. Newhouse School of Public Communications, Syracuse University, Syracuse, NY 13244.

CATHERINE N. DOUBLEDAY, Ph.D., Assistant Research Educationist, Graduate School of Education, University of California at Los Angeles, Los Angeles, CA 90024.

KRISTIN L. DROEGE, Ph.D. Candidate, Graduate School of Education, University of California at Los Angeles, Los Angeles, CA 90024.

MARGUERITE FITCH, Ph.D., Assistant Professor, Department of Psychology, Central College, Pella, IA 50219.

HANEY GEIOGAMAH, B.S.A., Visiting Associate Professor, Department of Theater and American Indian Studies Center, University of California at Los Angeles, Los Angeles, CA 90024.

SHERRYL BROWNE GRAVES, Ph.D., Associate Professor, Department of Educational Foundations and Counseling Programs, Hunter College, New York, NY 10021.

BRADLEY S. GREENBERG, Ph.D., University Distinguished Professor, Department of Telecommunication, Michigan State University, East Lansing, Ml 48824.

PATRICIA MARKS GREENFIELD, Ph.D., Professor, Department of Psychology, University of California at Los Angeles, Los Angeles, CA 90024.

DARRELL Y. HAMAMOTO, Ph.D., Visiting Professor, Department of Film and Television, University of California at Los Angeles, Los Angeles, CA 90024.

KRIS HORSLEY, Student, Communication Studies Program, University of California at Los Angeles, Los Angeles, CA 90024.

ALETHA C. HUSTON, Ph.D., Professor, Department of Human Development and Family Life, and Co-Director, Center for Research on the Influences of TV on Children (CRITC), University of Kansas, Lawrence, KS 66045.

PETER M. KOVARIC, Ph.D., Director of Educational Technology Unit, Graduate School of Education, University of California at Los Angeles, Los Angeles, CA 90024.

HOLLY KREIDER, Student, Department of Psychology, University of California at Los Angeles, Los Angeles, CA 90024.

DALE KUNKEL, Ph.D., Assistant Professor, Department of Communication, University of California at Santa Barbara, Santa Barbara, CA 93106.

DEBORAH LAND, Project Assistant, Department of Psychology, University of California at Los Angeles, Los Angeles, CA 90024.

GERALDINE LAYBOURNE, M.S., President, Nickelodeon/NICK at NITE, New York, NY 10036.

ELAINE MAKAS, Ph.D., Independent Research Consultant, 129 Nichols Street, Lewiston, ME 04240.

JOHN P. MURRAY, Ph.D., Professor and Department Head, Human Development and Family Studies, Kansas State University, Manhattan, KS 66506-1403.

EDWARD L. PALMER, Ph.D., Watson Professor and Chair, Department of Psychology, Davidson College, Davidson, NC 28036.

MAURICE PANTOJA, Student, Department of Psychology, University of California at Los Angeles, Los Angeles, CA 90024.

D. MICHAEL PAVEL, Ph.D., Assistant Professor, Graduate School of Education, University of California at Los Angeles, Los Angeles, CA 90024.

MILTON E. PLOGHOFT, Ph.D., Professor, Curriculum and Instruction, and Director, Center for Higher Education, Ohio University, Athens, OH 45701.

NANCY SIGNORIELLI, Ph.D., Professor, Department of Communication, University of Delaware, Newark, DE 19716.

DOROTHY G. SINGER, Ed.D., Co-Director, Yale University Family Television Research and Consultation Center, and Research Scientist, Department of Psychology, Yale University, New Haven, CT 06520.

K. TAYLOR SMITH, Student, Department of Psychology, Davidson College, Davidson, NC 28036.

HORST STIPP, Ph.D., Director, Social and Development Research, National Broadcasting Company, Inc., New York, NY 10112.

KIM S. STRAWSER, Student, Department of Psychology, Davidson College, Davidson, NC 28036.

FEDERICO A. SUBERVI-VÉLEZ, Ph.D., Associate Professor, Department of Radio-Television-Film, The University of Texas at Austin, Austin, TX 78712.

JOHN C. WRIGHT, Ph.D., Professor, Department of Human Development and Family Life, and Co-Director, Center for Research on the Influences of TV on Children (CRITC), University of Kansas, Lawrence, KS 66045.

EMILY YUT, Student, Department of Psychology, University of California at Los Angeles, CA 90024.